Hausfrau Honeymoon

Hausfrau Honeymoon

Love, Language, and Other Misadventures in Germany

By Beth M. Howard

MARGRETTA
PRESS

First edition
Published by Margretta Press
www.margrettapress.com
Cover design by Morgan Krehbiel
Cover image by Manuel Adorf, iStock Photo

This is a work of creative nonfiction. While all the stories in this book are true, some names and identifying details have been changed to protect the privacy of the people involved.

Printed in the United States of America

For Germany,

I love you more than I let on

und natürlich,

für Marcus

AUTHOR'S NOTE

I wrote *Hausfrau Honeymoon* twelve years ago. Publishers told me then, "If it were about France or Italy, we would buy it. But Germany isn't romantic enough."

"I know!" I replied. "That is *exactly* the point of my story!" The title might as well be *Why Couldn't I have Fallen in Love with a Frenchman or an Italian?*"

Germany may not be "romantic enough," but this book is full of romance. You will learn a lot about the country, both the good and the frustrating parts. And though it may not make you want to *move* to Germany, hopefully the story will make you want to at least visit. It really is a magical place, complete with enchanted forests and castles. And, remember, France and Italy are close by!

I recognize that *Hausfrau Honeymoon* may offend some. (And not just the people in it, even though I have changed their names.) It isn't exactly a love letter to Germany and likely won't be well received by Germans at all. They might not even let me back into their country! But it's my story, my own personal and unique experience, my own perspective, and in spite of the risks, I couldn't shake the desire to share it.

Lastly, if the ultimate outcome of my marriage to Marcus is already known to readers, I hope the story will still resonate because, location and language barrier aside, it is ultimately a love story about two people and their dogged determination to merge their disparate lives. Love may not conquer all, but there is nobility in the effort. I'd like to think that is worth something—at least the $14.99 cover price. (If you don't know the ultimate outcome, read my memoir *Making Piece*. And have your Kleenex ready.)

Thank you for reading and for believing in a happy ending—even when it's not a perfect one.

"There is always some madness in love. But there is also always some reason in madness."
—FRIEDRICH NIETZSCHE

"If the Romans had been obliged to learn Latin, they would never have found time to conquer the world."
—HEINRICH HEINE

Table of Contents

CHAPTER 1

You Can't Help Who You
Fall in Love With

AS THE PLANE DESCENDS, CLUSTERS OF RED-TILED
rooftops emerge through the summer haze. Lush vegetable fields, mingling with the brick-and-stucco houses, create a Christmas card patchwork of red and green. Beyond the fields are forested hills, too low to be called mountains but high enough to want to drive up, not walk. The hills brim with more red-roofed houses, church steeples, and meadows like an illustrated page out of *Hansel and Gretel*. With every lost foot of elevation, the landing strip comes more clearly into focus, along with the flurry of activity on the ground. Cars zip along next to the 767 on roads paralleling the runway, service vehicles with blue emergency lights on top and words like *Polizei* and *Unfalldienst* in blazing letters on their sides.

I've spent the entire flight imagining this new chapter of my life and how it will go. While I've lived and traveled all over the world, I have never moved anywhere for a man. Passion, however, is a powerful motivator and love can make you do things you said you'd never do. But will love be enough to make this work? I give my seatbelt an extra tug, as if it will secure me for what's to come.

The landing gear is set, the flight crew is seated, and, at last, fourteen hours after setting off from Los Angeles—ready or not—I have arrived.

Released from immigration, I claim my bulging blue duffel bags and wheel my cart past *der Zollbeamte* who gives me a nod that I'm free to enter my new country without paying customs on my freight of worldly possessions.

Heart racing, eyes wide, expectations as high as the television signal towers on the city's skyline, I scan the arrival area's waiting crowd: a military mother cradling a fidgety baby, several limo drivers holding up signs, a burly blond man holding a bouquet of pink roses.

He's not here.

Out on the curb, I search the line of double-parked cars for his 1988 white Volkswagen Golf. For the next thirty minutes, the steady stream of traffic includes many Golfs—though none of them his—dozens of tan Mercedes-Benz taxis covered in advertisements, and several smaller makes of Volkswagens not sold in the States. Surprisingly, I see no Beetles, but maybe it's just as well.

I sold my own Beetle just days before. It was my first new car, a silver one with leather seats, that I could finally afford after a dot com job rescued me from a lifetime of credit card debt; I'd driven it straight off the showroom floor.

"But you're moving to Europe. You are making room for the new," my sister told me as I watched my beloved Bug pull away with its new owner. "You're living your dream to get married and live overseas. You're going to have new adventures."

My co-worker Wendy had stated it more firmly: "You have to go for the whole thing. If you keep your car it's like keeping one foot out the door. Besides, you'll be in Germany. You can get a Mercedes."

A touch on my elbow causes me to spin around, coming face to face with the purpose of my journey: Marcus. His striking features—thick, brown hair, green eyes shaped like oversized almonds, full lips, a complexion hinting at a trace of Spanish blood, and a soccer build that fills out his hand-tailored wool suit—conspire to dissolve my apprehension. His hand on the back of my head pulls my mouth to his long enough for me to fall under his spell.

"My meeting went late," he says as casually as if we were meeting for coffee.

"That's okay," I lie. "I wasn't waiting long."

We reach the car—in immaculate condition for its age—and I grab one of my bags, preparing to heave it into the hatchback.

"No, let me do it," he says, prying my hands off of the nylon straps. While he's forcing my first bag to fit, thus too distracted to protest, I pull the second beastly duffel off the cart.

At the parking lot's exit, huge yellow signs point in three

directions—to Munich, Karlsruhe, and Stuttgart. Marcus steers the car toward Stuttgart.

The first time I heard of this city I was sixteen and living in Davenport, Iowa. My dad was driving me to school in the physical manifestation of his mid-life crisis—a cherry red Porsche 911. It was a week after my parents were summoned to the principal's office to resolve my "increasingly disruptive behavior" so that I might complete my Catholic education. The three-mile drive began with, "I don't think hanging around with that Troy Martin is good for you," referring to my bike-racer boyfriend.

I looked down at my wrinkled plaid uniform and ran my fingers over the "It's Better in the Bahamas" patch—sewn over the hole I burned from holding the iron down too long against the polyester. "How does Kathy Stemlar get *her* pleats so perfect?" I wondered as my dad continued.

"You're a smart girl and you like to travel; you could be a dental hygienist or an executive assistant."

I raised my eyebrows, but didn't utter what I was thinking: "Why not a dentist or CEO, Dad?"

Averting my attention to the dashboard, I fixated on a tiny metal plaque attached to the glove box. Closer examination revealed it was a coat of arms dominated by a rearing black stallion and the car's brand name painted in block letters above. I squinted to read the smaller letters above the horse's head, the name of the town where the car was made.

"If you marry some poor farm boy, Boo, you're gonna have your ass in a sling," he went on.

Stuttgart. The birthplace of the automobile. The industrial manufacturing center of Germany. The capital of the country's most conservative state, Baden-Württemberg. The bombing target of allied forces during World War II. My new home.

"I always forget how beautiful it is here," I say, opening the sliding glass door and stepping out onto the balcony. Marcus, who has already removed his tie and opened a bottle of pilsner, moves in behind me, wrapping me in his arms.

His one-bedroom bachelor pad sits on top of a vineyard; green, leafy vines cling to the sides of a steep valley whose bottom is a slow-moving, murky river called the Neckar. The river divides our village of Bad Cannstatt from Stuttgart's city center. On its near shore, the smokestack of the regional power plant puffs steam into the sky. On the far shore, high-rise offices and apartment blocks, along with a few historical remnants of churches and castles, cram together in a disorganized sprawl.

"I can't see your office," I say to Marcus, searching the cityscape for the giant revolving illuminated logo of his employer. "There's the factory, but I don't see your star."

"You can only see it in the winter from here." He guzzles half his beer and after a few more minutes of silent gazing—mutual wonder of what promise lies ahead out there—he says, "Oh! I have a present for you." He rushes inside and returns with an envelope. I pull out a certificate that reads *Deutsch für Anfänger, 1.Juli bis 1.August.* "It's an intensive German class, to help you get settled. Welcome to Germany. Or, I should say, *Willkommen in Deutschland.*"

"Thank you!" I say. "I was hoping to find a beginner's class exactly like this." I look at the card closer. "Wait, does that say it starts July 1st?" He nods. "That's next week. Well, I might as well dive right in."

A breeze from France rustles the leaves of the chestnut tree in front of the building. We kiss as the church bells clang eight times to mark the hour, then he whispers in my ear the words we've both been anticipating for a month: "Let's go to bed."

We met at Crater Lake National Park eighteen months earlier. I had just finished dinner in the Crater Lake Lodge, an imposing structure of stone and timbers built on the rim of the hollowed out volcano. I was on a soul-searching road trip from Los Angeles after September 11, accompanied by my shaggy, twenty-pound dog Gidget, my road bike, my tent, and my down comforter. My destination: Bend, Oregon. Sixty miles south of Bend is a fork in the road. One direction leads, of course, to Bend; the other—though I didn't know it at the time—to my destiny. I saw a signpost for the national park ten miles before the turn off and spent the next 9.99 miles deliberating whether or not to stop. When the fork appeared it was as if some spiritual force grabbed my steering wheel and spun me into the park.

I pulled into the first parking lot marked "Scenic Overlook" and there it was—a vision of pristine blue water nestled in an amphitheater of snow-capped mountains. All was silent except for the soft whoosh of the pine-scented breeze and my own voice that whispered, "Thank you, God, for preserving this peaceful place."

When I returned to my car, an SUV whipped into the parking lot, screeched to a halt, and a woman jumped out screaming, "Beth! Beth!"

I recoiled into defense mode as if she were a charging bear. No one knew I was here. I didn't even know I was coming here until five minutes earlier. After a moment of utter confusion, I realized it was my friend Kim from L.A.

"What are you doing here?" I panted, still recovering from the shock.

"I'm here to see my client in Sun River. We're sneaking in a side trip so Laz and Gabe can see the lake," she explained, pointing to her husband and one-year-old son in the car. "We're going to watch the sunset, then have dinner in the Lodge. Come with us. Get in."

After the sun dipped below the jagged ridgeline, leaving a chill in its wake at the 7,100-foot elevation, we drove to the Lodge. We hurried inside to warm up by the fire blazing in lobby's six-foot-tall stone fireplace, where other weekend travelers dressed in plaid flannel and fleece already occupied the oversized, Mission-style leather chairs and sofas. We found empty chairs—outside. A long row of wicker rockers lined the veranda, each supplied with its own wool blanket, and overlooked the lake where the moon was rising over the now-black basin.

"Merlot?" Kim asked when she saw a cocktail waitress in a down jacket taking orders.

"Definitely," I answered, pulling the scratchy blanket tighter around my neck.

As we reminisced about the days we used to work together in Hawaii, I was aware of a dark-haired man hovering near our chairs. He could have been eavesdropping or just searching the inky sky for shooting stars.

By the time we finished our wine, Laz had found us lobby chairs. We ordered french onion soup from the bar menu and talked way past the baby's bedtime. Meanwhile, in some other corner of the lobby lounge, a gay waiter was asking the dark-haired man if he needed a place to stay. "No, just the check, please," he replied, avoiding eye contact, his credit card already in his hand.

"Here, hold Gabe while we go to the restroom," Kim instructed and thrust her bundle of joy into my arms.

For the next five minutes I stood in the middle of the reception area twirling, bouncing, and—unaware anyone was watching—enjoying my motherhood fantasy. In reality, I was a road-weary car camper who at thirty-nine had recently been dumped by her latest boyfriend in a recent string of unsuccessful relationships. My blond hair was in a messy ponytail and I was dressed in an Ecuadorian wool sweater—orange with a giant daisy on the front and back—jeans, and trail running shoes.

"Who's a good baby?" I cooed to Gabe, holding him up to the ceiling as he smiled down at me.

"This is a beautiful place, isn't it?" the dark-haired man ventured, his voice confident with a hint of a British accent mixed with something else, something European.

I turned to look at him. "Yes, it is," I replied. He had a shadow of a goatee and inquisitive green eyes. "Are you staying here?" I asked, shifting Gabe to the other hip.

"No, I tried to get a room but they're sold out." He was wearing a funky combination of a traditional Austrian gray boiled-wool sweater with big silver coin buttons, surfer-style cropped jeans, and brown leather hiking boots that laced on the sides, and he had a book by Thomas Mann tucked under his arm.

"I know. I tried too. It's getting a little cold for camping."

"You're camping? I wish I had my camping gear," he said. "I would love to sleep by the lake."

"I'd love to sleep with *you* by the lake," I wanted to say, but instead I asked, "Where are you from?" to keep the conversation with this sexy stranger going.

"Germany," he replied.

"Where in Germany?"

"I was born in Bremen, but raised in the South."

"Bremen . . . That's where they import coffee for Europe," I remarked.

His eyes widened. "I caahn't believe you know where that is! I've been here for three months and find that most Americans don't know their geography very well."

I surprised myself remembering this tiny fact; I hadn't

thought of it since I worked on a Kenya coffee farm fourteen years earlier. "And what brought you here?"

He ran his hand through his hair. "An assignment in Portland with my company," he answered as Kim appeared.

"We need to get going," she announced.

"Hi Kim," I said, quickly passing her the baby. I looked back to my new acquaintance. "This is . . ."

"Marcus," he said. He extended his hand to Kim, but just smiled when he realized her hands were too full to shake.

"Nice to meet you, Marcus," Kim said, adding playfully, "I leave her alone for a few minutes and, what do you know, she meets a hunk."

He turned back to me. "And you are . . .?"

"Beth."

"By the way, Kim," he said, "you have a very nice baby." He looked back at me with a wink.

Laz joined us and we all walked out to the parking lot together. The night had turned colder, our breath visible underneath the dim streetlamps.

"Kim is giving me a ride back to my car," I told Marcus. "I'm sorry, I have to go."

With Kim and Laz observing, there was nothing more we could say. I watched him stroll back to his rental car, wondering if there could have been something more between us, if he was "the one" instead of the one who got away.

With a pang of resignation, I opened the car door and Gidget jumped out. Normally not one to stray, she ran straight to Marcus who was already at his car. He bent down to pet her, scratching her behind her gray and white ears, then scooped her up. We walked toward each other, meeting halfway. "Good job, Gidget," I said to myself, my hopes restored.

"This is Gidget," I said, holding her up to give him a closer look. Then we just stood there, eyeing each other, immobilized by a pull of energy. Until Laz revved the engine. In my unbarred, soul-searching state, I figured, what the hell, and handed him my card. "If you want to stay in touch, here's how to find me."

And that was it. The fifteen minutes and the fork in the road that would change my life.

"If you're ready, I can drop you off at the tram stop," Marcus yells from the bathroom where he stands in front of the mirror rubbing wax on his hair to keep it in place.

It's my second week of German class. My *Passwort Deutsch I* textbook lies open on the dining room table, my photocopied vocabulary of strong verbs next to it. My pencil taps impatiently on the glass tabletop, while my café latte grows cold.

"You might want a ride. It's already thirty-two degrees outside," comes his voice from the bathroom again.

I calculate the Celsius to Fahrenheit: eighty-nine degrees. It's 8:15 a.m., the sliding glass door is open its widest and, though there is a light wind, the rising sun—already high over Poland to our east—has begun its blazing assault. The month of my arrival coincides with the worst heat wave in history. Two hundred people have died so far and the number is expected to rise along with the temperatures. I pack up my books into my backpack, slug down the rest of my coffee, and wait by the front door.

"I thought you said you were ready," I say, beginning to pace.

Once in the car we roll down our windows immediately; he starts the engine. My watch reads 8:35, the exact time at which the scheduled tram pulls away from my stop, pushing my new ETA at the *Volkshochschule* past the class starting time of nine o'clock.

"Shit!" he says, turning off the ignition. "I forgot my I.D. I'll be right back."

The *Volkshochschule*—or People's College—is a government-funded school for adult continuing education. Summer classes listed in its phone-book-thick catalog range from wine tasting to jewelry making to computer skills to *Fremdsprache*—foreign languages. Housed in a sleek five-story glass and steel building with concrete walls, it sits on the prominent Rotebühlplatz corner in Stuttgart's city center. An inner atrium is filled by a massive open metal stairway. A handful of café tables fill one corner of the ground-floor lobby, where a pair of elderly men sits, concentrating on their newspapers. Glass elevators are accessible in both the front and back of the grand hall. My classroom is on the fourth floor. I take the stairs—two at a time.

Two weeks after Crater Lake—after visiting Bend, where I knew within five minutes it was not the town for me—I returned to

L.A. My email backlog contained mostly spam. I deleted one after another, but hesitated when I came to one with a strange address ending in dot de. I took a breath, weighing my chances of whether it would crash my computer or be the surprise job offer of a lifetime. I opened it.

> *I hope you enjoyed the rest of your weekend. I know*
> *I sure did. The sunsets were beautiful. If you're in Port-*
> *land maybe we could meet for a drink. Please say hello*
> *to Gidget from me.*
>
> *—Marcus*

That same day, a job offer did come—by phone. I moved to Seattle two weeks later to work as a web producer for the Winter Olympics. Only a two hour-drive from Portland, I emailed Marcus to meet up for that drink. He replied with a phone call, leaving a voice mail to say his project was over and that he had returned to Germany.

Five months later, after no contact, he called again. I recognized his accent immediately. "I'm calling you from the bathtub," he started off.

"Oh, really? Well, I'm pumping gas at a truck stop," I said. It was true. I was driving to San Francisco for a second date with Scott, a forty-year-old billionaire who made his fortune in voice mail technology. Scott flew to Seattle for our first date—a blind one. He picked me up in a limo and seduced me with his impeccable midwestern manners. It was my turn to impress him by driving thirteen hours just to have dinner at his favorite sushi restaurant.

"I watched the Olympics so I figured your assignment was over," Marcus said. "Germany won a lot of medals."

"Yes, but you lost one in the biathlon because of illegal doping," I teased.

"We deny he's German," he shot back. "He recently changed his nationality to Spanish."

I laughed. "Funny you should call," I said. "I'm going to be in Europe next month for my friends' wedding. It's in Tuscany."

"That's not too far from Southern Germany. Come visit me."

I replied quickly, "No, you come visit me in Italy."

Just as quickly he said, "Okay."

When I hung up, I had lost my hunger for sushi.

Seventeen students sit, sweating, at long tables arranged in a horseshoe. The windows are wide open, but only the sun's heat gets through. Two Turkish women are wrapped up in headscarves, but they aren't complaining. A craggy-faced Iraqi woman wearing a knit cardigan, wool skirt, and stockings doesn't seem bothered either—at least not about the heat.

Today's lesson is compound nouns—like *Hitzewelle* (*Hitze* + *Welle* = heat wave). Though not as complicated as they first appear, they are best taught when temperatures are not hot enough to melt your brain. Herr Keyser, our thirty-something, wannabe-actor teacher explains that nouns always start with a capital letter, and thus are easier to identify than verbs.

He deconstructs one—*Fussballweltmeisterschaftsqualifikationsspiel*—and segues into how German nouns are the bane of advertising copywriters. "Try fitting *that* into a newspaper column," he says, drawing vertical chalk lines on the green board to make his point. A Japanese classmate types the word into her electronic translator. "*Nein!*" Herr Keyser says. "First try to find the individual words in it. And if you're still unsure, *then* use your dictionary." We finally learn that the seven-word, supersize combo means "soccer world championship qualification game." Six words in English since foot + ball = soccer.

I returned to Seattle after my dinner date in San Francisco, where it became obvious that the billionaire and I didn't have a future. We just didn't have enough in common other than our midwestern upbringings and an appreciation for raw fish. I made my travel arrangements to Milan, Italy, where Marcus would meet me.

In spite of Malpensa Airport's poor napping conditions with florescent lights and impossibly hard plastic orange seats, I struggled to keep my eyelids open. Three hours had passed since my flight from Seattle landed and the slice of pizza I just ate was fueling my jet lag. It was nearing 10 p.m. and the waiting area had grown deserted. A man dressed head to toe in black leather, steel-toed boots, and a white motorcycle helmet entered. He looked around until a security guard chased him out, ordering "No helmets inside the building!"

Thinking it could be him, I picked up my duffel bag and followed his trail. I found him right outside the door standing next to a fully loaded black Suzuki.

"Marcus?"

"Hi," he said, removing his helmet to reveal his dark hair, green eyes, and wide smile.

"How was your trip? Did you have good weather?" I asked. In our phone conversation a week prior, he said he would come by motorcycle if there wasn't too much snow in the Alps. I packed light, cramming a black velvet dress, silk blouse, wool suit, strappy sandals, and black high-heeled boots into one duffel bag that could double as a backpack, just in case.

"Great! Excellent scenery," he said. If he was tired after his seven-hour journey of high-speed concentration, he did not let it show. "I had lunch on a mountaintop in Switzerland," he beamed.

We hugged to consecrate our improbable reunion. I waited for him to let go, but he didn't. He smelled of grimy leather and gasoline; his unshaven face was rough. He waited for me to let go, but I didn't. My scent was a combination of Givenchy perfume and airplane must. We pulled our heads apart for a light kiss that soon involved tongues. His mouth, as gentle and delicious as I had envisioned, tasted of chocolate. Mine still tasted of marinara sauce from the pizza. Our kiss went deeper and longer. I felt him getting hard against my jeans, even through the thickness of his leather motorcycle pants. "Displaying affection in public is impolite; it's socially unacceptable," ran the tape of my mother's voice in my head. "I didn't raise you kids to behave indecently!" If only she had seen how the Italian taxi drivers gathered to watch, and how they were cheering—for us. *Mama mia!* We needed a hotel room, quickly.

Herr Keyser's five-hour grammar session ends with a home-work assignment. "*Hausaufgaben für Morgen ist Kapitel Fünf zu lesen,*" he says. Chapter Five.

The entire class moves like a unit; we stuff our *Passwort Deutsch I* books into our backpacks and bags and shuffle toward the door simultaneously. The Iraqi woman, who knows I'm American, blocks my way. "What do you think about the war in Iraq?" she asks, though it's more of an accusation than a ques-tion. She brings her face so close to mine I can see the cracks in the plastic frames of her glasses.

Before I can answer, the two blond girls from Poland and Greece interrupt. "Come downstairs with us for a cappuccino," they insist.

"Yes, thanks. I'm coming." I brush past the old woman, but look back at her over my shoulder. I want to scream, "IT'S NOT MY FAULT! I VOTED FOR AL GORE!" Instead, I say to her softly, "I'm very sorry about it and I'm very much against it."

Marianna and Halina stir several cubes of sugar in their cof-fee. Halina met her German boyfriend while waiting tables in Warsaw. Surely he wasn't the first customer to fall in love with her long blond hair, blue eyes, and lean twenty-year-old body. Marianna, fair-skinned and more Northern Italian-looking than Greek, met her boyfriend when he was vacationing on Mykonos. "Is there anyone in our class who isn't here because of a relationship with a German?" I ask them.

Halina smiles, then shakes her head. "The two Turkish women are married to Turks who came here as guest workers for the factories," she says. "There's a whole population of them in Stuttgart and many, even those who are born a second or third generation after their parents immigrated, don't learn German."

"But they have to learn it to get jobs," adds Marianna. "Are you going to get a job?"

Marianna and Halina are both aiming to become *die Übersetzer*—translators. Already fluent in English, French, Polish, and Greek, they have a good shot at getting hired by one of the international corporations in town.

"I want to," I reply, "but my German will never be good enough to be a journalist here. I'll probably just keep writing for American magazines, maybe do some PR."

Halina chimes in. "But your husband has a good job. You won't have to work."

"I'm not giving up my career just because I'm getting married," I say a little too forcefully. We sip the last of our coffee. The girls light up cigarettes. I stand to leave. "Sorry, but I need to get going. It will take me the rest of the day to do my homework." They wave goodbye and continue puffing on their Marlboros.

The Milan morning was balmy, the Italian air fertile with spring. A layer of dew covered the Suzuki and its bulging travel cases.

"Look, everything fits," I said to Marcus, modeling the oversized hand-me-down motorcycle gear he brought for me.

He was wiping down the bike. "You'll be glad you have it. It's important for safety," he said. "Now are you sure you're not too tired?" We had spent the night in a hotel room in Milan but slept no more than two hours.

"There's no way I can fall asleep on a motorcycle," I insisted. But after the first hour of humming along on the expressway, when my helmet tipped forward tapping his as I dozed off, he pulled into an Autogrill fuel stop to buy me a double espresso.

"It should take about four more hours to reach Florence," he said, knocking back his coffee in one gulp. "Let me see the directions to your friends' place." He read the printout once and handed the paper back to me.

"Don't you want to hang on to this?" The route was complicated, listing multiple turns through tiny villages to reach their rented villa on a vineyard. The directions filled an entire sheet of paper.

"No. I'll remember them," he said.

"Really? Let me test you."

I held the paper so he couldn't see it and followed the words as he recited them. "From Florence, follow the A1 south. As it turns east look for Route SS67 and go northeast. After passing through the village of Pontesieve take Route SP2 to Rufina, then after crossing the bridge at the end of town turn right at the pizzeria onto Route SS556. Keep going for another five kilometers, then after the village of Londa you'll be climbing uphill, and after the fourth switchback look for a stone barn on the right."

"Oh my God! Do you have a photographic memory or something?" He grinned as I put the paper back in the pocket of my borrowed jacket. "I guess we should get going then. I need to call Laura before we get back on the road."

"You're here!" squealed the bride when she answered her cell phone.

"Yes, but there's one thing, Laura. I'm not alone."

"Oh? That's fine. There's plenty of room." Then she asked, as if she already knew the answer, "Are you going to want one bed or two?"

Marcus, tightening the chinstrap on his helmet, was safely out of earshot, but I turned away so he couldn't see the giddy look on my face. "Oh, definitely one!"

A *trennbar* verb is one whose prefix can be separated, depending on the verb's conjugation, and moved to the end of a sentence. Herr Keyser uses *abholen* as an example: *Ich* hole *mein Buch* ab. I'm *picking* my book *up*. In German, "to pick up" is one word. Apart from the twist of moving the prefix, this paring down of words might seem to simplify a language. But no. There are *seven* different German verbs to designate what *kind*

of picking up you are doing—are you cleaning up, collecting, fetching, meeting, calling for, claiming, or reclaiming? I follow along with his lecture, eagerly copying his chalkboard sentences into my spiral notebook. But then he adds a few adjectives in between the broken verb and it becomes a mind-bending memory test. "I'm picking my yellow German language book with the dog-eared pages and beer stain on the cover . . . up." I can't write fast enough. I'm scribbling illegible notes and am left behind in a Spirograph maze of ink as he moves on to the next topic.

He calls on Marianna to answer a question. "*Was ist* blah blah blah blah?" he asks.

"*Es ist* blah blah blah blah," she answers.

I'm so lost I can't even tell what they're saying.

"*Richtig!*" he says. She gets it right.

Halina is his next victim. "*Richtig!*" he says, applauding her correct answer.

I don't join the girls for cappuccino after class. My brain is so saturated I go straight home.

I'm still only half way through my homework when Marcus comes in the door. "Hi my love," he says, already removing his tie. "Have you eaten yet?"

My books and papers cover the dining room table. I look up at him. "Does it look like I've eaten?"

"Oh boy, what's wrong?" he asks.

"These stupid *trennbar* verbs are what's wrong," I say, glaring down at my notebook. "And I have to make ten sentences from the verbs on this list." I wave my handout at him.

"*Trennbar* verbs? I've never heard of them," he says.

21

"You know, when you separate the prefix from the body. Like *aus-steigen* or *ein-steigen* or *um-steigen* or *über*-fucking-*steigen*."

"Okay, okay, take it easy." He sets his briefcase down and grabs a beer from the refrigerator before sitting down next to me at the table. "I know what you mean, but I never learned the term because I grew up speaking the language."

"I just wish I would have fallen in love with a Frenchman."

"So he could cheat on you?" he asks.

"No, so we could speak a Romance language. French and Spanish were so much easier for me to learn. This German grammar sucks."

"Learning English is hard too. You have inconsistent pronunciations in your alphabet. Why do you say 'bow' like in ship but 'bow' like in crossbow? And how do you explain the difference between 'height' versus 'weight?'"

"Yeah, sorry," I reply. "You're right."

"Let me help you finish this, then we'll go out for dinner. I feel like having a steak at Mezzo Giorno."

I kiss him on the lips. "*Sì, grazie amore mio*. Italian food sounds great."

Sambuca is an Italian anise-flavored liqueur. It's also a flammable substance that can be poured onto a spoon, lit with a match, and swallowed while still burning. This is one of the activities that dominated our nights during the week in Tuscany. But the

wedding festivities were not only about drinking. Our days began at noon with a breakfast of *latte macchiatos* and *pane* with
butter and marmalade on the stone terrace overlooking miles of
vineyards. Our late breakfasts were followed by quick dips in the
swimming pool—quick because the water was the temperature
of snow melt. Afternoons were spent on the motorcycle tour-
ing the twisting roads of the Apennine Mountains. I ached with
envy when I saw so many athletes riding road bikes through the
canyons, wanting to be pedaling myself, but my yearnings were
quickly suppressed by wrapping my arms tighter around Marcus' waist. Late afternoons included naps, showers, and dressing
up for dinner. And evenings were an indulgence of food, with
dinners of lamb and penne, pecorino and olives, panna cotta and
tiramisu, red wine and limoncello. And sambuca. Until four in
the morning. Every night.

The wedding party grew to about sixty people. Friends and
family of the bridal couple traveled from San Francisco, Cleve-
land, Boston, and Vancouver. And Stuttgart. The wedding may
have been in Europe, but Marcus was the only European in the
group. But fitting in was hardly an issue. The night of the re-
hearsal dinner he dressed in a black suit and white shirt with
no tie. When we joined the rest of the group for champagne on
the stone terrace a roar of laughter erupted as the groom arrived
wearing the exact same outfit.

"You're looking pretty studly there, Marcus," John told him,
putting his arm around him.

"So do you," Marcus replied. The twins posed for pictures.

The villa was reserved for a week, but Marcus and I had

planned on spending only three days together. I hadn't invited him to stay for the wedding, but the mothers of both the bride and groom pleaded with him. "Please stay, Marcus," they insisted. "We love having you here. You have to stay for the wedding." I kept quiet and let them do the begging for me.

When Marcus called his boss to ask for the extra days off, it was the first time I heard him speak German. I pretended not to listen as he walked with his cell phone to the edge of the terrace. His voice, even in his mother tongue, sounded as smooth and soothing as a DJ's for a jazz radio station. When he hung up, he turned to me and smiled. The answer sat right there on his raised cheekbones.

Yes!

The fifteenth-century stone castle, perched on a hilltop in Fiesole, stood guard over the red mosaic of the Florence Cathedral and brick towers. On its sweeping manicured lawn, a string quartet played Pachelbel to announce the bride and groom. Marcus rubbed his hand on the back of my velvet dress, occasionally running his fingers along my pearl choker and up into my ponytail, as a minister chanted, "John, do you take Laura . . ." I dabbed my wet eyes with a handkerchief. "I now pronounce you . . ."

Following the post-ceremony commotion, Marcus found me on the castle's terrace. "Here, you need to eat something," he said, placing a bacon-wrapped hors d'oeuvre in my mouth. "Grease is the best cure for a hangover."

"So is champagne," I said. "Cheers." We clinked glasses as the ancient city prepared to draw its velvet curtain on another day. The sky glowed in dusky hues of pink and blue. The villas on the hills opposite radiated the sun's Mediterranean warmth in earthy yellows and oranges. Even the sharp edges of the arrow-like Cyprus trees softened. I had visited Florence three times before, but its beauty had never resonated like this. I dabbed my eyes again.

"Hey you two love birds, let me get a picture of you." Using the stone balustrade and red geraniums as a background, John's friend Andrew snapped a photo of us—Marcus had his arm draped around me and I, wrapped in a black cashmere shawl, was snuggling into his embrace, our faces illuminated by the setting sun. "Gorgeous," Andrew said, holding up his camera.

Dinner was an event for nobility in a round room with baby-angel frescoes covering the walls and ceilings. In between sips of Brunello di Montalcino, I left my body and viewed the scene from above. The loud voices and clanking silverware became a mere hum. The crowd blurred and only our table was in focus: Marcus laughing at someone's joke, his head tipped back, his teeth gleaming white, his hand gracefully poised on a Cuban cigar. I was laughing too, my fingers wrapped around the stem of my wine glass, the other hand resting on Marcus' thigh. "I haven't seen you this happy in a long time," I told myself. "But don't get ahead of yourself. Just enjoy the moment."

With every week of German class—three down, one to go—my comprehension of the language grows exponentially less. In English there is one way to say "the." In French and Spanish there are two (feminine and masculine); four if you include the plural versions. In German, there are sixteen. The article used with a masculine noun is *der*, as in *der Mann* (man); *die* is for feminine nouns, such as *die Frau* (woman); and *das* is for words of neuter gender like *das Kind* (child). But that's just Herr Keyser's introduction; the logic stops there. The remaining five hundred million German nouns have no rule to designate their gender or which article to use—bread (*das Brot*) is neuter; a loaf of bread (*der Brotlaib*) is masculine; and a slice of bread (*die Brotschnitte*) is feminine—and therefore each one must be memorized.

Along with the gender changes, noun endings change, depending on how the noun is used in a sentence. Herr Keyser scribbles a chart on the board as fast as he talks about the four noun cases—nominative, dative, accusative, and genitive. From what little I gather from his discourse—not easy when the class is taught entirely in German—the varied word endings designate whether you're giving or taking, pointing at, staying in one place, or possessing something. The complexities involved in creating just one sentence—the correct combination of article + subject + verb + preposition + object + perhaps, a *trennbar* verb ending—make me think I'm back in the hell of Sister Margaret's algebra class. "I didn't sign up for math," I want to cry. "And I got straight As in English!"

"How on earth am I ever going to learn all these?" I complain to Herr Keyser after class.

"There's no secret formula. It will only come with practice," he says.

When Marcus strolls through the door at 8:45 p.m., my first words to him are, "My teacher says we have to speak German at home."

"That's a good idea. We should," he says—in English.

"If we speak German then I'll never get to talk to you. I barely see you as it is," I say.

"Herr Lehman needed my help preparing slides for his meeting with a board member tomorrow."

"Herr Lehman! The guy is your own age. You drink beer with him. And you still call each other 'Mister?'"

"He's my boss. I don't mind it; it helps us keep our professional distance." He carries on with his nightly coming-home ritual: remove shoes and tie, open beer. "What are you working on?" he eventually asks.

"Don't ask," I reply. I close my textbook.

"Do you want me to check your homework?" He comes over to the table where I'm sitting. I don't answer him. "Oh, my cute little thing, I know you don't think so, but your German really is improving. Be patient with yourself." He pulls me out of my chair and leads me to the bedroom—the *Schlafzimmer—der, die, das, dem, den, des Schlafzimmer.*

"Are we going to have pillow talk?"

"Yes."

"In German?"

"Ah ja, meine geile Schlampe. Ja."

The magical week came to an end; the wedding party dispersed, flying back to their respective American homes. I was going to visit friends in Bern, Switzerland whom I had met twenty years earlier during my first trip to Europe; Marcus was riding his motorcycle back to Germany, alone.

The parking lot of the Florence train station was jammed. Car horns honked and Vespa engines sputtered as Friday night commuters arrived from, and departed to, Rome and Bologna. My train was scheduled to leave in a few minutes. With Marcus' motorcycle helmets and my duffel bag bouncing against our legs, we sprinted to the platform.

"Thank you for this very nice time," he said, breathing hard.

"I had fun too," I panted as sweat ran down my back.

"Okay, you better get on board." He reached for me and we kissed like it was the last kiss of our lives, because for all we knew, it was.

I stood at the window in the narrow hallway outside my sleeper car. When Florence, along with my motorcycle man, disappeared from sight, the dam burst. I was crying so hard a conductor offered me a tissue after punching my ticket.

When I stepped off the train the next morning Uschi greeted me. "Bethli, darling, it's so wonderful to see you!" she cried. But upon seeing my eyes, swollen to the size of golf balls, she said, "Oh, what's happened to you? Tell me all about it, honey."

After regaling her with the stories of my romantic interlude— ending with the melodrama of how I found my true love only to watch him ride off into the sunset on his motorcycle with no talk of seeing each other again—I took a nap. When I woke, Uschi drew me a hot bath and cooked me dinner. The phone rang while we were still eating. Uschi answered it and said, "It's for you."

"I'm at a fork in the road. I can either keep going to Germany or come see you in Bern."

It was his voice.

Before he could say another word, I pushed the phone back into Uschi's hand, shrieking, "He's coming to Bern! Give him directions!" I jumped up and down while she talked, ecstatic that he found the note with her phone number that I'd slipped into his motorcycle tank bag.

When Uschi hung up she smiled at me and said, "There is no fork in the road."

Marcus arrived at 45 *Effingerstrasse* with hands stiff and frozen from his Alps crossing. We prepared him a plate of leftover pasta and poured him a beer.

"I missed you on the back of my bike," he said later as we laid down on the futon together. My heart raced as he spoke. "That's never happened to me before."

We fell asleep with our bodies locked and stayed that way for the rest of the night.

The boxy yellow *U-Bahn* ride takes twenty minutes from the Obere Ziegelei stop to Rotebühlplatz. The electric tram has green velour seats, large windows, wide aisles, and is graffiti-free. It travels above ground until it crosses the Neckar River and passes the mile-long city park—sensibly named Stadtpark (City Park)—before submerging beneath Stuttgart's city center. My last day of German class, I use the air-conditioned time to increase my vocabulary. My dictionary—whose plastic yellow cover matches the tram—gets no rest from its boot-camp workout.

"I am not going to live here and feel like an idiot every day," I accidentally blurt out aloud. A woman with hair dyed a popular shade of magenta glances my way, but keeps talking to her friend; the mechanic in blue coveralls doesn't look up. I go back to my notebook and write down today's new words—*Hochzeitseinladungen* (wedding invitations) and *Hochzeitskleid* (wedding dress). With my German course finished, I can start building my *neues Leben*—new life—one gender-specific noun and separable verb at a time.

CHAPTER 2

Settling into German Life

"I'VE JUST DISCOVERED WHERE ALL THE GERMAN housewives hang out," I tell Marcus over the cell phone. Sitting with my plate of Swedish meatballs, I survey the cafeteria tables occupied by young women with baby carriages parked next to them. "They're all here at Ikea."

"Did you find your way okay?" he asks in a whisper from his desk.

"Uh-huh. Your directions were good. The traffic wasn't bad except for in the tunnel. It wasn't too heavy on the Autobahn but, God, some of these people drive like frickin' maniacs." My jabber continues. "Oh, and I saw the Mercedes-Benz plant. It's huge! Cars as far as the eye can see! Think of how much money is sitting there in that parking lot."

"Did you get the closet?"

"Yep. Same kind as yours. White with the glass doors. I got you something too. It's . . ."

"I can't talk right now," he says. "I'll call you later." Click.

"Bye," I reply, the line already disconnected. The housewives are chatting and tickling each other's babies, laughing. I pick at the last of my meatballs with my fork.

I weave my way around the rest of the home-furnishing maze. There's my parents' gray and black rug. There's my sister's white slipcovered chair. That's the bookcase I just sold at my garage sale. With all this familiarity, I know where to come if ever get homesick.

My boxes hanging out the back of the hatchback, I retrace my route—to my new home.

Screwdriver? Check. Allen wrench? Check. Forty-two screws? Check. I spread the open boxes and wooden panels out on the living room's parquet floor, pushing my six dented boxes that arrived from the U.S. out of the way, and begin assembly. German apartments don't have built-in closets, so our six hundred-square-foot space is crowded by armoires—three and a half for Marcus, and half, plus a whole new one, for me. After six weeks, I can finally unpack the few things I didn't sell.

"Are you sure you don't want to leave Grandma Genny's silver and Ida's china behind? We can store it for you," my mother had said almost two months earlier as she watched me wind bubble wrap around each delicate coffee cup, saucer, and silver teaspoon.

"No, Mom. If I don't use it now, when am I ever going to use it?" I told her.

"'Use the good today,' as you always say. I'm learning," she teased.

"Besides, for once in my life, I want everything I own to be in one place, not in someone's garage." I was kneeling on my parents' guest room floor, the glass patio door closed to keep out the sand that was whipping up from the beach. I sealed another box with packing tape and pushed it over to the stack of others. "I'm tired of being such a nomad. I want to settle down and make a home."

She was standing next to the armchair, not sitting, as if she was unsure how long she planned to linger. "You can wait. See how things go, and then ship your boxes later."

I kept wrapping. I wasn't sure if her concern was about the two broken engagements I'd already suffered or about Marcus. Without looking up, I said, "It's going to be fine, Mom."

"Well, Sigrid said . . ."

It was about Marcus.

"Muh-therrr!" I sighed. She fingered the neck of her sweatshirt, casting me an innocent look. I met her gaze and insisted, "I am going to be fine."

"Okay, well then, I'll leave you to your packing," she said and scurried up the stairs.

Sigrid was my mother's one German friend—an elegant redheaded woman who, back in the fifties, had met an American soldier stationed in Berlin, married him, and moved to Iowa where they had seven kids. Sigrid impressed the small-town Iowan mothers with her refined European cooking—German *Kaffee und Kuchen* in the afternoons and French *Coq au Vin* dinners—and with her strict rules—"Children are not allowed in the dining room!" Even though she hadn't lived in Germany for forty-five years, she held on to strong opinions about her countrymen. But it wasn't until after Marcus' first trip to L.A. to meet my parents—upon realizing that my new beau was more than a fling—that the emails started flying between these old friends.

My mother: "He's domineering. He was giving me laundry instructions, told me to shake out my clothes before putting them in the dryer to keep the wrinkles down."

Sigrid: "*Ja, ja*. German men are chauvinists."

My mother: "And he smothers her. When Beth brought him down from Seattle to meet us, the vet called to say that Gidget died from heart failure. Beth was devastated, of course, but he wouldn't leave her side. He just kept holding her, stroking her hair; he wouldn't let her go."

Sigrid: "*Ja, ja*. German men are chauvinists."

I finally intervened, a few months before I moved, from the safe distance of Seattle. My stomach tightened as I spoke, even though my sister had coached me on what to say before I called. "Mom, what you see as domineering, I see as decisive. And what you see as smothering, I see as affectionate and caring. I would not have survived my grief over Gidget if not for Marcus." My mother wasn't going to hold my head in her lap and stroke my hair—and, more poignantly, dig Gidget's grave—like Marcus did. "I'm sorry if you don't approve, but I love him and I'm going to marry him."

When Marcus and I said goodbye in Switzerland, it wasn't a repeat performance of the Florence train station. There were no tears, because I didn't fly back to Seattle; I boarded another train a few days later—to Stuttgart.

In my eighteen years of traveling in and out of Europe—including living there for a year when, at age twenty-two, I studied French in Switzerland, worked on a yacht in France, and ate my way through Italy—I had only been to Germany once. I went to Hamburg in the north to visit Matthias, a strapping news reporter I met in Thailand while staying at the Embassy of Switzerland (where Uschi's dad was the ambassador.) Matthias' apartment was sparsely decorated, except for the framed pictures sitting prominently by his bed—of his girlfriend. I left after twenty-four hours.

I arrived in Stuttgart expecting the city to be swarming with 911s and Boxers, but from the lack of them I deducted all the Porsches must have been shipped to Beverly Hills. Marcus picked me up near the train station in his old Volkswagen. We drove past a glut of 1960s high-rises, past the old part of the city where a few surviving blocks of stone buildings from the sixteenth and seventeenth centuries stand, and up a steep hill lined with subsidized apartment blocks, to his tidy street of trees and beige townhouses. He had come from work. I wanted to rip his gray suit and black turtleneck right off of him. Seeing no evidence of other women's pictures in his apartment, I did.

Over the next few days, he introduced me to his food.

At Stuttgarter Stäffele, decorated with red-checkered tablecloths and matching curtains, we ate traditional Southern German fare like *Maultaschen* (salty pork ravioli) and *Spätzle* (tiny egg noodles fried in butter.)

"Try this," Marcus said, lifting his fork to my mouth. "It's another local Swabian specialty." I chewed the rubbery meat slowly, wrinkling my nose at its vinegary flavor. He waited until I swallowed to tell me, "It's called *Kutteln*; it's cow's stomach. Here, you can wash it down with a sip of beer."

He introduced me to his recreation.

"The saunas are co-ed, and everyone's naked. Don't worry, it's not sexual; everyone's used to it. Just make sure you sit on your towel. And when the sauna master pours the water and essential oils on the rocks, lift your arms like this." When the water hit the rocks, the temperature soared along with the aromatic steam. The master, as if performing some sadomasochistic ritual, propelled the boiling air around with a towel. Surrounded by strangers in their birthday suits, I obediently held my arms above my head as sweat surged out of my pores.

He introduced me to his culture.

"Do you see those grates?" He pointed at the tiny metal openings all along the country road leading to the ditch. "They're frog tunnels. So when the frogs migrate back to where they were born, they won't get killed crossing the road. People used to scoop them up with buckets and carry them across, but there were still so many getting run over it became dangerous to drive. The Green movement was worried about them becoming extinct, so they built these."

And he introduced me to his parents.

Forty-five minutes outside of Stuttgart is the quiet village of

Steinegg, population one thousand. Sandwiched in between a crumbling sheep-filled barn and a shiny new kindergarten stands his parents' four-story home built of solid wood beams and white stucco. We rang the doorbell.

Inside, the house countered April's damp and dreary elements with its Tiffany lamps, ceramic fireplace, and heated tile floors.

"*Hallo, Papi; hallo, Mutti,*" Marcus said.

Wolfgang, silver-haired with silver-wire-rim glasses, wore a pale yellow cashmere pullover, plaid pants, and white Birkenstock sandals with dark socks. Andrea, bottle blond with brown eyes, high cheekbones and plucked-off penciled-in eyebrows, was dressed in jeans, a pink V-neck sweater, and accessorized with giant emeralds.

"Please, come in and sit," they said, though I only understood the gesture, not the words.

We took our places on Queen Anne chairs around the dining room table, sipped coffee out of antique, gold-trimmed china cups, and ate strawberry cream cake with miniature silver spoons.

"*Noch mehr Kaffee, Bess?*" Andrea asked me, holding the coffee pot over my cup.

"Yes, please. Thank you," I answered in English, nodding and smiling.

"You . . . are . . . welcome," she replied in stilted but effortful speech.

Marcus recapped the Italian wedding for them, but other than "John" and "Laura" I could only pretend to understand what he was saying. Wolfgang, deciding this was something to celebrate, opened a bottle of *Sekt*, Germany's version of champagne; Andrea handed me a crystal flute.

"*Zum Wohl*," they said as they raised their glasses.

I allowed a taboo thought to enter my mind as I clinked my glass with theirs. *I'd love to have these people as my in-laws.* "Cheers."

At the end of our four days, before I flew back to Seattle, Marcus made an announcement. "Guess what?" he said. "I have to travel to Portland on business. I'll be coming over once a month for this new project. And I'll be able to see you next week."

Thirteen months, 140,000 transcontinental air miles, 260 phone calls, and 198 emails later, Marcus and I stood next to a waterfall in a dense forest one hour south of Crater Lake, the place where fate introduced us. In front of a moss-covered rock wall, with a river of water cascading down it, steam still rising off our bodies from the Umpqua Hot Springs water, he presented me with a question and a ring. The question was one I had dreamed of since our time in Tuscany, one we had discussed, one I could answer without the slightest hesitation. I had been engaged twice, true, but I had never gotten married. I had never felt this certain, this connected, this *committed*. The ring, in a tiny handmade wooden box, was simple but heavy, made of two layered bands; a gold band on the outside with a steel one on the inside. Connected yet separate, the ring jingled when it moved. I held the box in my hand, savoring the moment.

Fiancé No. 1 had given me a flashy two-carat diamond after I had insisted I didn't want him to waste money on an overvalued rock, especially not one mined by slave laborers. Fiancé

No. 2 had given me a twelve-dollar cubic zirconium solitaire and a promise of fidelity worth as much. Marcus had our matching rings designed by a goldsmith friend in Pforzheim, Germany's famous jewelry-making city. "The gold is for the elegant things we like, like our week in Tuscany. The steel is for the rugged things, like getting there by motorcycle," he said. "It represents us." He reached for my hands. "In Germany, you wear it on the left hand to show you're engaged, then move it to the right hand when you're married," he explained.

I took the band from him and slipped it on my right hand. "I hope you don't mind," I said, "but when we're married I want to wear it the American way."

The waterfall, relentlessly gushing out from the rocks, serenaded us with a symphony of white noise. Puddles of spring water formed in the tangled web of roots around our hiking boots. I looked into his eyes and had a crystal-ball vision: I saw my future forty years on, Marcus with gray hair looking even more handsome, me marked with age spots but still spunky, us sharing the kind of peace that comes with growing old together. I had never had that kind of clairvoyance with anyone else.

"Is that a yes?" he asked.

"Yes, man of my dreams," I said, pulling him down onto the muddy ground. "Yes."

With "Buy Closet" checked off my to-do list and my German course completed, I can begin wedding preparations.

Chris Brautmoden is a modest, cramped boutique across the Neckar River on the busy Mercedesstrasse. It sits beneath two sky-scraping neon marquees advertising Stuttgarter Hofbräu and Schwaben Bräu beers. The shop is filled with towering racks of pouffy white wedding dresses—all with varying degrees of ribbon and lace overkill—hanging in plastic bags. I flip through them, uninspired. Surprisingly, there are no *Dirndls*, the traditional German-style pinafore dress with the lace-up bodice and the low-cut ruffled white blouse underneath. It's the dress depicted on the St. Pauli Girl beer label, where the model looks like a Hooter's waitress. (Marcus informs me this German beer is sold in America, but not in Germany! It's a marketing gimmick, he says. I used to drink it, but decide I no longer want to.) I walk over to the bridesmaid section—to the colored dresses—and stop when I come to a light gold silk top embroidered with daisies and tiny pearls. It's accompanied by a floor-length gold skirt with a fishtail train. I search inside for the tags. My size. My price. It's so affordable I could buy ten of these dresses for what my friend Trish in L.A. paid for hers. I call Marcus at work. "I think I've found my dress. Can you come and see it?"

"I'm just wrapping up for the day," he says. "I'll be right there."

The summer's heat wave is unrelenting. We've had six weeks of temperatures that have never dropped below eighty-five degrees. Even in the air-conditioned bridal shop, sweat continues to drip from Marcus' brow while he waits for me outside the dressing room.

"Tah-dah!" I step out from behind the curtain and twirl around for my prince in my Cinderella gown.

"It's so you," he says. "It matches the color of your hair."

The shopkeeper smiles at us. "So you buy dis den?"

I look in the mirror again. The silk drapes over my curvy hips, the bodice hugs my narrow waist, the neckline reveals no cleavage. My mother would approve of the dress. If she were here, she would insist I get shoes and a purse to match. But knowing how she feels about me moving here, it's a wonder I can go through with a wedding at all. I hand the shopkeeper my credit card.

"Yes. I'll take it."

"She's just upset because you're moving to Germany," my sister said when I had called her for yet another pep talk while I was still living in Seattle. "It's one thing that you moved to Seattle, but moving to another country . . ."

"That's ridiculous!" I interrupted. "I've spent a lot of my life overseas and she was always supportive of my travels. She was always telling me I should marry a European. Didn't she ever consider that might mean I actually *live* in Europe?" I twisted the phone cord around my fingers and propped my feet up on the arm of the couch. The wood-burning stove blazed, vanquishing the Pacific Northwest sogginess from my cabin.

"Mom and Dad moved to L.A. to be closer to us, Bethacita," my sister replied, calling me by the Spanglish name she invented for me. "They like spending time with you; she's afraid they'll never get to see you."

"I like hanging out with them too. And you, and Miguel," I said, referring in Spanglish to our brother, Michael, who also lives in Southern California. "It's not forever, and I'll visit as often as I can. We're only planning on being in Germany two years, so he can get his promotion. Doesn't she get that it was my choice? He's not forcing me to go. She acts like he's going to hold me hostage. I told him I want to get to know his grandmothers while they're still alive, and learn his language. And we'll get to spend weekends in France and Italy."

"Don't worry about her. She'll come around. And Dad is really supportive. He's already talking about coming over for your wedding."

The wide counter at Copy-Tech separates the customers from the photocopy machines. Behind the counter, Herr Westerwelle, a small man with round black spectacles and a gray mustache, is supervising a print run.

"*Guten Tag*," I say to him.

He looks up with an expression of "Oh, it's you again." "*Tag*," he replies.

"*Die Wetter ist fruchtbar*," I comment.

"You mean *das Wetter* not *die*, and it's *FURchtbar* not *FRUchtbar*," he replies.

"What did I say then?"

"You said, 'The weather is fertile.'"

"Oops." I laugh. "Thanks for letting me practice on you," I say.

"Guess I need to spend more time with my friend here." I pat my German dictionary that I've set on his counter.

"What can I do for you today?" he asks in English, impermeable to my repeated attempts to humor him.

"I need more invitations. Color copies of the photo, plus the inserts." I hand him my folder containing a print of the photo Andrew took of Marcus and me on the terrace at the wedding in Tuscany. I show him a sample of a completed invitation—our picture under a vellum cover, tied with organza ribbon. Two printed cards, each written in German and English, are tucked inside listing details for our two weddings—a picnic-style celebration in Seattle and a black-tie church wedding in the Black Forest—in case people want to come to both. "But unless you're going to charge me less than five euros, I'll cut them myself."

"You pinch pennies like a Swabian," he says taking my folder.

"I guess I'm more German than I thought," I say, winking at him.

He puffs out his chest. "These machines cost a lot of money. You want your cards to look nice, no?"

"Okay, go ahead and cut them," I say. "I'll come back for them tomorrow. *Tschuss!*"

"*Tschuss!*" he says back.

All six lanes of the A-8 are at a standstill, going both east and west. Every bumper of every car and truck is nearly touching the next, eager to move a millimeter closer toward its destination. The trucks—bearing license plates from Turkey, Poland, Lithuania, and other countries on the European Union's waiting list—form an endless caravan, anxious to deliver their perishable cargo wilting under tied-down tarps. The pop-rock station is automatically interrupted at unpredictable intervals with the latest traffic update on the *Stau*. Pronounced "shtouw," it's the word for traffic jam, which is used with great frequency in Germany.

"I thought it would only take two hours to get to Munich," I say. I tap my fingers on the outside of the passenger door, as the hot wind drifts through the open window. "Too bad your car doesn't have air conditioning. We're never going to make it if the stores close at two. I can't believe you don't have longer store hours. Six o'clock on weeknights, two o'clock on Saturdays? How does anyone ever get their shopping done?"

Marcus ignores my whining. "You know what they say about this Autobahn?" he asks. I shake my head. "It's the best part about Stuttgart."

"Why? Because it's the way to Munich?" I ask. He smiles, proud that I get the joke, and pushes in a cassette into the Golf's stereo.

Nestled back on a cobblestone street, only slightly removed from the crush of tourists gathered on the Marienplatz, is Lodenfrey—the Saks Fifth Avenue of Munich. At least it would be if Saks sold traditional folk-costumes in America and people still wore them. The name, spelled out in gilded letters above a series of stone archways, marks the entrance. The men's clothing is divided into sections and we head to the one for *Trachten*. The word comes from an old version of the word *Tragen*, to carry, bear, or in this case, to wear—as in Bavarian-style garments. Originally worn by peasants in the Alps and adopted around the eighteenth century by the noble class as a *Landhaus Stil* or "country house style," *Trachten* is best known as the uniform of Oktoberfest. Given Lodenfrey's inventory of embroidered suede jackets, *Lederhosen* (leather shorts and knickers), wool trousers, leather suspenders and belts, felt hats, and hiking boots that lace up the sides, this section could pass for the wardrobe department of "The Sound of Music."

Marcus, who looks more like Ewan McGregor than Christopher Plummer, takes his turn modeling wedding clothes for me. "That looks amazing on you!" I gush of the dark green suede jacket and the green wool pants. "I love the buttons on the jacket. What are those made out of? Sawed-off antlers?"

He turns around. "And look at this stitching on the back. It's brilliant." The jacket is a definite purchase, but he's not sure about the pants. "These are going to be too hot, even in September," he says, rubbing his hands on the fabric, heavy enough for hunting in the Alps, which is what they were originally designed for.

"They'll be fine. They complete the outfit," I insist. "Let's get them. I'm ready for lunch."

The object of my culinary desire is an outdoor oasis known as a *Biergarten*. Five-minutes and a world away from Lodenfrey, is Munich's city park where joggers and inline skaters are making laps around a huge green lawn. In the middle of it, soccer players and geese share open patches of the freshly mowed grass. Well-dressed elderly couples in sensible walking shoes stroll around a pond filled with paddleboats. It's no wonder the park is named "English Garden" as Munich's *grüne Lunge*—green lung, as it's referred to—with all its flowerbeds resembles London's Hyde Park.

Across the street from the park's quiet perimeter is Osterwald Garten, where tables covered with blue-and-white-checkered tablecloths—the pattern of Bavaria's flag—pack the restaurant's courtyard. Each table is set with cardboard beer coasters and baskets of salty, doughy pretzels.

"*Zwei Weissbier, bitte*," Marcus tells the waiter. I know that *Weissbeer* is a compound noun that means "white beer," but what is that? When he sees my puzzled look, he explains, "It's wheat beer. It's not called Hefeweizen in this part of Germany."

"I wonder if our waiter from last time is here," I say, scanning the garden for signs of the *Lederhosen*-wearing surfer dude we met the previous spring. "I still can't believe I guessed right that he was a surfer. It was the suntan on the back of his neck that made me think it. He had just gotten back from Bali. That was such a fun weekend. Remember that?"

"I remember the picture I took of you," he replies. "You were sitting with a glass of beer, your hair was in braids, and you were wearing your new *Lederhosen*."

I laugh, remembering how he emailed me the JPEG upon my return to Seattle. He had titled it: "Your Mom's Worst Nightmare."

"That was back when I thought the pretzels were free," I say, reaching into the basket knowing now that we'll be charged fifty cents for one. "I still haven't figured out how they keep track."

"They always start with six in a basket," he says.

"Well, now there are five. Want a bite?"

The traffic moves faster on the way home. We pass through Munich's outlying farmlands and cross the rocky plateau of the Swabian Alps. As densely populated as Germany is, it also has an abundance of breathing space with generous stretches of lush, rugged, and ancient landscape worthy of *National Geographic*. But descending at ninety miles per hour allows us only a quick glimpse of the 900-year-old Roman Helfenstein Castle and its crumbling turrets on the distant peak. Approaching Stuttgart's city limits, the deep valleys, dark forests, and smokestacks closing in around us, the "best thing about the Autobahn" joke comes to mind. Maybe Munich—with its elegant shops, trendy restaurants, and stunning view of the Alps—would be a better place to live.

The main road leading west out of Stuttgart's urban basin climbs past the busy Marienhospital and through a neighborhood of renovated villas—built for the factory barons in the 1800s—before entering a forest preserve. "Are you sure we don't need to bring anything?" I ask Marcus.

"I ran into Matthias at the factory this morning; he said they have everything they need. They're all looking forward to meeting you."

We park the car and hike along a trail until we come to a clearing in the trees. A noisy group of people surrounds a picnic table, their paper plates piled high with sausages, potato salad, and fruit. Beer bottles consume every inch of remaining space in between the serving bowls and platters. More meat smokes on a park-service-maintained grill inside a brick pavilion.

A tall curly-haired blond with freckles and a wide grin that accentuates his dimples jumps up to greet us. "*Hallo*, Marcus. And you must be Beth. Good to meet you. Nice *Lederhosen*," says Matthias, looking down at our legs. "Let me introduce you to everyone." Matthias stands at the head of the table. "This is Silke, my wife." She's a petite blond with blue eyes and freckles that match her husband's. "Silke is an architect. And these are some of her coworkers. Mark and his wife Bibiana—Bibiana is from Mexico." The cute brunette couple smiles and nods at us. "And this is Steffi and Ralf. Steffi is from Italy; she and Ralf got married last weekend." The newlyweds don't take their eyes off each other. "Okay," says Matthias, taking the cue to leave them be. "Let's get you a beer."

I squeeze onto the bench between Silke and Bibiana. Bibiana, who could be Salma Hayek's little sister, asks, "Where in the states are you from?"

I give her the simplified answer, instead of explaining how I was born in Iowa and have been zigzagging all over the planet since I left there at seventeen. "I count L.A. as my home—Venice Beach, actually—since I've lived there longest. Where in Mexico are you from?"

"Mexico City."

"How is that you speak German so perfectly? How did you learn it?" I ask, desperate to know—desperate to speak it as perfectly as she does.

"I grew up in Belgium; my dad was an executive with a phone company. My first languages were Spanish and Flemish, but I learned German too, because we lived on the German border. My family moved back to Mexico, and I went to university in Germany." Bibiana's moving history is almost as complicated as mine. "That's where I met Mark.

We both look over at Mark who is talking with Marcus and Matthias in German. Mark, a broad-shouldered young teddy bear, smiles back at us.

"That's so interesting," I tell her. "I'm always so fascinated when people grow up learning all these languages. My friend Uschi in Switzerland speaks five languages fluently. It makes me feel so uneducated."

"Oh, stop!" she says with a sweet laugh. "I'm sure you'll learn quickly."

"It doesn't feel like it. They teach High German in school. I thought I was catching on, but outside of the classroom I don't understand a word!"

"Yes, I see what you mean. Out of all the German dialects, the *Schwäbisch* dialect is the hardest to understand." (*Schwäbisch*, or Swabian, refers to Swabia, the southwestern region of Germany, which includes the state of Baden-Württemberg and its capital, Stuttgart.)

Germany has between fifty and 250 dialects, depending on how you define dialect. In broad terms, dialect means that spoken words vary from the standard language; different words are used for the same things—a maddening prospect when you are trying to learn a new language.

"But why is Swabian harder?" I ask.

"They slur their words together and drop syllables, or add different word endings. Even I don't understand it all the time." Bibiana's brown eyes convey sympathy for me. I take another bite of sausage.

Silke, who is German, leans over and says, "I love your *Lederhosen*! I've never seen any like that, with lace around the hem. They look so cute on you. We'd never think to wear them in Stuttgart, but now I want to get a pair."

Wearing *Lederhosen* when not at a beer festival or in an Alpine town is the equivalent of wearing a kilt to the office or the grocery store.

"Thanks," I say. "Marcus thinks we're going to start a new trend wearing them with flip-flops." I point over to Marcus who is wearing his leather knickers with the flip-flops he bought in Venice Beach. Joining the mutual admiration society, I add, "I love that blouse you're wearing. And your necklace. Very chic."

As the forest thins out and the road heads downhill, Stuttgart's city lights come into view. "Everyone loved you," Marcus says from the driver's seat.

"Yeah, I had a great time. Thank God, everyone spoke English. I'd like to see Silke and Bibiana again. I didn't get their numbers though." I look out at the glowing cityscape, my mind wandering outward with it as I try to imagine the future in my new environs. Snapping back to the here and now, I add, "I loved those spiral-shaped sausages. Yum."

"Do you still have room for dessert?" he asks.

"Always."

"Good." He turns the car to climb another steep hill. "You're going to thank me for this."

From behind an open window cut out of the stone wall, a jolly-looking round man—the owner of Eis-Bistro Pinguin—scoops ice cream into a cup. My German lessons continue with real-life visual cues instead of through textbooks, because with fifteen flavors in front of me, the meaning of *Eis* is clear. *Bistro* is universal for café. And the cartoonish statue of a penguin out front makes *Pinguin* obvious too. Not wanting my ice cream to melt, I take my first bite before the man finishes Marcus' order.

"Ohhh, gianduia! God, this is soooooo good!" I exclaim, my eyes widening as the chocolate-hazelnut flavor fills my tongue. "This is as good as any gelato I've had in Italy."

The man hands Marcus his three-scoop waffle cone and makes a comment to him about me. "What?" I ask, looking back and forth between the two smiling men for a clue.

Marcus translates. "He said he loves that Americans express their enthusiasm."

I note that he says *that* and not *how*, implying that Germans are not known for being demonstrative.

"I hadn't really thought about that," I say. "But yeah, Americans tend to be pretty enthusiastic."

Marcus continues. "There's an expression in Swabia: '*Nicht geschimpft ist schon gelobt genug.*'"

"What on earth does that mean?" I ask.

"Not criticizing is praise enough."

"Jesus. That's charming."

"Yes, even Germans from other regions have to get used to that."

"In other words, people in Stuttgart don't get excited about good ice cream."

"No, they do," he says. "They just don't *show* it."

We walk across the street from Pinguin's carry-out window to a tiny park just big enough for a gargoyle fountain and a few stone benches, all of which are filled with other ice-cream-eating couples. We find a place to sit on the stone wall that hovers above the side of the cliff.

"Thank you," I say, licking my plastic spoon. "This is incredible." I scoop up another spoonful to give him a taste. "So is this view!" The downtown lights of the Königstrasse below twinkle like little beacons. To the right of the shopping avenue is the Stuttgart *Hauptbahnhof*, the train station with steel train tracks leading out of it like an unraveling cable. And on top of the station's clock tower is Daimler's star logo, exactly like the one on the factory in our neighborhood, lit up in white. An international status symbol, this star is more recognizable than any Hollywood celebrity. It was the star on the Swiss Ambassador's (Uschi's dad's) limousine in Bangkok. It was the star on the five broken-down cars parked on the Kenya coffee farm where I worked in my twenties. It's the star that brought Marcus to Oregon for work. Watching its slow spin, I make a wish on it—but not for a Mercedes. "Hey lucky star, please let us live happily ever after."

CHAPTER 3

Two Weddings and a Dry Cleaner

THIRTY MILES EAST OF SEATTLE, ON AN EARLY-September afternoon, a cloudless sky offers a view of Mount Rainier, radiant with its snowfields reflecting the sun. My dad, following in the wake of my sister and two nieces who are tossing rose petals in our path, leads me by the arm through the fallow fields of a friend's farm. Our mini-procession passes a red barn, traverses a dry field—scorched by a record-breaking seventy-nine days of sun—and weaves through a canopy of cedar trees to a free-standing stone fireplace-cum-altar where Marcus is waiting—sweating in his embroidered suede jacket and green wool pants.

"Marcus is a good man, Boo," my dad says as we approach, my silk train dragging through the dust and pine needles. "I'm happy for you." He gives me a bear hug before stepping aside to let Marcus take my hand.

"Thanks, Dad," I say, pushing the wreath of fresh daisies higher up on my forehead. Yes, my father must be happy. I've survived a hurricane in Mexico, amoebic dysentery in Africa, minus-twenty temperatures in Alaska, countless bouts of unemployment, thirty some address changes, and hundreds of attempts at lasting love. Hell, he's just happy I survived high school. Now he can relax knowing his younger daughter is marrying a corporate executive—a stable, wage-earning, highly educated automotive engineer who can provide me with health insurance—even though it means his "Boo Bear" is living in Germany.

Though my mom was the main objector to my move, my dad brought up the subject too—without my mother around—over martinis before I left California.

"I don't know about you living over there," he said, picking the last of three gin-soaked olives out of his empty glass. "It's such a different culture; you may find it limits you. And the language will make it more difficult."

I'm not sure how he knows this since he's never been to Germany.

"It's not going to be that bad, Dad. And you know me; I'm very resourceful. I meet people easily. I always find my way," I told him. He has always supported my choices, provided I make a compelling argument—and so I stated my case. Then, I gave him the same insistent line I gave to my mother: "I'm going to be fine."

I squeeze Marcus' hand until my knuckles whiten as Judge Hayek, a short, gray-haired woman dressed in a black robe and white collar, recites, "It is right and proper for a bride and bridegroom to welcome and celebrate their wedding day with a unique sense of triumph. When all the difficulties, obstacles, hindrances, doubts, and misgivings have been, not made light of, but honestly faced and overcome."

That we have overcome *everything* on her list is an exaggeration, given we are still in the early stages of our relationship, but I take it as a promise that we will prevail when issues do arise. And they will. I am not entering into this marriage naively.

Looking toward the small but attentive group of friends, four siblings, and my parents, all seated on white folding chairs, I see only my mother is crying. *Are those tears of joy?* A deer wanders through, stopping to watch the ceremony for a moment before disappearing into the forest.

Our picnic reception is a meal of grilled salmon, salad, and Black Forest cake, or, as I learned, *Schwarzwälder Kirschtorte.* We ordered the triple-layered chocolate cake, filled with and topped with cherries and whipped cream, from a nearby German bakery. Of the rare guarantees life offers, one is that you will find a German bakery in every one of the United States.

"How does it feel being married?" my friend Alayne asks, breezing by to pour more champagne into my glass.

"I don't know yet. Good, I guess, but I don't feel any different," I tell her. "Ask me again after my next wedding. I'm so excited that you're coming to it."

Bad Cannstatt, an incorporated part of Stuttgart, is the name of our village. About a mile from our apartment, on the village's busy corner of Überkinger Strasse and Marktstrasse, is Lange *Reinigung*. The rotating rack of crisply pressed, plastic-wrapped business shirts hanging in the window negates the need to look up the word for "dry cleaner" in my dictionary.

The clerk, a pale and thin woman, studies my dress, turning the gold fabric inside out, her fingers feeling along the seams. I don't know how to ask her in German if she's searching for the tags I cut out, the scratchy ones that said "Made in China" and contained the cleaning instructions, so I just stand there and wait.

She asks me something, but, like the dog in Gary Larson's *Far Side* cartoon, "Blah, blah, blah, blah, blah," is all I hear. When I don't reply, she casts me a look of disapproval and calls out toward the back room for her colleague. A beastly woman with short and spiky black hair, wearing five coats of even blacker mascara, appears.

Together, they scrutinize the dress. Discovering the dirt and grass stains on the skirt's hem, they talk excitedly between themselves. The black-haired woman glares at me and then points to the smudge of Black Forest cake she's just found on the top.

"BLAH BLAH BLAH BLAH BLAH BLAH!" she barks with hurricane force.

"*Schokolade Kuchen*," I say, shrinking back, my heart beating faster.

"YOU SHOULDN'T BE EATING CHOCOLATE CAKE IN THIS DRESS!" is what I'm pretty sure she shouts next, as she stabs me with her dagger eyes.

My brain reels as I file through the logic: I'm at a dry cleaners, a place that wouldn't exist—in Germany or anywhere—if not for a spot or two on nice clothes. Though the dress looks expensive, it is made of silk-like polyester; there's nothing unusual or exotic about this fabric. Surely this requires only a standard cleaning process.

And yet, for all the rational arguments going through my head, adrenaline surges through the rest of my body. What good were those long hours of intensive German classes? I can't speak her language. I have no fighting words, no ability to explain myself. At least not in German. So in my most articulate, loudest English, I shout right back at her: "IT . . . WAS . . . MY . . . WEDDING!"

She mutters something to the skinny clerk, turns her back to me, and storms off. Filling out a form, the clerk declares, "*Nächsten Mittwoch.*"

Next Wednesday? "*Nein! Freitag,*" I say. At least I know my days of the week. Even if I knew how to explain that I'm getting married again in a few days, I wouldn't dare broach the subject.

"Okay," she relents with a grimace. But, determined to have the last word, she points to the dress and shrugs her shoulders to convey, "No guarantee about these stains, *Fräulein.*"

"*Danke.*" I take my receipt and, forcing a Goodwill Ambassador smile, bid her farewell. "*Tschüss.*"

"*Tschüss,*" she replies.

The second I'm out of sight of Lange's big window, I lean against the side of the building and burst into tears.

The Black Forest is named for its color, its trees so densely packed not even a ray of light can penetrate the canopy of its branches. In spite of an air pollution-acid rain scare in the 1980s and a rare tornado in 1999, the wooded mountain range is a thriving, environmentally protected region enjoyed by hikers, ham lovers, and cake bakers.

Deep in this fabled forest, only an hour and a half south of Stuttgart's smoke-spewing factories is the village of Alpirsbach where we're having our German wedding. Alpirsbach isn't a well-known Black Forest destination, not only because it's overshadowed by the nearby spa and casino city of Baden-Baden, but also because it's just one of hundreds of tiny villages in the region. While Baden-Baden reeks of worldly James Bond glamour, the rest of the Black Forest is all about "Little Red Riding Hood" fairy-tale cuteness. It's also where a priest-friend of Marcus' has his parish.

Descending to the bottom of a sharply V-shaped valley, clusters of historic timber-frame farmhouses and stucco chalets sit nestled on the forested slopes. Signposts for hiking trails appear regularly alongside the roadside. One almost expects the cloaked girl, or any one of the Brothers Grimm characters, to step out of these dark woods any minute.

Dominating the heart of the village is an immense bell tower connected to a pink stone cloisters church. The design of this walled church, and its adjoining Benedictine monastery, is plain compared to Europe's other famous cathedrals; there are no flashy spires like Cologne Cathedral or heaven-reaching domes like Saint Peter's Basilica—and no throngs of tourists. Yet

Alpirsbach's *Klosterkirche,* having just celebrated its one-thousandth birthday, stands solid, regal, and fully intact, like Petra without the sandstone cliffs—or the camels.

Surrounding the church are *gemütlich* inns, cozy guesthouses with woodsy names like Waldhorn, Schwanen-Post, and Adler Gästehaus, which our families and friends fill up during our weekend-long wedding celebration.

"These checkered curtains are very cute," my mom says when I show my parents their room in the Schwanen-Post. "Oh, and the bedspreads match."

"Look, Mom. You can see cows from your window." I point out the grazing herd in an open meadow high up on the steep hillside that's so storybook-pretty it looks like a page ripped out of *Heidi.* "I hope they don't keep you awake with their bells. Although, it's the church bells that will probably wake you. You have to get used to that here."

"I love the sound of church bells," she says.

"Not when they ring every fifteen minutes all night long, and do their full chiming at the top of the hour—no matter what the hour," I say. "Combine that with the fact there's a church about every six blocks. The worst is when you have insomnia, you're reminded every fifteen minutes of the sleep you're losing."

My dad has already started unpacking. "I brought my martini bar," he announces. He pulls out a square case that holds a metal shaker and two glasses, a couple of flasks, and a jar of olives. "I thought we could set it up in your room."

"Tom," my mom starts off in her scolding way, "Beth and Marcus are going to want their privacy."

"No, that's okay," I reply. "Our suite will make an ideal Party Central. From our balcony we can see everyone who's coming or going so we can just yell down to invite them up for cocktails."

Horst Schmelzle, the resident Lutheran priest who will conduct our Lutheran wedding ceremony, offers us a behind-the-scenes tour of the church. He's small with graying hair and jumpy, as if he has other things on his mind besides our orientation. Marcus and I, along with John and Laura (our American friends who got married in Tuscany), Alayne (from Seattle), and my parents, fall in line behind Horst.

"This used to be a Catholic church," Horst begins. His English is a little hard to understand since he tries to speak it too quickly. "We still share part of the monastery with them. There is a small Catholic chapel in the south wing."

I don't have to look at my mother to know her interest is instantly piqued. She may have dreamed of a Catholic wedding for me, but discovering that I'm getting married in a former Catholic church is, well, close enough.

"Right. Let's go," Horst says, whisking us through a side door into the monstrous cathedral. He stops at a small-scale model of the church depicting the architectural plans for the new organ he wants. The instrument, which will consume an entire wall, looks modern, elaborate . . . and expensive. "We are selling sponsorship of pipes to raise funds," he says, his eyes beaming through his spectacles.

"My parents bought one," Marcus tells everyone.

Horst nods. "Yes, here," he says. He points to a graph showing the stage of fundraising efforts. "Look, there's their name." *Herr und Frau Eisen* is written in magic marker on a strip of construction paper.

"And they bought a pipe for us too, for a wedding present," Marcus adds, putting his arm around me. "Look, here's *our* name." And there we are, destined to be a part of Alpirsbach history—as pipe patrons—provided Horst's attention stays focused on the project for the remaining two-thirds of funding required.

We follow Horst into a rarely visited barn-like wing of the church. "Up this way," he calls, already zipping up a ladder. "Here are the monks' quarters," he chirps, darting like a hummingbird from one tiny cell to the next. "This place was converted in the fourteenth century and has been left in its original state since then. The monks slept in here on hay with no heat and they didn't have shoes."

Remnants of hay are still visible in rooms barely big enough to hold a single bed. And though you could wear shorts outside, the air inside these stone walls is wool-sweater cool.

"No shoes? How could they survive the winters? It would have been so cold and miserable!" Laura voices what everyone else is thinking.

"Think about it, they couldn't talk to anyone either," says Alayne.

"That would have been the death of you," I tease her. "Unless you got kicked out first."

"No, I would have been knitting wool sweaters for everyone and handing out echinacea," she quips back.

"Ha! That's true," I laugh.

Horst, ignoring our banter, leads us back down the ladder, through the long stone archway paths circling the inner court-yard, and back into the church. We enter a small room behind the altar. The stone room, painted white, is filled with flat rocks and candles. "This area is for meditation," he announces, push-ing his glasses back up on his nose. "I started having groups come in once a week here. Marcus, you remember the medita-tion groups I held in my last parish."

My mother perks up again. "I teach meditation in the U.S.," she tells Horst.

"Really? What kind?" he asks her, suddenly capable of con-centrated attention.

"Centering Prayer," she says. "I work with a Catholic monk from Colorado named Father Thomas Keating. He revived an old form of Sufi prayer. He's created a new movement and has written several books about it."

"Yes, yes! I've heard of him," Horst replies.

My mom puts her hand on Horst's arm as she gushes on. In our wedding preparations, I didn't take so quickly to Horst; he spoke only German and only directly to Marcus. But right now I love this man. He is making my mother feel at home—in the hor-rible foreign land of chauvinists that stole her daughter away. I wish Sigrid could see this.

As the two of them delve deeper into their common interest, the rest of us—now led by Alayne—wander off to the part of the monastery that is still working: the *Klosterbrauerei* or cloisters brewery. The beer made here—called Alpirsbacher—has been brewed in this original location since the year 1095.

"That's four hundred years before America was even discovered," Marcus boasts. He has already educated me about German beer purity laws that have been around almost as long. There's a five-hundred-year-old rule that beer may only contain hops, barley, water, though later they allowed yeast to be added. This rule even has its own name: *Reinheitsgebot*. It applies to every brand, bottle, and stein, no matter what style of beer, and there are many. Hefeweizen, Kölsch, pilsner, lagers, bocks, dark beers, ice beers . . . there are more than twenty styles.

Alpirsbacher beer is no longer brewed by Benedictine monks, but by Carl Glauner, whose family has run the business for a hundred years. We head straight for the brewery's sampling room, an inviting space renovated in the best of European ways: merging the medieval with the modern. The roughness of the old beam and stone structure, preserved and left exposed, contrasts with new sleek, stainless steel countertops and halogen lighting.

It's only 11 a.m., but Alayne insists, "Just two tablespoons, everyone." We obey and down sample-size glasses of pilsner, Hefeweizen, and an unfiltered spicier brew called *Naturtrüb*.

"You may turn me into a beer lover yet," I tell Marcus. "I like this."

The bartender refills our glasses.

"What I meant was two tablespoons three times a day," Alayne says. "Here's to Wedding Number Two." Clink, clink.

Standing in front of the bathroom mirror I apply a second coat of mascara. Laura zips me into my gold dress and tucks pink roses into the bun at the nape of my neck. In the adjoining room, Marcus reties his bow tie for the third time and John helps him fasten his cuff links. "It's 12:40," Marcus calls from the doorway. "We're going over to the church now."

"Okay. See you over there," I call back from the bathroom.

It's a sixty-second walk to the *Klosterkirche*. I'm ready, but twenty nerve-wracking minutes remain before the ceremony starts. Laura eyes the traveling martini bar sitting on the desk in our room. "Do you want a shot?" she asks.

I laugh. I haven't done shots since high school. "Sure. Why not?" Laura pours a jigger of vodka into each glass.

"Here's to you, Miss B. The beautiful bride." We slam our glasses back and Laura pours us another. "It's one o'clock," Laura says. "Don't you think we should go?"

"People are probably still filtering in," I say, grossly unfamiliar with German punctuality. "But, yes, we better go."

Laura and I amble across the village's main courtyard, passing the fountain in the center, from which spring water has been spouting nonstop for centuries. When we are in sight of the church we see Horst by the church's double bronze doors. He's jumping up and down in his black cassock, waving his hands frantically at us.

Laura and I look at each other and laugh. Without a word, we break into a run across the cobblestones.

"Where have you been? The opening hymn has already been played three times," Horst wheezes.

We don't answer.

"Where's your dad?" he asks.

"I have no idea," I say. But just then, my dad, oblivious to any sense of urgency, appears outside the church doors.

"I had to use the bathroom," he says.

"Okay, okay, now follow me," Horst instructs, his heart attack narrowly averted.

For the second time in two weeks, I hook arms with my dad for a walk to the altar. This time he is wearing a tuxedo and I'm teetering on rhinestone-encrusted stilettos. And instead of a dirt path through Pacific Northwest pine trees, we tread on uneven stones past rows of towering Roman columns. Sunlight penetrates the windows high above the altar, beaming down through the stained glass, shining a spotlight on the stage—my destination.

"Thanks for being here, Dad," I tell him before I let go.

He smiles his Wise Buddha smile back at me, his blue eyes twinkling. "I wouldn't miss it," he says.

Horst blathers on in German and I don't mind not understanding my own wedding vows. For one, we're already married; nothing Horst says will change that. But also, I'm more entranced with the lone sunbeam that continues to illuminate only us in its light. I'm convinced it's a consecration from the gods, a holy ray telling us that our union is not of two people but of two *spirits*, and that our marriage has been approved by higher powers. I'm also tuned into the vibrating cello strings playing Bach's Suite No. Four, moved to tears by the music's deep resonance. We may be in a church but I've drifted off into my own private pagan ceremony. I squeeze Marcus' hand and when he returns the squeeze I feel his love pulse all the way to my heart.

After Marcus and I kiss in front of the congregation, our wedding party moves further inside the monastery walls to a champagne reception in the grassy courtyard. Marcus' mom, Andrea, has prepared party favors—decorative bags filled with a split of champagne and flutes engraved "Marcus + Beth."

"Das ist ein sehr gut Überaschung!" I tell her, acknowledging her nice surprise. She smiles back at me and continues to pass out glasses.

With glasses of champagne in hand, we pose for photos with our families creating a rainbow against the ancient pink walls. Marcus' mother wears peach chiffon, his grandmother, Oma Inge, is in purple sequins, Oma Hilde is draped in emerald green silk, and I'm in my shiny gold. And my mother? My mother is in funeral black. After an hour of sipping champagne, the whole pack of us traipses back across the cobblestones to our next appointment: *Kaffee und Kuchen* at the Hotel Schwanen-Post.

Whoever made up the line "Life is uncertain; eat dessert first" must have been German. We barely ate breakfast and we missed lunch completely, but by God we're going to have cake. And not just one; we have a dozen. Cheesecake, plum cake, apple tart, and, as in Seattle, Black Forest cake, only this time it really is from the Black Forest. There is no white-frosted tiered-tower with plastic figurines on top, no cake-cutting ceremony, no smushing anything into the groom's face. Just a big dessert buffet and very strong European coffee. I like this German approach very much.

We take a *kleine Pause* (my favorite words during German class for "short break") before returning to the church in the early evening for the Stuttgart Symphony's performance. Like the magical light beam streaming through the stained glass, it is another godlike sign that the concert is scheduled for our wedding day. "And how fitting, my cute little thing!" Marcus says. "They're playing Dvořák's *From the New World.*" What's even more fitting is that Dvořák's symphony was inspired by his time in my home state of Iowa!

Dinner is served at the Lowenpost Hotel, so our group once again moves like an ocean wave from the church back to Party Central. Andreas, the hotel chef, has set the wooden tables in crisp white linens and dimmed the bright lights to let candlelight from the silver candelabras warm the room. Bowls of red roses draped in strands of pearls, designed by my mother-in-law, adorn the tables. The otherwise casual café looks as if it's had an extreme makeover by Ralph Lauren.

"Your table decorations are beautiful," my mother tells Andrea sitting directly across from her.

Andrea seems to understand her perfectly. "Sank you, Marie," she beams.

I marvel at how our parents have been able to communicate. Apart from my mother learning *"Guten Morgen"* and Andrea saying "Thank you," neither speaks the other's language and yet I watch them build a bridge to each other's side, nodding, smiling, pointing, sipping my dad's deadly martinis, and toasting. A lot of toasting.

Marcus and I stand up, lightly clanging knives on our champagne glasses to get our guests' attention. *"Ein herzliches Willkommen an alle, unsere Familie und unsere Freunde."* He welcomes everyone—about sixty people total. I get the gist of what he's said, thanking everyone for being with us to celebrate, and

I repeat the sentiment in English for my side. Then Marcus demonstrates old-world manners, announcing, "Gentlemen, you may remove your jackets," and wriggles out of his tuxedo coat. A flurry of arms and chairs move as the others follow his example.

Chef Andreas starts us off with pumpkin soup, served in individual, small pumpkins, followed by freshly caught grilled trout, and ending with crème brûlée and espresso. "Andreas," I tell him when he comes to check on our table, "no one would ever believe that this restaurant normally serves sausage and sauerkraut."

"We prepared this special for you," he says with his hands placed on his rotund belly.

Trays of champagne, wine, and Alpirsbacher beer, carried by waitresses in traditional *Dirndl* dresses, regularly circle the room. The beer disappears fastest.

Skits and slideshows follow dinner. This kind of "home entertainment" is a custom in Germany and was assumed to be part of the evening's festivities. Except that no one ever mentioned it to me. But I'm excited to see what unfolds. Marcus' four cousins reenact the play they performed throughout their childhood: "The Wizard of Oz." Dressed in their original costumes, stored in an attic all these years, Claudia is the Wicked Witch, Martina is Dorothy, Daniel is the Lion, and Tobias is the Tin Man. They push Marcus into a chair and begin to recite their lines reading from the tattered notebook paper, also retrieved from the attic. "*Es gibt keinen Platz wie Heim,*" says Martina as she clicks her heels together three times.

There's no place like home. I don't yet know how much this

classic line foreshadows for me, for us, but I muse over it for a moment. What is home? A physical place? A state of mind? The town where you were born? Anywhere as long as it's with your partner? We will be in Germany for two years, and then . . .? Marcus' company is a global one; he could get transferred to any country in the world. My thoughts are interrupted by applause.

Performance over, the actors laugh and take their bow.

Siggi, a forty-something former co-worker of Marcus, takes center stage next. Short but very fit, Siggi's special skills include inline skating, Hefeweizen consumption, and, as he demonstrates, multimedia presentations. A PowerPoint deck set to pop music ranging from U2 to Duran Duran, Siggi's photos take us through a journey of Marcus' past. Marcus in diapers. Marcus drinking his first beer. Marcus on a hiking trip. It's the most generous kind of wedding gift. But Marcus' friends are not done giving. They present us with a gift certificate for a weekend on a vineyard in France's Alsace. The Alsace is a region on the German border along the Rhine River and, given it has exchanged hands several times between the two countries, it has a blend of both cultures and it's bilingual. You say liverwurst, I say foie gras.

"You didn't register anywhere for gifts," Siggi says. "We thought you'd rather have a trip to France than a new blender anyway."

I barely know Marcus' friends, but they already seem to know me very well! Whenever the opportunity arises to go to France or Italy, my policy is Just Say Yes.

Chairs are repositioned back to the tables and barmaids with trays of beer circle the room again. "Your friends drink beer like water," I comment to Marcus.

"That's because it's cheaper than water," he teases.

"That's good, since we're paying for it," I tease back.

Michael Jackson's "I Want to Rock With You" blares over the loudspeakers. "Who brought the disco music?" I ask.

"I went to the bar down the street and borrowed some CDs," Matthias says flashing his dimpled grin. "Disco was all they had. Let's go!" He pulls Laura and me onto the makeshift dance floor. My parents join in, doing the bump and the hustle with us until two a.m. I double over with laughter as Wolfgang twirls Laura around and around at high speed. Laura grins, her hair flies in her face.

"Did you know your dad could dance like that?" I ask Marcus.

"Yes, he's good, isn't he?" Marcus replies, gently spinning me around with commanding grace. I have never seen myself as the belle of any ball, but my husband makes me feel like a bona fide princess in glass slippers.

"Dad, I have to run some errands. Do you want to come with me?" I ask. My mom had to fly back to California for a meeting and because Marcus and I will take a belated honeymoon over Christmas, my dad stays on for a week in Stuttgart with us newlyweds.

He's lying on the inflated mattress in the living room reading a John Grisham novel. "Sure, Boo," he says, crawling out of his nest. "I just need to get my shoes on."

We pack Marcus' VW Golf with an empty crate of beer bottles, several canvas shopping totes, and my wedding dress. I spilled champagne on it, so, like it or not, a trip back to Lange Dry Cleaners is necessary.

We enter the dry cleaner, walking past the racks of freshly pressed business shirts to the counter. I look for the clerk who waited on me before, but she's not there. The mascara-caked brute isn't there either. A woman with a stocky build, cropped gray hair, and thick-framed glasses asks, *"Was können für sie tun?"* It's the standard question of "What can I do for you?" that comes out slightly less welcoming than the American version of "May I help you?" In this woman's case, much less welcoming.

"Ich habe ein Kleidung für Reinigung," I reply in German so rough it would sound something like, "I have dress for clean."

She takes the dress and turns it inside out to look for the missing tags. She shakes her head and frowns. My pulse quickens as her displeasure becomes apparent. "Blah, blah, blah, blah, blah," she grumbles.

Oh, great. Here we go.

"I just had this cleaned her last week," I immediately protest. "Surely, you can do it again."

She is unfazed by my attempts to speak her language. She hands me a pen and an orange form to sign. "You must sign this."

It appears to be a release-of-liability form, but, since I can't understand it—or her—I panic. I push the pen along with the form back to her and shake my head to say no. I'm not going to sign the life of my dress away, especially when it wasn't required before.

She pushes the orange paper back to me.

I push it back to her, holding my hand over it this time. My heart races.

"BLAH, BLAH, BLAH, BLAH," she snaps, glaring at me through her glasses. She makes the Mascara Monster seem like Wanda the Good Witch. I take it she is saying, "Sign this, or else."

My dad stands there watching, helpless. My world spins out of control. I freeze for a moment, unable to speak or move. Then, I come to my senses. I snatch my dress off the counter, wad it up into my arms, and say, "I'm taking my business elsewhere!" as I rush out the door. My dad follows right behind me.

"I'm proud of you, Boo," he says once we're out on the sidewalk.

"What for? I handled that badly," I reply, staring straight ahead, waiting for the Don't Walk signal to change when all I want to do is run.

"You maintained your dignity," he says. "You don't need to take grief from people like that."

"I've got news for you, Dad. There are a lot more people like that who live here."

We walk to the corner and I stop to use my cell phone to call Marcus at work. I tell him what happened. "Why don't you go to the other Lange Dry Cleaner?" he suggests.

"What other Lange?"

"There's another one about two blocks down the main street. Sometimes I take my suits there. I'm sorry I didn't tell you about it before. If you want to wait, I can take your dress there the next time I drop off my suits."

"Thanks, my love, but as long as I'm in town, I might as well just go now."

We change direction. We walk down Bad Cannstatt's Market Street, a pedestrian zone bustling with commerce. We navigate past the apothecaries, clothing shops, and bakeries, through mobs of shoppers and baby strollers, until we reach the *other* Lange.

An Italian woman with a long tangle of brown hair greets us with an easy smile. She examines my tagless dress and nods her head. "*Ja*, no problem," she says. "We can clean this."

There is an Eastern philosophical expression—one I cannot specifically quote but often employ—about how if your view is blocked, simply take one step to the left or to the right to get a new perspective. One step may apply to other places; in Germany, it takes two blocks.

CHAPTER 4

Grocery Shopping, German Style

"THIS CAR IS IN GREAT SHAPE FOR ITS AGE," MY DAD observes as we pull out of the public parking garage.

"Yeah, Marcus is proud of this little thing. He can even tell you the exact date he bought it; it was the day before the Berlin Wall came down. November 8, 1989," I say. "Pretty funny, huh?"

I shift the VW into second gear and we turn the corner, passing the first Lange Cleaners. Possessed by forces beyond my control, I lift my middle finger and wave it vigorously at the shop.

"Hey Dad, see this?" I laugh, pumping my hand up and down. I manage to catch a faint glimpse of the gray-haired clerk through the glass storefront.

"You tell 'em, Boo," he says, laughing with me as we wheel around the corner.

As we drive up Schmidener Strasse toward the grocery store,

my dad's car fascination continues. "There are quite a few old cars here, but none of them are rusted or dented."

"That's because they have strict laws here. You have to get your car inspected every two years and the standards are very tough," I explain. "They won't license a car with so much as a cracked mirror or burned out blinker, even if the car is brand new."

"I think of all those big clunkers on the farm roads in Iowa. You don't see any of those here," he says.

"Did you also notice how clean the cars are here?" I ask.

"I did."

"That's because Swabians have a reputation for being compulsively clean. It's a ritual to wash their car every Saturday, but I'm not sure if that's before or after they sweep their sidewalks."

He laughs his hearty belly laugh. "Good luck living here, Boo," he says.

Aldi, an international chain of more than seven thousand grocery stores, opened its first location in 1948 in Essen, Germany—fitting since *essen*, both a noun and a verb, means "food" and "to eat." Its German founders, the Albrecht brothers, became billionaires, and up until their deaths they were listed just behind Bill Gates and Warren Buffett on Forbes' annual list of the world's richest people. Aldi also owns the American chain Trader Joes. The first U.S. Aldi store was, ironically, in Iowa and my mom used to shop there. It opened in the mid-seventies, long before there was such a thing as warehouse stores like Costco or Sam's Club. There's an Aldi in Bad Cannstatt less than two blocks away from our apartment. Most often I walk, but when I drive I give thanks for their spacious parking lot, a luxury in this tightly packed urban region.

I park the car, reach in the back for my canvas shopping totes, and rummage in my purse for the shopping list. Milk, corn-flakes, wine. And gin. For my dad's martinis. He is here on vacation, after all.

I lead my dad over to the outdoor corral of shopping carts and show him how the system works. "See? I have this special token that Marcus gave me. It's the same size as a one-euro coin; it's supposed to work if you use a U.S. quarter, but I've never tried it. You put the token into this slot and it releases the chain that secures it to the next cart." I demonstrate, pulling my cart free. "It seems kind of pointless though since I could still steal the cart for just one euro, but they do it so people will bring their carts back to the storefront. I get my token back when I return the cart."

"That's sure neat, Boo. You're really learning the ropes here," he says.

Marcus tells me later that the reason for the shopping cart system is indeed to keep them organized. "Your labor is cheaper in the U.S.," he explains. "We don't have jobs like you do for high school students to bag groceries or collect shopping carts."

"Well, from what I've learned about your country so far, you probably have to have a college degree and then do a five-year apprenticeship to get a grocery-store job," I reply.

Marcus just laughs. I may be sarcastic in my comment to him, but in reality I'm impressed with how Germans are so highly educated.

I was first introduced to grocery shopping in Germany—and

the German Aldi—a year earlier, at Thanksgiving. I flew over from Seattle hauling an oversized duffel bag loaded with ingredients in order to cook a traditional American Thanksgiving meal for my future in-laws and ten of Marcus' co-workers. "It looks like you violated some customs regulations," Marcus said when I unpacked fresh cranberries, pecans, yams, brown sugar, and pumpkin pie filling.

"It was worth the risk," I said. "You'll see."

To supplement my ingredients, Marcus took me to Aldi. We loaded up the shopping cart with flour, sugar, butter, organic green beans, Italian chestnuts, Spanish oranges, California walnuts, heavy cream, and wine in quantities to stuff the bellies of fourteen people. I was prepared to spend over a hundred euros, but when the total came to only thirty-five, I became an instant Aldi fan.

There are many things I love about Aldi. And some I don't.

My dad pushes our cart up to the checkout and I unload the items onto the conveyor belt, long by American standards at around ten feet. The length allows for several customers at a time to empty their carts. Unfortunately, at this moment, I am one of them.

"Blah blah blah, *Ihre Flaschen*!" the clerk shouts toward me across the three people ahead of us. I glance around. Everything goes silent except for her voice still thundering in my ears. *She's talking to me, right?* All I understand is the last word: bottles. *What's wrong with my bottles?* I survey my assortment of cornflakes, milk, and liquor bottles lined up neatly on the belt; everything appears in order to me.

A line starts to form behind us. It's late Friday afternoon and people are shopping for the weekend; all stores are closed on Sunday, and some close as early as two p.m. on Saturday, so there are already at least eight people in line now. I don't know what to do, so I just stand in my place—innocent until proven guilty—and leave my things as they are.

"BLAH BLAH BLAH BLAH!" shouts the clerk again, louder this time, aiming her gaze unmistakably at me.

I cower away from her and catch the eye of the man behind me. He says, helpfully, in English, "She wants you to lay the bottles down."

Well, how was I supposed to know?! I have shopped here at least thirty times in the three months I've lived here and no one has ever told me the rules, *this* rule. German Rule No. 341: Bottles must be lying down on the conveyer belt.

I glimpse over at my dad. His blue eyes are fixed in a wide gaze; he is too stunned himself to console me.

One week earlier, when John and Laura were staying with us for a few days prior to our Black Forest wedding, we took them to the local mineral baths, even though it meant the four of us would all be . . . naked. We went into a crowded sauna and couldn't find seats together, so Marcus and I went up to the top bench where it's hotter, while John and Laura found seats together on the middle bench. Marcus and I placed our towels lengthwise giving us enough terrycloth to reach under our feet. I know this rule. German Rule No. 485: Bare skin must not touch sauna wood.

The sauna master, dressed in a T-shirt and gym shorts, arrived with a bucket of ice water and orange-honey aromatherapy scents to do "the pouring." Just as he was about to dump the first scoop of ice onto the hot rocks, he stopped abruptly. "*Sie MUSSEN* blah blah *FÜSSE* blah blah blah!" he bellowed directly at John and Laura.

In a 190-degree dark room crammed with more than forty naked, sweaty men and women, he managed to single out our American friends for having their bare feet resting on the wooden bench. After the reverberation of the sauna master's voice died down, Marcus translated the reprimand—quickly, but gently—across the crowded cedar room and they immediately pulled up their feet. Appeased, the *Saunameister* continued with his work, swatting at the steaming air with his towel.

"That was crazy! That guy is insane," John and Laura said afterward. Then they laughed—and laughed.

"Yeah?" I said. "You guys think it's funny you got yelled at, but you're just visiting for one week. You don't have to live here!"

"Oh, Beth, you just need to keep your sense of humor," Laura said.

"Don't take things so personally," John said.

"But this *is* personal," I replied. "This is my life."

"Keep your sense of humor. This is not personal," I coach myself internally as the clerk waits for me to obey. I lay the gin and wine bottles down. I even lay the milk cartons down, just to be safe. The crowd stops staring. The clerk, satisfied at last, returns to her immediate business. Even with my dad standing by my side, I have to will myself not to cry.

When we reach the cash register we come face to face with—I sneak a look at her nametag—Barbara. Plump like an overcooked bratwurst, with magenta hair and red lipstick, Barbara sits on a stool, looking at me expectantly. I give the cart a 180-degree turn so the front of it pushes up against the end of the check-out stand. I take my position, ready to place the items back into the cart as they fly pass Barbara's scanner. Checking out at the grocery store is like driving on the Autobahn, only faster. My adrenaline surges as I grab the bottles, trying not to break them as they land in the cart. She barks out the total due: "Dry-oond-zwan-tsig-zwi-oond-fear-tsig." It's such a mouthful I can't deci-pher it. My body tenses up until I can identify the numbers on her electronic display: twenty-three euros and forty-two cents. I hand her a fifty-euro note and she hands me the change, which I don't dare take the time to count.

My dad starts to walk toward the door. "Wait a sec, Dad," I say, pushing the cart over to the bagging area. "We have to bag our own stuff, that's why I brought these tote bags."

After we load the car and return the cart, my dad says, "Boo, I don't know how you're going to last two years here."

I don't answer him. I'm still too rattled. I inhale deeply and start the engine. After we leave the parking lot I finally say, "You need to make me one of your martinis when we get home."

"You're on," he says.

"It's so clean here," my dad comments as we pull onto our street, Ferdinand-Hanauer-Strasse. He's right. The neigh-borhood has a sense of controlled orderliness—every bush is trimmed, every tree pruned, every leaf is swept and put in its proper place, in the biodegradable trash bin. "There's no graf-fiti," he adds.

"Oh, there is, just not on this block," I say, parking the car in front of our apartment, which spans the middle floor of a three-story building. In Germany, this is called a house. Ours is part of a block-long row of attached houses, each similar in materials (brick covered in plaster) and color (varying shades of beige). For all of my dad's observations, he doesn't comment on the blandness of the architecture and lack of color.

"Can you carry the bottles, Dad?" I ask. "I'll get the rest."

I unlock the house's outer door, metal-framed with circa-1970 textured, brown-tinted glass. The prevalence of doors like this is the reason you don't see posters touting "Charming Doors of Germany" like you do for France and Italy. Maybe it's a rule. Rule No. 62: House doors must resemble an office entrance. Even many of the houses in cute Alpirsbach subscribe to this commercial door syndrome.

There are six empty wine bottles sitting on the landing of our indoor staircase. "Looks like your landlord had a party," my dad says.

"Shhhhhh! They're probably home and they'll hear you," I tell him as we walk past their door, our voices echoing in the marble stairwell.

We continue up one more floor to the second floor, or what Europeans call a first floor. (What we know in America as the first floor, they call the ground floor.) We live directly above the Schindlers, a retired couple who has owned the building for forty years. "Dad, try not to knock over Frau Schindler's plants on your way up." Spider plants and ferns fill the stairwell. "I've had to sweep up spilled dirt more times than I care to count. And, believe me, I don't need any more trouble with our landlords."

Me? In trouble? In Germany?

It was during my third visit to Germany during our yearlong transcontinental courtship—several months after I had been introduced to his food, his recreation, and his parents—that I was introduced to Marcus' washing machine . . . and his landlords.

BAM! BAM! BAM! Herr Schindler pounded on the door. It could only have been him because he locks the building so tight it's a fire hazard, and he and his wife are the only other tenants since his 102-year-old mother died a year earlier. Marcus was at work.

"You stupid girl! What have you done? There is water coming into our living room!" His sharp words were laced with spit. His thick black eyebrows furrowed together and his ruddy complexion pulsed red. He pushed past me into the apartment and headed straight toward the bathroom. His wife, short and round with a beehive hairdo and goggle-size glasses, followed behind him.

Don't you people have to ask permission to come in?

"What have you done?" Frau Schindler repeated, as if I hadn't understood the question in her husband's thickly accented English the first time.

"The door of the washing machine came open," I explained, cowering into the corner of the entryway, my own face burning red. The machine was a front-loading relic, installed around the same era as the Schindler's front door, and its latch finally gave out—while I was using it. "I already mopped up all the water," I told them.

Minutes before their intrusion I was on my knees developing an intimate relationship with the patterned brown, orange, and black tiles as I sopped up the sudsy mess. With each twist of the towel I wrung out in the goldenrod bathtub, I dreamed of the ways I would update this *Mod Squad* decor.

Herr Schindler shouted something to his wife causing her to rush back downstairs, presumably to call the plumber.

I stayed in the corner, too scared to move. While he inspected the washing machine and the bathroom floor, I silently pondered questions like, "Isn't grout supposed to be waterproof?" and "Why don't you use top-loading machines?" After weighing my options—making an escape or risking his further wrath—I snuck out of the building. I walked laps around the freezing vineyards, bawling, and didn't return until after dark when I was sure Marcus was home from work.

"Have you heard?" I asked, scooting in next to him onto the sofa, reaching for his hands to warm mine, aching from the cold.

"Heard what?" he asked.

I burst into tears again. "I ... sniff, sniff ... got ... sniff, sniff ... yelled at." I sobbed as I recapped the story of Old Man Schindler.

"He should not talk to you that way," Marcus insisted, his British-accented voice firm but soothing. "In fact, he should not talk to you about apartment matters at all. He should have called me at work. I'm going downstairs to speak with him."

Marcus returned with bad news. "We have to pay to have his wall and floor repaired. He estimates it will cost around two thousand euros."

"But he owns the building, and the washing machine came with the apartment," I argued. "You're just renting."

"There's nothing in the lease that says he is responsible for the washing machine," Marcus said.

"Well, if you're renting an apartment in America . . ." I started, but Marcus quickly interrupted.

"My love, we're not in America."

My dad and I carry the groceries into the kitchen, a cheerful, bright-orange-tiled room about the size of a sailboat galley. While there's a full-size stovetop range and oven, the refrigerator is the size of a hotel mini-bar. Though big enough to keep a bachelor's beer supply cool, it can't contain the food needed for two adults—and a houseguest. Which means frequent trips to Aldi. Where Barbara works.

In addition to a space-constrained refrigerator, we have a lack of kitchen cupboard space. But we're lucky to have cupboards at all since, when you move into a German apartment, all you get is a bare, raw shell. No built-in cupboards, no stove, oven, or refrigerator. Not even a sink! But ours is a unique set-up. Because Herr Schindler normally rents out to single automotive executives who don't have the time—or the wife—to build out a kitchen, he rents the place with the cabinets and all the big appliances already installed. This includes the washing machine. After the flood, we bought our own. It has a sensor that stops the machine—and the water flow—if anything goes awry. We also took out renter's insurance.

"This place isn't really big enough for two of you, is it?" my dad asks as he watches me try to cram the cornflakes box into a cabinet.

"It's fine," I tell him, leaving the cornflakes on the counter. "We're not home that much, the view is great, and it's so cheap we can spend extra money on traveling." I don't tell him about the washing machine incident and how badly I've wanted to find a new apartment ever since.

"You've done a good job with what little room you have," he adds. "I like those closets you have in the bedroom."

"Yeah, we're keeping Ikea in business," I say. It's true. Europe's lack of built-in closets is why Ikea's founder, Ingvar Kamprad, was just ahead of Aldi's owners on *Forbes'* top-ten wealthiest individuals list. "We did talk about looking for a bigger place, but you have to give three months' notice whenever you move," I continue. "I just don't want to go through the hassle, especially knowing we're not going to be here that long."

"At least you'll be saving me space in my address book," he says. "Do you know how many pages I've used up because of you?"

I raise my eyebrows as if to say I have no clue, though it's a subject he brings up often. "They were all good places," I say.

He rattles the ice in the silver shaker and fills my glass. "Here's your martini."

I take the drink from my dad and slugging back a gulp.

"Ahhhhh," I sigh, feeling the gin and vodka mixture travel down my throat. "It burns so good."

"Here's to you, Boo," he says, holding up his glass to mine. "I have to hand it to you. You're doing great."

I roll my eyes. "Yeah, thanks, Dad."

"You can always come back to L.A.," he adds. "You know we miss you."

I try not to cringe. "Dad, I'm married now. I love my husband," I say. "And how many times do I have to tell you? We're not going to stay in Germany forever."

"I've seen how much Marcus loves his country. And he's an only child. His parents have a tight grip on him and aren't going to let him leave," he says, sounding suspiciously like a mouthpiece for my mother.

"Oh, he'll leave," I insist. "He lived in London for four years. He's made his break from his parents; he's very independent. And we have an agreement. Two years. That's one year and nine months from now."

"I'm not so sure," he says, popping an olive in his mouth. "You saw what happened with Anne and Peter."

The gin combusts into flames in my stomach. I saw exactly what happened to my sister, an actress, and her investment banker husband. He promised to move from New York to Los Angeles when they got married because she landed a starring role on a soap opera in L.A. "Just one more business deal," he kept promising as the months passed by. He did finally move to the West Coast, but not until it was too late, and they divorced soon after.

"Don't worry, Dad. Marcus is not Peter," I say.

"If things don't work out between you two . . ." he starts off.

"Dad!" I interrupt him. "I just got here. And I'm determined to make a go of it." I slam back the rest of my potent cocktail, glad at least that this conversation is with my dad mitigated by alcohol and not with my mom who doesn't drink.

He sits quietly for a moment, apparently contemplating my situation. And then he simply says, "I love you, Boo."

"I love you, too, Dad." I point to his empty glass and ask, "Are we going to have another one?"

He smiles at me and says, "Of course."

CHAPTER 5

The Path to Domestic Bliss

M Y DAD FLIES BACK TO L.A. AND WITH HIS DEPAR-
ture my married life officially gets underway.

Hausfrau is a simple compound noun—house + wife, though to read about its usage in the *Random House Unabridged Dictionary of American English* is to be reminded of the more sensitive nature of the word. "Housewife is offensive to some, because of an implied contrast with career woman (*just* a housewife) and because it defines an occupation in terms of a woman's relation to a man."

As for my "relation to my man," I want to make my husband happy, even if that means ironing his clothes. But I want him to make *me* happy, too.

"Dinner's been ready for an hour," I say. "You said you'd be home at seven."

Marcus goes through his open-beer-remove-tie routine before answering. "You know I'm trying to get this promotion. Dr. Unser needed some slides for his presentation."

From the dining room chair where I sit fuming with a glass of red wine, I call after him as he heads to the bedroom to change his clothes. "Doesn't it ever bother you that your work is so intangible? You make all these PowerPoint slides about process and best practices, but what do you actually have to show for it? Do these ideas ever get implemented?"

No answer.

The door to the balcony off the bedroom opens; the hanger clinks against a hook as he hangs his wool suit and trousers outside to air overnight. His wooden shoe trees creak as he pushes them down into the toes of his Italian leather oxfords. Finally he comes back. "Hi," he says cheerfully, either ignoring my mood or wanting to start the evening over. He sits down across from me. "How was your day?"

"Fine."

"What did you do?" he asks.

"Bought groceries. Did three loads of laundry. Ironed two of your shirts. Cooked dinner." I don't disguise the resentment in my voice. "I need to eat. I've been waiting for you and I'm beyond hungry." I dish up two plates of ravioli and green salad. Just when I lift my fork to dig into my food, he jumps up from the table. "Now what?" I ask.

"I want to put some music on," he says, combing through three shelves of CDs as the food grows cold. "I know you like this one." He puts on a *Café Del Mar* jazz CD, sits down again, and reaches for my hand. "Thank you for this beautiful meal, my love. Thank you for being," he coos.

Across the candlelight I give him a slight nod of acknowledgement and then stab a piece of ravioli. After a few bites, I set my fork down. "I'm sorry for being such a bitch," I say. "I'm feeling out of sorts. My German classes are over. Our wedding is over. My dad just left. I moved my whole life over here and now I feel like all I am is a . . . a housewife."

He doesn't say anything, so I go on. "My purpose in life is not to be someone's domestic servant. I can't speak this damn language so I can't get a job. And it doesn't help that you're working so late."

Still no response. He takes another sip of beer and sits back in his chair. I count to ten, willing myself not to get worked up by saying anything more. "You just need to give it more time," he finally says. Then he changes the subject. "I was talking to Anton in the parking lot after work . . ."

I pretend to listen, but my mind wanders to the dark side: *You're home late because of Anton? Anton only stays late because he's unhappy in his marriage and avoids going home to help with the twins.* And even darker: *Maybe Germany is not the problem.*

I tune back in without him noticing my absence. "Really? And then what did he say?"

Dinner over, Marcus goes into the living room and sits down in his leather armchair, propping up his feet on the ottoman. While I clean up the kitchen he reads his new issue of *Motorrad* magazine and opens another beer.

After he leaves for work in the morning, I spot his cereal bowl and coffee mug sitting on the counter next to the sink—rinsed but not washed. I know that if I don't wash them myself they may sit there for the next four days. But instead of a sponge, I pick up the phone to call my sister. It's almost midnight in California, but she's usually up late.

"How's the *Hausfrau* honeymoon?" Anne teases.

"Not that well," I tell her.

"How so?" Anne asks.

"I expected him to help more with the housework. He leaves his stuff lying around and if I want our apartment to be tidy, I have to pick up after him. I wouldn't mind, except that I feel like he assumes it's my job."

"Oh, Bethacita," she says. "The situation will change. Life evolves. In two months things will probably be completely different. Just let it be for now."

"I can't!" I tell her. "Why shouldn't it be a given that he pitch in with the cleaning? I don't want to set a precedent that I do all the housework. Once we establish a pattern it will be more difficult to change it."

I have to wait until late afternoon, when it's morning again in L.A., to call my friend Trish in Santa Monica. "You've invested tens of thousands of dollars in marriage counseling. Tell me everything you learned," I beg.

"He'll only do as much as you let him," she says.

"Let him?!" I snap at her. "You think I'm not *letting* him do the dishes? You think I wouldn't let him help with the cooking? Oh, and I'm *letting* him stay late at the office?"

"You knew what he was like before you moved there," she continues. "You knew he was going for this promotion. You need to support him in getting it."

"Oh my God, you're the last person I thought would sound like a 1950s housewife," I say, forgetting that her husband is the definition of a chauvinist—and he's not even German. But she accepts his lack of domestic participation—along with his sports-television obsession—due to the fact he earns a million dollars a year.

"Maybe I didn't *really* know what he was like," I continue. "I want to support him, but I didn't realize it would be so hard to settle in, that I would need so much support myself. And now I've turned into nag."

"Get a dishwasher," she says.

"There's no room," I reply.

"Hire a maid."

"That's ridiculous," I say. "It's just the two of us in a tiny apartment." She's not the best person to ask for advice on the subject given she and her husband have had a housekeeper, a gardener, a car washer, and a dog walker—all before hiring a full-time nanny for the baby.

"You can always leave him," Trish says.

"Thanks," I reply with a half-laugh. Silence fills the international wires for a second.

Finally, she says, "I think you just need to get busy. Get out of the house more."

"You don't know what it's like out there," I reply. "Every time I set foot outside, I get in trouble for something."

I am not going to find the sympathy I'm looking for from her, so I ask, "How's Emily?"

"She's good. She's getting a new tooth."

"How's Max?"

"I took him to the beach this weekend," she says.

"The beach by Olivia Newton-John's house?"

"Yes," she answers. I picture the miles of white sand, the expanse of shimmering blue ocean, the whitewashed mansion surrounded by pink and purple bougainvillea on the cliff . . . "Max is good, but he's got fleas." She pauses. "Oh, sorry, I have to call you back. Emily just woke up."

"Okay," I say. I hang up and stare out the sliding glass door at the city below.

Sitting around a wide, square table are five women—two from Sweden, one from Malaysia, one from Japan, and me—and one German man, who is our instructor. Fokus, a private language school in the Stuttgart suburb of Möringen, offers something *Volkshochschule* does not—short-term intensive German courses in the fall. By looking in the Yellow Pages, I've found a way to spend the next month—out of the house. I look at the clock. 10:20 a.m. Ten more minutes until our *kleine Pause* or coffee break. Two and a half hours before class is dismissed for the day. Three more weeks until we leave for our tropical honeymoon.

Karin, a thin, blond beauty from Stockholm, reads from the

textbook. I'm following the text word for word as she delivers it so fluently. "Excuse me," I raise my hand when she's done. "It says 'u.s.w.' in the book. But she said something else when she read that part."

Uwe, our elfin, tousle-haired, unshaven instructor, answers in English. "U.S.W. means '*und so weiter*.' It means 'and so forth.'"

"But how did you know what that meant?" I ask Karin directly.

She looks back at me sheepishly. "I studied German in Sweden for six years."

"Oh, okay. I was just wondering why I missed that. Thanks," I reply, also wondering how we ended up in the same class since she's clearly beyond my beginner level.

"You go next," Uwe tells me, his accent Americanized from a year spent in San Francisco. "Begin with '*Ein Auto hat*.'"

During the break, Jun, my petite Malaysian classmate whose husband was just transferred from Singapore to Stuttgart, pours a cup of coffee from the pot in the break room. "Would you like some?" she asks in clipped British-English.

"Yes, please." I hold out a school-issue porcelain cup.

"I'm going to have lunch for our class at my house next Tuesday," Jun says. "Can you come?"

I quickly scan my mental to-do list: Learn German, Find work, Get Marcus to help more around the house, Get a life. "Yes, I can make it."

After class I make the daily forty-five-minute journey back to our Bad Cannstatt apartment, looking out the window instead of starting my homework. The tram passes through onion fields, where mist hovers above dark soil and protruding green shoots, before easing down the long, steep hillside toward Stuttgart's city center. The same sea of red rooftops and church steeples I first saw from the airplane fills the valley below. From the distance the city appears preserved from centuries past, helped by the fact there are no factories on this side of town. "It's so old, so European, so beautiful . . . but what exactly am I doing here?" I muse, until another voice takes over in my head. It could be my mother, but maybe it's my own voice. Either way, I get a good ol' midwestern pull-yourself-up-by-the-bootstraps talking-to. "You need be more grateful, missy. You have a smart and sexy husband who loves you. And living in Germany is an experience many people dream of, so make the most out of your time here. If it's not working then you need to try harder, make it work." The tram finally reaches the bottom of the valley. As it enters the subway tunnel, the voice, along with the view, disappear in the blackness.

Trish calls later in the afternoon. "How's the new German class going?" she asks.

I look over at my course book and my industrial-size dictionary lying open on the dining room table. "Good," I answer. "My teacher is nice and I think I might actually make some friends."

"How's Marcus?"

"Busy," I say. "He's working longer hours than ever."

"At least you'll be out of there in a few weeks," she replies. "I'm glad you're coming to L.A. before you go on your honeymoon. We can go to yoga, just like old times."

"I know. I am desperate for Vinnie's class, so definitely count me in."

Jun's neighborhood, Degerloch, is built along the edge of Stutt-gart's largest forest preserve, a quiet sanctuary thick and green with pine trees. This area has the highest concentration of wealth in Stuttgart, apparent by the large stand-alone homes be-longing to CEOs and entrepreneurs—manufacturers of screws, seat belts, and other uncelebrated but indispensable car and ma-chine parts. "Are there hiking trails in these woods?" I ask Jun as our school group walks from the tram stop.

"Oh, yes. That's where I go jogging every morning," she says.

"Before German class?" I ask.

"Oh, yes. Otto, my husband, leaves for work early, but I still have time to run and get Lucas ready for school when I get back," she explains. "Lucas is our son, he's nine. Do you run?"

"I do."

"You should come with me sometime," she says. We turn the corner and walk along another tree-lined block, passing chateau-style villas in pink, yellow, and brick—all with deco-rative wooden photogenic doors—before stopping in front of a pale four-story modern building. "Here we are," she announces pointing to the glass, office-like entrance.

Jun's apartment spans two floors and is more than quadru-ple the size of ours. In the living room that's like a big solarium, sun radiates through the sliding glass doors that open up into a spacious grassy backyard. "You all sit," Jun says. "I'm going to prepare lunch." I follow her into her sleek, narrow, all-gray kitchen. "No, I'll do this. You go talk with Karin and Lena." So I take a seat next to them on the rattan sofas.

"How did you two end up here?" I ask the Swedish goddesses.

"My husband got transferred here. He works for Bosch," Karin says in her quiet way. She tucks her blond hair behind her ear and looks down at the floor.

"My boyfriend has lived here for ten years," says the perkier Lena, who is half-Indian. Her skin and hair are dark, but her broad cheekbones and freckles convey her Swedish half. Her pierced tongue conveys something else altogether. "He's a dental technician."

"Why Stuttgart?" I ask, continuing to poll everyone I meet. I want to ask, "Why not Paris? Why not Rome?" but my manners keep my mouth in check.

"The dentist he works for is Swedish," Lena says.

"Oh," I reply. "And how do you like it here?"

"I love it!" she says. "There are great clubs here. We dance all night. And there are fun bars. The best one, Die Bar, is in our neighborhood. You should go there sometime."

"I was there once," I tell her without adding that once was enough. While it draws the younger, hipper residents of Stuttgart, this place is not for the claustrophobic. I can handle narrow spaces, but the bar, in the basement of a pre-war building, was more crowded than a New York City subway car at the height of rush hour—and everyone was smoking.

Jun appears from the kitchen and instructs us to take our seats at the dining room table. I sit with my back to the windows and face a painting of Buddha-cum-Godzilla kicking down the

World Bank. In between bites of steamed halibut, the discussion hones in on the one subject we have in common.

"German is easier for us Swedes to speak because many words are the same," Karin explains.

I think of English words similar to German. I can only come up with kindergarten, bratwurst, sauerkraut, and beer—which, in German, is spelled *Bier* with a capital B.

"And we learn it when we're in grade school," Lena adds.

"I started studying it ten years ago when I first met Otto," Jun chimes in. "This is really just a refresher course for me. Except that I've never lived in Germany before. Now I have to speak it."

"What about your son?" I ask.

"He's been going to German schools since preschool," she says. "He's fluent."

"I just find German so harsh," I say. "And the sound of the words don't correspond to their meaning. Like *ausgezeichnet*. Aus—geh—TZIKE—net!" I bark out each syllable doing my best Colonel Klink impersonation. "How can you describe something as 'excellent' using a word like that?"

Lena giggles. "That is so funny," she says. "I never thought of it that way."

By the time we've filled up with fish, Swedish butter cookies, and conversation, it's dark outside. Karin and Lena leave; I stay to help Jun clean up. Using my chance to do some first-hand research on a subject more pressing to me than learning *Deutsch*, I ask her, "Your husband is German. What is he like? Does he help out around the house?"

"He's a banker," she says. I guess that partly explains the

Buddha painting. "We met when we were both working for a bank in Sydney."

"Sydney, Australia," I confirm.

"Yes. I was a vice president, but when we had Lucas, I quit. I haven't worked since, so I do the cooking and cleaning. I love to cook."

"I guess it would help if I liked to cook," I say without explaining further.

"Lucas is over at a friend's house, but Otto should be home any minute. If you stay a little longer, you can meet him."

"Home?" I ask with great surprise. "What time does he usually get home?"

"By six, every night, so we can have dinner together as a family," Jun says.

I get it. She accepts his lack of domestic participation because he makes the family schedule a priority. My heart sinks a little thinking of the cold dinners and not seeing Marcus sometimes until nine or ten.

Otto slides his house key into the front door at six p.m. on the dot. He's tall, strong-boned, and wears a V-neck sweater and gray trousers under his trench coat. "Nice to meet you," he says warmly, kissing me on each cheek. Then he pours himself a glass of wine and heads straight for his armchair to watch the soccer game.

When I get home to our apartment (dark and empty) I check my email (none), pour myself a glass of wine (a Spanish Rioja), and plop down in Marcus' leather chair. I scan the handful of my books on the shelf that didn't fall victim to my garage sale.

I pick out one—whose title does not amuse Marcus—*How to Make Your Man Behave in 21 Days or Less Using the Secrets of Professional Dog Trainers*, by Karen Salmansohn. I, however, think this little gem of a book is hilarious down to its simple but clever illustrations.

"*Remember the Four Cs*," Salmansohn writes. "*Always be Consistent about your demands, Clear in how you express yourself, Confident in your authority, and Complimentary about good behavior.*"

I implement the advice that evening. "I need you to help me wash the dishes after our meals," I announce to Marcus during dinner.

No. 1: Be consistent about your demands.

"I would, but I don't have the time," he says. "I have my job."

"Excuse me? I make you breakfast to help you get out the door on time, I drive you to work to save you twenty minutes in the mornings. The least you can do is to wash your own dishes."

"Well, right now, since you're not working, you have the extra time to do more around the house," he says. "Eventually, when you get a job and I'm not as busy, I can pick up the slack and do more."

No. 2: Be clear in how you express yourself.

"Bullshit!" I hiss, calling his bluff. "It'll be ten years before my German is good enough to get a job. And even if I could get one, there's never going to be a time when you're not busy at work. You are not being respectful of my time."

No. 3: Be confident in your authority.

"The only thing I am asking is for you to wash a few dishes, even if they're just your own," I continue, suppressing my inclination to include a few swear words. *(Don't make a habit of yelling, or in time he'll never listen to anything you say*, instructs the dog trainer.)

He washes the dinner plates. We go to bed without speaking.

The next morning he calls to me through the bathroom door. "Can you drive me to work? It will keep me from being late to my meeting."

I calculate the forty minutes it will take me round-trip and whether or not I can still make it by tram to Fokus on the opposite side of the city without being late for German class. Close, but possible. "Yes, okay."

When I come back into the kitchen his clean cereal bowl drips in the drying rack.

We walk out to the Volkswagen together. Marcus, loaded down with his briefcase, coffee mug, and suit coat slung over his arm, hands me the keys. I shift the car into gear and head toward the factory, past the endless rows of bland, soot-stained apartment blocks. I look for the mobile speed camera, sometimes hidden behind the bridge to catch morning commuters. Marcus turns his head too. "It's not there," he says. "You can speed up."

When we are half way to the factory, where the apartment buildings give way to warehouses and assembly plants, we stop at a red light. I turn toward him and in a soothing voice say, "Thank you for doing your dishes this morning."

No. 4: Compliment good behavior. I am heeding the dog advice impeccably.

"Well, I won't always have time to do my dishes," he replies. "Some days I'm just going to be too busy."

I squeeze the steering wheel. I clench my teeth. I count to ten. (*Never treat aggression with more aggression – you'll only aggravate the situation,* the book states. *Always strive for partnership and understanding.*)

"God, these stoplights are long," I say.

"They are," Marcus replies. "The stoplights in Stuttgart are so notoriously long, we hear frequent complaints from Germans visiting from other cities."

"Then why don't they reset them?"

He doesn't answer.

We start moving again. "I was just trying to give you a compliment. I wanted to let you know I appreciate your listening and making an effort, and being an equal partner in this relationship. Your helping with the dishes makes me feel loved."

We pull up in front of the company gate, parking in front of the security guardhouse between a delivery truck and another wife dropping off her husband in a shiny black Mercedes. "I'm sorry," he says as he gets out of the car. "I'll try to help out more."

He kisses me goodbye, then he turns and waves. He files into the factory with the other briefcase-toting dogs . . . um, I mean pigs . . . um, I mean *men.*

I'm not alone on my drive home. My mother's voice is with me, and she's joined by Sigrid: "We told you so," they taunt in unison.

"No!" I tell them. "Marcus is different, evolved, even progressive. I just know he is. I promise, you'll see." I don't admit how confused I am, how I thought Germany would be more like America—it had seemed that way during my visits, making me think adjusting would be a breeze—and how Marcus had seemed to be more of a free-spirit. Every time he visited me at my Seattle cabin he helped out with the dishes and drove *me* to work. He was not a chauvinist. Not at all. But I was on a different side of the world now, and seeing a different side of Marcus.

Anyway, I couldn't possibly have married a chauvinist. I already learned my lesson by being "married" to one in Christian Marriage Preparation, a required course my senior year in high school. At the beginning of the semester our entire class gathered in the auditorium waiting for Father Phillips to draw names to pair us as couples. My reputation still clung to me from the previous year during which I didn't shave my legs or armpits to express my equal-rights views, views I've refined in my married life to "If I cook, then you clean." It was the same year I caused great controversy by discovering a loophole in the dress code that until then stated nothing about having patches on our plaid uniform skirts. "But it's covering the hole I made when ironing my pleats," I told Sister Elizabeth who eventually gave up in exasperation. So when Father Phillips drew my name pairing me with Sean O'Donnell the class went wild. The Alex P. Keaton of Iowa, Sean made his own political statement by wearing a suit and tie to school every day, though the only boys' loose uniform requirement was No Jeans. "Girls should not be allowed to play on the boys' baseball team," he argued against me. "And absolutely not football." We made it through the semester, got a B on our report cards—barely—and never spoke again.

Marcus is no Sean O'Donnell. If German schools had sports teams, he would have been cheering for the girls who were playing baseball *and* football, and giving them rides home on his motorcycle. But if our marriage were graded—based solely on effort in our first semester—I would give myself an A and Marcus a C-minus.

"Die Sekretärin soll eine dynamische Persönlichkeit haben." Jun reads from *Themen Neu 2*, whose content has progressed from basic grammar to practical subjects like how to read job postings. According to this one, a secretary should have a dynamic personality.

During the break I mention to Jun, "Did you notice how all the jobs listed for women were clerical? I mean, don't you find that just a little sexist? In some ways this country seems so progressive, but in others it's like it's fifty years behind America."

"The German system is set up for women to stay home and raise the children," she says.

"But Jun, doesn't that bother you?"

"My days are so busy—I have to take care of Lucas, I have my German classes, my art classes, and I try to keep up with reading the *Financial Times*. I don't have time to think about it."

A Fed Ex package is waiting for me when I arrive home from school. I rip open the box and six books tumble out. I read a few of the titles: *When Things Fall Apart, The Places That Scare You: A Guide to Fearlessness in Difficult Times*, and, worse, *The Wisdom of No Escape*, all by an American Buddhist nun named Pema Chödrön, an author I've never heard of.

I open the enclosed card. "Thought these might help. Love, Trish."

"How sweet," I think. Then it occurs to me, "Boy, do I seem that bad off?"

I skim through a few pages.

According to the Buddha, the lives of all beings are marked by three characteristics: impermanence, egolessness, and suffering or dissatisfaction. Recognizing these qualities to be real and true in our own experience helps us to relax with things as they are.

Yeah? Well, according to me, life is too short to suffer. And there is no way I am going to relax with "things as they are." I try another chapter.

For an aspiring bodhisattva, the essential practice is to cultivate maitri.

What? No, no, no, this is not a good time to learn Sanskrit. My brain is already confused enough with German.

I put aside *108 Buddhist Teachings* and Pema's other titles, swapping them for another little publication on my shelf titled, more to the point, *100 Ways to Stay Together* by Ben White. Why hadn't I seen this earlier?! Numbers one, two, and three on the list: *communicate, communicate,* and *communicate.*

Good in theory, but try having a conversation about feelings with a German engineer. I move further down the list.

No. 4: No matter what you do, be equals at home.

Exactly!

No. 12: Share housework and swap chores. In a poll that asked women whether they'd rather watch a man dance naked or wash dishes, 61 percent chose dishes!

Yes! Finally, someone speaks my language!

I make a copy of the list and prop it up next to Marcus' coffee cup at breakfast. I pretend to be busy with my homework as he skims the list while shoveling spoonfuls of cornflakes into his mouth. When he's slurped the last drops of milk from his bowl, he washes, dries, and puts his dishes away. He doesn't say anything about the list—or his clean dishes—so I don't either.

Uwe sits at the square table in the same baggy green sweater he's worn all week; a bakery sack holds his daily butter croissant and next to it sits a carton of chocolate milk. "I want you to write five sentences using the *Indikativ, Präteritum,* and *Konjunktiv II* forms of modal verbs," he says. "Remember what we talked about last week, this is the conditional form and needs a conjugated verb at the end. You can use either coordinating or subordinating conjunctions."

The girls around the table eagerly pick up their pens while I stare out the window hoping to be abducted by aliens.

Uwe swallows a sip of chocolate milk. "And I want examples with both singular and plural forms of *Sie* and *Du*."

Karin's handwriting is too small for me to see so I try calculating a sentence on my own.

"Time's up," Uwe says after three minutes, wadding his bakery sack into a ball. "Let's see what you've come up with."

I stare down at my notebook. Numbers two through five are still blank. I keep my eyes cast down, hoping he won't call on me.

"Beth," he says. "Give us your first sentence."

"Okay." I shift in my chair and clear my throat. "I would be happy if German so difficult to learn not was."

"Good. You got the structure right. Okay, Jun. You go next."

I let my breath out, unaware I had been holding it.

"Dr. Zimmerman got promoted to E-1 . . ." Marcus begins his nightly monologue of corporate gossip as we linger over our empty dinner plates.

Swirling my red wine around in my glass, I try to listen, but my mind keeps wandering to the question, "Will he do the dishes?"

When he finally pushes back his chair to leave the table, I swallow hard. I will myself to stay seated and "let him" do his part. He picks up our plates and carries them to the kitchen. The faucet running, I restrain from making any comments about the importance of water conservation as he cleans up.

When he's done he comes into the living room. Puffing up his chest, he says, "See? I *am* a good husband." We both start laughing.

"Oh, you are," I reply. "Now sit. Lie down." I push him onto the couch and climb on top of him. "Do you know how much an obedient man turns me on?" I purr in his ear, "Good husband, good husband . . ."

CHAPTER 6

Belated Honeymoon
in Costa Rica

H ORST INVITES US DOWN TO HIS VICARAGE IN
Alpirsbach where members of his congregation are
gathering for the annual fall *Schlachtfest*, a "slaughter festival."
Tradition goes that in earlier times, before refrigeration or fast
food, when an animal was killed, the parts that couldn't be preserved—smoked, canned, or dried—were made into sausages.
And because the sausages had to be eaten right away, the Germans found yet another food-related excuse to throw a party—
like they do for the harvest seasons of asparagus, onions, straw-
berries, cabbage, and grapes, and, naturally, *any* season for beer.

We step out of the car into the crisp Black Forest night. "It's
nice to be back here," I tell Marcus. "Hard to believe we got married here just two months ago." He pulls me into his arms and
as he kisses the back of my neck, I melt into his chest. We linger
a moment to look up at the *Klosterkirche's* pink stone tower, its

blue and gold medieval clock lit by a spotlight, before entering the warm vicarage where the party is already in progress. Vats of potatoes boil over propane burners and a keg of Alpirsbacher beer flows steadily in the corner. Marcus and I squeeze in between the other noisy guests at the long tables and benches set up in Horst's ample hallway where laughter and chatter echo off the stone walls.

Horst's seventeen-year-old son, Joe, carries baskets of brown farmer's bread out from the kitchen. His younger brother, Ben, follows with a steaming bowl of boiled potatoes. The sausage, loaded onto platters, is passed down the long line of tables by German-speaking parishioners of all ages. The white-haired man to my right asks me something I cannot understand—the Black Forest dialect is even more convoluted than the Swabian one. I just smile at him and nod, accepting the meat platter he hands to me.

Before I can take my first taste of freshly slaughtered pig remains, I need instructions for approaching the gastronomical experience. "First, you cut open the casing," Marcus says, poking his knife through the thin, rubbery exterior that looks like a condom but is made of intestines. "Then you scrape the meat out, like this." He holds the outer casing in place with his fork while using his knife to pull the soft, greasy pork-blend free. "Next, you mash up your potato a bit." He goes at it with his fork. "And then mix the meat together with the potato."

I follow his lead, but am interrupted by the old man to my right again. This time he passes a bowl of sauerkraut. "*Danke*," I say and set down the bowl between Marcus and me. I scoop out a spoonful of the dripping wet cabbage for each of us.

Horst spots us filling our plates, swoops over, and says, "The ladies from the next village over made this. It's a special white cabbage from this area. They marinated it for six weeks. Renate's kitchen is going to smell like the stuff for days."

"Where is Renate? We want to say hi to her," Marcus asks about Horst's wife, but Horst has already scurried away to chat with some of his other guests.

I take a bite of the sausage-potato combo, saving the sauerkraut for later. "Mmm, it's very . . . rich," I mumble with my mouth still full. "But it's tasty." It really is quite good. It's the kind of fill-your-belly food made for cold weather, a hearty meaty indulgence I would never speak of to my vegetarian friends back in L.A.

"It's liver sausage," says Marcus. "It's good for your iron count."

"I suppose that's a comforting thought," I reply. Sometimes, when it comes to certain German delicacies, like the pickled cow's stomach he fed me during my first visit, I'd rather not know what I'm eating.

"The sauerkraut is good for you too," he says when he sees me sniffing it and wrinkling my nose. "Its enzymes are very good for your digestion."

"Marcus and Beth, how are you two?" Carl Glauner, the CEO of Alpirsbacher Beer, approaches our table. Redheaded with wire-rim glasses, he looks more Bostonian than German in his navy blue sport coat, plaid shirt, and khaki pants. He carries two pitchers of beer, leans over us, and refills our glasses. "Glad you could make it down tonight."

"How's business?" Marcus asks.

"Good, good," he says. "Pretty tough competition with more than twelve hundred other breweries in Germany. We've gained some market share in the last quarter. We're exporting to China now."

"We're loyal customers," I say.

"I'm happy to hear that," he says, then wanders off to fill more glasses.

"What a nice evening," I tell Marcus on the drive home. "Alpirsbach is such a friendly community. Renate is so adorable. And Carl's wife is very cool. Katherine, right? She's gorgeous."

"She reminds me of Trish," he says.

"I know. Sounds like she's an incredible athlete."

"You should call her up. Go biking or hiking with her sometime," he says.

"I should." I don't tell him I probably won't, how fumbling with the language in the presence of a highly educated German sends my self-esteem into the toilet.

"Jun, do you ever get intimidated speaking German in front of other Germans?" I ask as soon as our coffee break starts.

"No. I don't care what they think about me," she says, pouring coffee into her cup. "And you shouldn't either."

"I envy your attitude," I say. "I don't know how living here doesn't get to you like it does me."

She's quiet for a minute then says, "You just need a break. Take it easy on yourself. Go enjoy your honeymoon with your husband and forget about Germany for a while."

A sea breeze rattles the closed blinds, letting intermittent rays of California sun into the dark guest room. I lift my head from the pillow just high enough to blow my nose. I wheeze, cough, and then drop the wadded up Kleenex onto the growing pile on the floor. Marcus rolls over, leaving a pool of sweat behind. He moans.

My mother stands in the doorway. "You've been sick for a whole week already. You're going to have to cancel your trip," she insists.

It's been six days since we left Germany. My excitement about being back—my plans for daily yoga classes, seeing friends, and last-minute Christmas shopping—are all stymied by some tenacious strain of the flu. "Stay here with us for a while," she continues, "then you can go to Palm Springs or Santa Barbara when you're better."

Marcus and I just lie there, too depleted of energy to argue her point. I had been looking forward to exploring a new country, someplace tropical, exotic. It would take some emotional wrestling to scale back my idea of exotic to a Moroccan-style hotel in Palm Springs. But the way we are feeling, we'll be lucky if we can even get that far. As it is, we barely muster enough strength to make it to the E.R.

Dr. Watson, the attending physician at the Marina del Rey Medical Center, saunters back to remove the thermometers left in our mouths. "Your fever is down to a hundred and one," he tells me. To Marcus he says, "But yours is a hundred and two. You have lung congestion and redness in the throat. I'll write you a note so you can get your airline refund. Where was it you said you were going?"

"Tamarindo, in Costa Rica," I answer.

His slouched back suddenly jerks upright. "There's an awesome surf break there! Let me tell you about this killer spot just south of there you should try."

"You mean you think we can still go?" Marcus asks.

"Oh yeah. You're fine." He leaves us sitting on the gurney, next to a ninety-year-old woman wearing an oxygen mask, and comes back with a blank piece of paper. "Now here's Turtle Beach," he says, drawing a map on the paper. "Just five miles down from here is Playa Avellena where they filmed *Endless Summer II*. The waves are usually good here."

"But won't we infect other passengers on the airplane?" I ask.

"Naw," he says.

"What about infectious diseases in Costa Rica? Maybe we'll get even sicker," I say, remembering the acute amoebic dysentery I picked up in Africa.

"You'll be fine. Now, if you go further south to Santa Teresa, there's another great surf spot . . ." He is so excited to have someone to whom he can administer his salt-water prescription, he practically follows us out to the car.

"Some honeymoon this is. You won't even talk to me," I say to Marcus from my lounge chair next to his. We've parked ourselves at a beachfront bungalow in Tamarindo for four days, taking time to recover.

"Just let me get to the end of this chapter," he replies, turning another page of *Angels and Demons*.

"Dan Brown has ruined my vacation," I tell him. "I'm a Dan Brown widow." I chatter on to his deaf ears as he continues reading and look back at my own novel. "Too bad I got stuck with this book. It's about a woman who is unhappy in her marriage and cheating on her husband. I don't know why my sister thought I would like this."

I stop talking and watch a pair of giant green iguanas walk by. They're inches from our chairs, but since we were told they're harmless I stay still and study them with fascination. As big as a human baby, the male moves slowly, one webbed foot at a time, his tail dragging on the sand behind him, his tongue slithering in and out of his mouth; his mate saunters along beside him. They look like a happy couple; maybe they're newlyweds too.

"Okay," Marcus says setting his book down. "I'm done with the chapter."

"Do you want to go surfing?" I ask.

"I don't really feel up to it yet," he says. "How about you?"

"No, and I'm so bummed," I reply. "One of the main reasons I wanted to come to Costa Rica was to surf, but I still feel so weak."

"Do you have enough energy to walk up to that day spa and get a massage?" he asks.

"Do you think you can part with Dan long enough?" I ask back.

"Just wait until you start reading it," he replies. "Then you'll understand." He flashes a smile at me that makes me smile back. This is the kind of banter I love with him.

With our energy restored, we head further south to a town called Montezuma and check in to a small hotel, a collection of thatched-roof huts called Los Mangos. "Look, they have yoga here," I tell Marcus as he hands over his credit card to secure a three-night stay. I pick up a flyer announcing a two-hour Christmas Eve class, and sign us up for it immediately.

If we were in Germany, we would be in downtown Stuttgart, at the Christmas Market. It runs for a month during advent up until the twenty-third of December, so I was able to go with Marcus the year before, when I visited for Thanksgiving. Several squares in the city center are transformed into a holiday wonderland with millions of twinkling lights strung around the buildings. Christmas trees, garlands, nativity scenes and an ice skating rink bring life to the old castles and churches, and make the more bland post-war architecture glow with a magical elegance. Wooden huts and stalls pack the square, with vendors selling everything from nuts and nutcracker figurines to heart-shaped gingerbread cookies called *Lebkuchen*, Christmas ornaments, sausages and cheeses, wooden toys, and other gifts of all kinds. On an icy night, dressed in our thick wool coats, our bodies pressed together by the throng of shoppers, Marcus and I ate bratwurst and drank Glühwein (hot spiced wine) and Mead (hot honey wine, a beverage that's been around since at least 2,000 B.C.), and took in the festive atmosphere. Everyone was smiling. And nice. Christmas in Germany really is, like the song goes, "the most wonderful time of the year." But not as wonderful as being in Costa Rica.

We are in Los Mangos' open-air yoga pavilion where, instead of Christmas lights, pine boughs, and snow, we are surrounded by lit candles and red bougainvillea, and warmed by the tropical breeze. I lay my mat down on the polished mahogany floor next to a man sitting in lotus position, his eyes closed as he breathes in and out. I work my legs into a pretzel while watching Marcus unroll his mat. His black bike-style shorts cling to his thick thighs and a black tank top accentuates his broad shoulders. A warrior-style red headband holds back his brown hair. The intense guy in the suit I'm used to seeing every day has morphed into a laid-back cover model for *Men's Health* magazine.

"Hey, gorgeous," I say. "Welcome to your first yoga class."

Marcus follows along easily receiving only a few adjustments; the willowy instructor, Dagmar—who is from Germany!—hikes up his hips during a high lunge and gently straightens his arms in Crescent pose. We chant oms, and after a deliciously long, relaxing final Savasana, we're served juicy slices of watermelon.

After class Marcus walks toward me, gracefully, mindfully, practically levitating from his newfound yoga high. "Merry Christmas, my love," he says, kissing me tenderly.

"You did great," I tell him, tasting his sweat on my lips. "You took to it so naturally."

"I got a black belt in Tae Kwan Do when I was young."

"I didn't know that! Aren't you full of surprises?"

"I'm sure I have a lot more to learn about you too," he says.

Across the street from Los Mangos is a beachfront restaurant called Playa de Los Artistas. With sand for a floor and sky for a ceiling, it is completely outdoors and lit only by candles. We kick off our sandals, sit on asymmetrical driftwood furniture, and are served a whole fish so big its head and tail hang off the ends of the platter.

"Besides last year at my cabin in Seattle—remember when it snowed and you shucked all those oysters?—this is the best Christmas I've ever had," I say, holding up my gin and tonic to clink glasses.

"Mine too," he says. "And don't forget, it's also our honeymoon." In the candlelight I can see his eyes well up with tears. "I am so happy to be married to you."

I'm happy to be married, too. Married to Marcus, *this* Marcus—the Marcus on vacation. This is the man I fell in love with, the man with time for adventure, laughter, and sex. Here, away from the stress of German life—him from the demands of his work, me from dirty dishes and my *Themen Neu 2* textbook—we reconnect. It may only be for a few weeks, but I'm grateful for the reminder of how good we are together.

A few days later, on Costa Rica's southern Península d'Osa, we cram into the bed of a pick-up truck—a *colectivo* taxi—with eight other passengers including locals wearing gum boots and carrying machetes, and backpacking tourists like us. Bouncing along on a rutted dirt road, the deeper we drive into the rainforest the more Technicolor the colors become. Zip-a-dee-doo-dah, baby! It's like Uncle Remus in that 1940s movie, *Song of the South*—we are real but everything around us is animated.

Screeching cries come from above and we look up to see our first pair of scarlet macaws, the unmistakable parrot breed with flamboyant red bodies and rainbow wing feathers, gliding in tandem.

Two and a half hours later the *colectivo* drops us off in the town of Carate. What they call a town, we would call an intersection. A rickety wooden shack selling only bottled water and crackers sits at this junction of two dirt roads. Opposite is an airstrip where several horses graze on the grass growing between cracks in the asphalt. Our *colectivo* is met by a group of jungle-weary travelers who seem suspiciously anxious to make the return trip to Puerto Jiménez. In their mud-caked Teva sandals and ragged khaki shorts, they can barely wait for us to unload our gear before they clamber into the truck.

We are heading to the Corcovado Lodge Tent Camp. Without a reservation. At Christmas. It's a place I had seen on the cover of *Travel & Leisure* years earlier; set against a backdrop of a lush jungle were romantic safari-like white canvas platform tents illuminated from within by lanterns. Glamping by the sea.

Shouldering our backpacks, Marcus and I begin the trudge up the wild beach. We walk for forty-five minutes seeing only sand, sea, and palm trees. There is not a soul in sight, let alone a store, a telephone, a light bulb—or a hotel. It starts to rain.

"Are you sure it's this way?" Marcus asks, his mood dimming along with the darkness. It's times like these I remind myself his Zodiac sign is Cancer; he can't help his desire to retreat to the comfort of his shell.

"This is the direction the taxi driver pointed," I say. I wipe the rain from my eyes as it comes down harder.

"We don't have any food with us," he reminds me.

"I know," I say, still plodding along with determination. "I thought the store in Carate would actually be a store." Just then a man passes us in a horse cart; he is heading in our same direction and he's hauling luggage. "Hey, that's a good sign," I say perking up. Marcus looks only slightly encouraged.

We walk another ten minutes in silence when lights come into view ahead. "Maybe that's it," I say. We get closer. "It *is* it!" There are the white tents whose image I carried in my mind for so long. The tents are indeed aglow, but the white canvas is graying and weathered, and they are *much* closer together than they appeared in the magazine photo. Wet towels and T-shirts hang on clotheslines between the tents, and cheap plastic chairs, some tipped over, are scattered on the lawn. We climb the stairs to the main lodge. There are wooden tables and a full bar, and though it's approaching dinnertime, there is no sign of any meal preparation. There is no sign of any life at all.

"It smells bad," Marcus says.

"Yeah, it does," I reply.

"Like ammonia mixed with dead fish."

We can't find a reception area, but we finally spot a young woman sweeping rainwater off the steps. *"Hola! Tiene una habitación libre?"* I ask her, reading the question straight off the back page of my Spanish pocket dictionary.

"No. Is full," she answers in abbreviated English. "No room until February."

"Maybe you will still get a cancellation tonight?" She looks at me with uncomprehending brown eyes. I persist. "Do you know of anything? Any place?"

"*Esta* new camp," she says. "Five minutes down beach."

We continue in the dark toward the national park, the *wilderness*. "You wanted to get away from Germany," Marcus says. "This is as far as you're going to get."

I would laugh, because his comment is funny, but right now I'm more worried about the predicament I've gotten us into.

We walk no more than thirty seconds before spotting another camp. A freshly painted wooden sign announces La Leona Lodge and a lantern-lit trail marks our way. "That was a short five minutes," I say brightly.

We pass by pristine canvas platform tents. The rain has stopped and guests are dining outside at picnic tables, their plates heaping with fish, rice, and salad.

We are instantly welcomed by Mario, a jovial, round man in a white chef's jacket worn with shorts. "You're on your honeymoon? In that case, I have a special tent for you." He shows us to a brand new white canvas tent, built on a platform with floor-to-ceiling mosquito-net windows.

The next morning, relaxing on our front porch in the sun, drinking coffee, Marcus says, "I'm sorry if I doubted you. This is paradise."

"Um, excuse me, but can't you see I'm reading? Please do not disturb me." I smile without looking at him and put my nose back in *Angels and Demons*.

"Now you know what it feels like," he says, laughing.

We both look up as yet another pair of squawking scarlet macaws flies overhead. Corcovado National Park has the highest concentration of them in the world, since deforestation and poaching has diminished their numbers elsewhere. "It sure is hard to read here," I tease.

We are soon interrupted again. "The monkeys are back," Marcus says. A gang of Capuchin monkeys scrambles out of the trees. These clever little black-bodied, white-faced cuties are on a mission. We watch as they sneak through the kitchen's lattice window coverings, knowing that Chef Mario has left his banana stash unguarded.

"Look!" says Marcus. "Look at what they're doing." The monkeys, back up in the trees with their booty, are peeling the bananas and throwing the skins onto the lodge's roof. "Audacious little buggers."

"Almost as entertaining as a Dan Brown novel," I say. "I have to finish this damn book or I'm never going to know I was here."

Mario makes us a big tropical fruit salad for lunch. Afterward he gets on his hand-held radio, putting out a signal to Luna Lodge. We read about this pricey eco-lodge—and their yoga classes—in our *Lonely Planet* guidebook. A woman answers Mario's crackly call.

Mario: "Did you say 4:30 p.m.? Over."

Luna Lodge: "Roger."

Mario: "Thank you. Over and out."

"Okay, you're in," Mario says to us.

Daily yoga classes at sunset. Perfect.

The fer-de-lance is the most dangerous snake of Central and South America, and is said to cause more human fatalities than any other American reptile. A member of the pit viper group, it can sense the body heat of a passing victim to strike at the warm-blooded prey. A fer-de-lance can reach up to nine feet in length and the species is very common in this part of Costa Rica.

To get to yoga, we walk in the steamy afternoon heat the mile back to Carate and another mile up a mountain road. In this seemingly uninhabited jungle sits Luna Lodge, a secluded collection of thatched-roof huts, luxurious by jungle standards. We negotiate with Lana, the perky blond lodge owner from Colorado, for a ten-day package of yoga classes that will include dinner afterward.

Higher up on the mountain, above the huts, a yoga platform supported by stilts juts out over the treetops. "Okay, we can pause for a moment," the instructor says when he sees that everyone has already broken the Warrior One pose to watch a pair of orange-beaked toucans nesting at eye level with us. "I don't normally do this, but go ahead and look," he says, pausing the class again when a family of orange squirrel monkeys swings through the branches. By the end of the session, the sun has set over the ocean, the sky darkens to orange then black. We dine on fish and organic vegetables before beginning the trek home.

The journey back to our La Leona camp is much different at night. We have only the thin beam of light from our headlamps to navigate back down the dirt road. The jungle, alive with foreign sounds, closes in around us. Shrieks of howler monkeys echo through the trees. Flapping wings of vampire bats whoosh by our heads.

"What was that?!" I gasp, instinctively grabbing Marcus' arm for protection.

"It was just a leaf," he says.

"It sounded like a large animal."

"I thought you were a nature girl."

"I'm out of practice," I reply.

We keep walking, ticking off the twenty or so crossings of the meandering river, stopping at each crossing to soak our feet and splash the cool water on our faces. The moon lights our way down the mile-long stretch of beach until we see the torchlights of La Leona camp where Mario is waiting up for us.

"You walked in *those* shoes?" he asks, looking down at our flip-flops. "You need to be more careful. The snakes come out at night; they hunt by the river. We have some knee-high rubber boots back in the shed. Help yourselves to a pair."

"We wondered why all the locals were wearing those big boots in this hot weather," I say.

"And watch yourselves with those headlamps," he continues. "Snakes equate light with heat and they'll come toward a flashlight."

We listen with new interest to the local snake lore, stories that dominate the conversation at every meal, stories of people who were bitten. We hear about the Luna Lodge groundskeeper who accidentally stepped on a fer-de-lance a year earlier. He screamed in agony as the *colectivo* bumped along the dirt track, a two-and-a-half hour drive to the nearest anti-venom. The rain had washed out the road in several places and, on the brink of death with poison burning through his puffed-up body, he had to get out and help push the truck! Once he reached Puerto Jiménez, they stabilized him enough to fly him to a bigger hospital and after three weeks of treatment he is now a living legend.

For the next few days, we complete the four-mile round-trip hike in gumboots.

"Are you scared?" I ask Marcus as we pick our way down the dirt road in the dark.

"No," he says. "Are you?"

"Are you kidding?" I say, bursting out in nervous laughter. "I haven't been this terrified since Miguel and I were camping in Kenya." I don't elaborate about the lions and how they killed a warthog a mere one hundred feet away from where we slept in our camp cots, and how our only protection from the man-eating wildlife was a thin layer of mosquito netting—and an armed safari guide who slept with ear plugs. My heart races just thinking about it.

On the seventh night, we see a snake on the road, a small one. It slithers away rapidly into the thick, leafy undergrowth. "Do you think it was a fer-de-lance?" Marcus asks.

"I think so. It had those black triangle markings."

"But it was small," he says.

"Yeah. You know what that means," I tell him. "The younger the snake, the more concentrated its venom."

We have three more pre-paid nights of yoga and dinners

scheduled, but our enthusiasm to continue the routine is suddenly diminished.

When we hike up to the lodge again the next day we talk with Lana. "Yes, there are plenty of snakes out there," she says. "They come into the lodge sometimes. We had a jaguar come through here once, too."

She's not helping any.

"Your chances of getting a snakebite are as high as getting struck by lightning," she continues, sensing our discomfort. "But I'll get Stefano to drive you down the hill tonight. He can take you as far as the beach."

After dinner, we climb onto the back of a quad bike, the lodge's all-terrain vehicle. Marcus and I grip the frame as Stefano speeds down the bumpy road. "Hello there, snakes! Ha, ha, ha!" I yell to the river as we whiz through it, water splashing over the bike. I look over at Marcus; the wind is blowing his hair back and he is laughing. "I LOVE YOU!" I shout over the sound of the wind and the motor.

"I LOVE YOU, TOO!" he shouts back.

Stefano drops us off at the mouth of the river where it meets the beach. We cross the river down by the ocean's edge, out of snake range. And because it's so shallow, we don't have to worry about the crocodiles either. But hundreds of small crabs rush in and out of little holes in the sand, so we leave our gumboots on for the sandy walk back to camp.

The sun rises over the coconut palms. While we're sipping our morning coffee we see a commotion over at the woodpile between our tent and the dining hall. We join the other camp guests and staff members huddled together, peering down at something—a black and brown snake curled up on a log. "You have a fer-de-lance living next door," Mario reports. "And see this?" He points to a higher spot on the woodpile where there's a tiny bright enamel-blue frog. We look without coming any closer. "It's a poison-arrow frog," he says. "The Indians used to put its poison on the ends of their arrows to kill their enemies. Don't touch it. If you get its poison in your eyes you'll go blind."

Our Poison Species List grows a few hours later when Marcus finds a scorpion in the bathhouse. For the remainder of our stay, I don't set foot outside the tent at night, no matter how badly I have to pee.

For our last night in Costa Rica, Mario has insisted on preparing us a special honeymoon dinner. He sets up a table for two, away from the main dining area, surrounded by a wall of palm leaves for privacy. He has placed hibiscus flowers everywhere; red blooms cover the table, hang from the palms, and carpet the ground. "Dinner will be ready in one hour," he says.

"Okay, then we'll go for one last swim," Marcus tells him.

Corcovado's waters are wild and temperamental. I'm a strong swimmer, but my instincts tell me to stay inside the whitewater zone. Marcus goes further out to body surf. I dunk a few times to cool off, holding on tight to my bikini to keep the waves from ripping it off. Even in calf-deep water, I have to fight against the undertow to get back to the black-sand beach. "I should go get one of those boogie boards up at the camp, in case Marcus needs it," I think. But since I get glimpses of him in between the troughs, I ignore my instinct and savor the sunset.

About twenty minutes later, Marcus staggers onto the beach and flops down next to me, his chest heaving up and down. "I almost drowned!" he pants, his eyes wide, his voice shaky. "I've been trying to get to shore this whole time."

I move close to him and stroke his cheek. I say softly, "That's so strange, because I just had this scary feeling that I could lose you."

"I need a few minutes to recover," he says, shaking his head.

"Take your time."

As we sit in stillness, the sea continues its relentless roil. The heaviness of salt, humidity, and near-death settles on our skin. The coastline of coconut palms fades into a silhouette as darkness falls. Marcus' breath slows to a gentler pace, his muscles surrender their tension. I say silent prayers of gratitude to whatever God is out there: "Thank you for keeping my husband alive."

We gorge on Mario's feast of macadamia crusted fish and grilled prawns. "Who would ever guess we'd eat such a gourmet meal in the jungle?" I rave to Mario.

"I used to be the chef for the Belgian ambassador in San José," he says. "And now for dessert." He sets down a chocolate cake decorated with a plastic bridal couple on top.

"I wasn't sure I was going to live to see this dinner, Mario." Marcus tells him about his death-defying swim.

"There was a lady from Switzerland who drowned in that same spot about a month ago."

"You're telling us this *now*?" I exclaim.

Mario continues, "Helicopters came, and boats, but they couldn't find her. A week later, they found half of her body. They think a shark might have gotten her."

We return to our tent to find our king-size bed decorated with more red hibiscus flowers, laid out in a heart design on top of the white sheets.

"That was so cute of him," Marcus says.

"Yes," I reply, "but if Mario thinks we're going to make any babies tonight, well . . ."

"I know," Marcus says wiping sweat from his arms with a bandana. "You don't have to tell me. It's still ninety degrees."

"And 100 percent humidity."

"Did you see how wet my clothes are? Nothing ever dries here." He re-seals his backpack and lies down. I lie down next to him, but keep my distance to avoid any extra body heat.

"Did you check under the bed before you turned off your headlamp?" I ask.

"Yes. All clear."

"I'm ready to go back to civilization," I tell him as we lie there in the dark. "I want to be able to get through a day without fearing for my life." I have a sudden flashback to our arrival in Carate. "Now I know why those people were so anxious to get in the *colectivo* that day we got here."

"You read what it said in the guidebook, didn't you?" he asks.

"Don't go to Costa Rica on your honeymoon because it's too hot to have sex?"

"It says this area is the most biologically intense place on Earth."

"And whose idea was it to come here?" I reply.

"Yours," he says.

"Oh, yeah."

In spite of the stresses of the Central American jungle, the break from all things German has been restorative. We return to L.A. together in good health, still savoring the melodies of the Spanish language and the gracious Costa Rican hospitality. Upon our return, L.A. presents its own surprising form of hospitality: my mother. On Sunday morning when mass is over, she returns home with a bag of Krispy Kreme donuts—just for Marcus. "You didn't get to try these before you left for your trip," she coos to him. "But now that you're feeling better, I thought you'd like to see for yourself what everyone's been talking about. Here, try one." She sets a plate stacked high with glazed donuts in front of him on the dining room table. He's still in his pajamas and he has a full-blown case of bed head. "Let me get my camera," she says. "You look so good with that suntan." She rushes off to her bedroom and comes back to take a picture of him holding up a donut. "Let me make you some coffee," she says.

I must have a fever; maybe I picked up malaria, because what I'm witnessing cannot really be happening. My mother has gone from disapproving to doting. No, really, I must be delirious. I put my hand to my forehead. No fever. Either we've passed some test of hers by surviving our first six months together or she just hasn't talked to Sigrid for awhile.

"I'll make the coffee," I offer, getting up from the table. "You two just sit there and enjoy yourselves."

Marcus flies back to Stuttgart for work and I stay an extra week in California with my family. I fill my time with my usual energizing, action-packed routine: lunch with my mom, a manicure/pedicure with my sister, the latest movies with my dad, surfing with my brother Miguel—and power yoga classes with my friend Trish.

Sweat pours from my eyelids. My quadriceps, locked in a particularly long Warrior Two position, are on fire. "Take it deeper now," instructs my favorite yoga instructor, Vinnie, talking above Sting whose music blares through the speakers. "Pretend you have a silver tray with a stevia latte balancing on your thigh." The whole class bursts into laughter, but no one breaks the pose.

"What the hell is stevia?" Trish whispers from her mat, still snickering.

"I have no idea," I whisper back with a smile.

Standing outside on the busy Santa Monica sidewalk after class, Trish says, "I wish you didn't have to go back to Germany."

"I know. But at least I got to stay here an extra week. And as much as I want to stay, I miss Marcus," I say. "Do you have time to go out for a glass of wine?"

"I can't."

"How come?"

She pauses. "I'm pregnant."

"What?" My eyes widen. Last I knew she hadn't forgiven her husband for his affair.

"I know. I was surprised too."

"That's great!" I lie. "It will be so nice for Emily to have a sibling."

"I didn't want to tell you before, because I know you've been trying," she says.

"No, no," I say, shaking off her comment. "I have enough to adjust to without adding a baby to the mix." It's true. Marcus and I have been trying to conceive since *before* we got married. Eight well-timed ovulations so far, but still nothing. I may be forty-one, but I'm not panicked. "Besides," I continue, "we've talked about it and we've agreed that having a baby isn't our ultimate goal. If we get pregnant, great. If we don't, we're okay with that too."

"That's a good attitude," she says. She gives me a sweaty hug. "It was great to spend some time with you."

"You too."

I watch her drive away in her Range Rover. To her Santa Monica mansion. To her household staff. To her unfaithful husband, who is surely at the moment sitting in front of the huge plasma screen TV watching a football game. As her car disappears into the traffic, it occurs to me that my life in Germany—workaholic spouse, language classes, grumpy store clerks, and all—is actually pretty good.

CHAPTER 7

Munich

THE AIRBUS 340 CUTS THROUGH A THICK BANK OF dark clouds covering Stuttgart's skyline like a wooly military-issue blanket. I hand my American passport to the immigration officer clad in his muted green uniform. He turns each page, stopping when he reaches the one with my German residency stamp on it, then without a trace of emotion or even a passing glance of eye contact he waves me through.

The baggage claim hall is bone-chilling cold and filled with the stench of cigarette smoke. People with pale, pasty winter complexions wear black or gray coats and sullen expressions.

I can't find my token for a luggage cart deposit. I dig in every pocket of my purse until I find a one-euro coin and wheel a cart over to the baggage carousel, but after thirty minutes my duffel bags never show up. I keep the cart anyway to haul my laptop and purse, and follow the signs to Lost Luggage, which, oddly, route me to a back door. I poke my head inside. A woman's voice erupts immediately. "You cannot come in here! Dis is not zee entrance. You must go to zee front door."

"But the sign said . . ." I protest.

Grumbling to myself out loud, I return down the long, dimly lit hallway, back into baggage claim area and out the other side, through customs, to the *front* door of the office. I don't get stopped by *der Zollbeamte*, but if my bags were here I could be fined for bringing in two pounds of Costa Rican coffee, which I admit to knowing is one pound over Germany's legal limit. *Does decaf count?*

I wheel the cart inside Lufthansa's customer service office and take my turn with the airline representative—a young brunette in a blue uniform. "Your bags vill come on dee nextes flight from London," she says.

From behind, an older man growls at me, "Can't you read the sign?" He points to the tiny *Gepäckwagen verboten* icon on the window. German Rule No. 799: Luggage carts must be left outside the customer service office. Every head in the room turns to look at me.

The honeymoon, as they say, is over.

"You were very brave to move there," Trish has told me more than once. "I could never do it."

I turn her words into a mantra: "You're so brave. You can do it. You're so brave. You can do it." I repeat it over and over, the rhythmic chant gaining momentum, as I wait outside in the cold for Marcus to arrive.

I don't consider myself brave. I just have a love for travel, for foreign places (even difficult ones), and for shunning routine as soon as it sets in. And yet, I also have a love of returning home. In my previous globetrotting days I could return home whenever the time felt right, even if it meant quitting a job or leaving a lover. Now I'm committed to Marcus. I'm committed to his country—and to his career schedule. Seventeen more months and we're out of here.

You're so brave. You can do it.

I sit down on the edge of my luggage cart, pulling my coat tighter around me. A man in a black leather jacket walks by and tosses his smoldering cigarette butt. It lands right by my feet.

You're so brave. You can do it.

A few weekend outings with Marcus ease me back into Stuttgart life. I savor the time with my husband, especially as my role as *Hausfrau* hasn't resumed. Yet. We go out for a drink Saturday night at Bistro 21, a piano bar on the top floor of the eight-story train station tower. We take a Sunday morning walk down to Bürkle, our neighborhood bakery. (This is a treat as bakeries are the *only* businesses besides gas stations allowed to be open on Sundays. Even so, this law was only passed several years earlier when bakeries successfully argued that gas stations sold fresh *Brötchen*—bread rolls—on Sundays, thus cutting into their Saturday business, so they should be allowed Sunday business too.) We bring home a loaf of *Hefezopf*, a sweet, yeasty, braided egg bread to eat with our breakfast of boiled eggs, cheese, yogurt, and café lattes. After an afternoon walk in the ice-covered vineyards, we stop at our favorite Turkish snack bar and eat Germany's version of fast food—*yufkas*, like lamb burritos. And we resume our Sunday night routine of eating Vietnamese take-out in bed while watching the weekly crime series *Tatort*. With the TV's subtitle function I can read the German words as they're spoken.

"What are you thinking of doing, now that you're back?" Marcus asks as he gets ready for work Monday morning.

"I don't know," I say. "Ask me again in three weeks when I get over this jet lag."

The German word for "happy" and "lucky" is the same: *glücklich*. The word for "if" and "when" is the same: *wenn*. This makes it difficult to be precise about what you want to convey. "If" means it *could* happen, but "when" means it will or already did happen. "Happy" is a feeling, but "luck" is chance. I feel *happy* when my husband does the dishes. I feel *lucky* I was born in America, not in Kosovo, Iraq, or Afghanistan, lucky that learning German for me is purely a choice and not a desperate means to get a job, feed my family, or pursue religious or political freedom.

I take the U-Bahn downtown to the *Volkshochschule* to register for yet another intensive German course. (This will be my fourth, after taking the two courses in Germany, plus the community college "Introduction to German" semester I took in Seattle.) I have a certificate from my last *Volkshochschule* summer course that says I am eligible to sign up for *Deutsch Intensiv IV*. I do not, however, have the certificate *with* me.

"Can I just fax it to you later?" I ask the woman behind the glass window, already regretting not going back to the more expensive Fokus, in spite of being triple the cost.

"*Nein*," she says through the speaker box.

"Can't you check your computer records and see that I took Level Three this past summer? The teacher's name was Thilo Keyser. Just check."

"*Nein*. You must come back with the document."

"Fuck you," I say. No, I don't say that. Well, I *do* say it, but I wait until I am outside on the street. A bundled up bicycle messenger hears and scowls at me, which makes me want to say fuck you to him too. But I don't.

German Rule No. 552: All documentation must be presented at time of registration.

One thing you never do in Germany is joke about Jews. Ever. Besides being in very poor taste, anyone speaking derogatorily about them will be considered a Nazi sympathizer and will likely be detained. Moreover, anyone publicly denying the Holocaust will go to prison. Marcus didn't hear his first Jewish joke until he moved to London and he was shocked, until he realized it was only taboo in Germany, but not in the U.K. Germany takes its history seriously, so seriously it has established Days of Remembrance and erected numerous memorial monuments in city centers—so no one will forget. (No one will forget as long as Steven Spielberg is still making films.) In spite of this zero tolerance *for* Nazis, it is surprisingly acceptable—even welcome—to make jokes *about* Nazis. When *Seinfeld* aired in Germany, I would have thought the recurring character, the abrasive New York deli cook called the Soup Nazi, would be censored, but his name was merely translated to *der Suppen Nazi*. I've found the perfect mate for him: the School Registration Nazi.

It starts to snow. I call Marcus. I complain about the *Volkshochschule* woman and about the snow. "It's not snowing at my office," he says.

I get the hint. He can't talk from his open cubicle space. Still, his inability to soothe me stings like the snowflakes hitting my face. Will he get a private office when he gets promoted so we can talk during the day? And will that even make a difference?

I go over to Café Nescafe to ease my defeat. "I'll have a *Schokolade heiss, bitte*."

"You mean *Heisseschokolade*," replies the teenage German cashier.

"*Ja*." Who am I to sign up for Intensive IV? I can't even order hot chocolate.

I go back to the *Volkshochschule* the next day with my certificate. The same woman is working, her hair pulled into a tight bun, her plastic rim glasses pushed close to her ruddy face. I hand her my papers, avoiding any eye contact. I am calm and confident. I have everything I need now. Except the name of the bank.

In Germany, you don't write checks, and credit or debit card use is still uncommon in many places, particularly at government institutions like *Volkshochschule*. To pay for things like German classes you transfer money from your bank account, called a *Konto*, directly to theirs. You need your account number, your bank routing number, and the name of your bank. The *exact* name.

Our bank account is in the village next to Marcus' parents' village, about thirty miles from Stuttgart. This bank recently merged with another and its new name does not appear on my papers, nor is it recognized by *Volkshochschule's* computer system.

With the Registration Nazi waiting, I call Marcus from my cell phone. He doesn't answer. Defeated again, I leave, returning to Café Nescafe for a *cappuccino*, thank you, and wait for him to call me back.

I contemplate the months that lie ahead. The winter intensive semester lasts four months. That's four hours of grammar a day for twenty weeks. Twenty! Plus homework. Plus commuting time. By the time Marcus calls—and suggests meeting me for a drink as long as I'm downtown—my calculations have blown into an existential quandary: What the hell am I doing with my life?!

I don't want learning German to be my *raison d'être*. I don't want to be a perpetual student of this difficult, foreign language. No one warned me that learning German would be so much harder than French. I am more fluent in French after forty hours of lessons than I am after four hundred in German. Even my high school Spanish is better than my German.

After three cappuccinos I smear on a fresh layer of Viva Glam lipstick and make my way over to meet Marcus. Shuffling through the thin layer of snow, the resolution hits me just as I reach for the school's door handle: *"Ich muss sprechen!"* I have to speak! For God's sake, communicating is what I do for a living. I let out a deep sigh before going inside, my foggy breath shooting out into the cold air like dragon fire. Yes, German is hard, but I have to stick with it. Learning the language is the only way I will ever feel at home here.

The Treffpunkt Café lies on the second floor of the *Volkshochschule*. By day, the place is a basic school cafeteria with the ultra-modern, public-building décor of cold gray concrete. But by night, it's transformed into a romantic bar with thick white candles glowing on every table.

Marcus strides in with the air of a man about to get a promotion, his gray wool suit and white shirt looking as crisp as they did first thing in the morning. He sits down and peruses the drink menu, even though there's no question he will order a pilsner. Before the waitress even reaches our table I launch into yet another rant about my frustrations with school. It takes me mere seconds to get myself worked up into a frenzy. "I'm never going to adjust to living here," I cry. "I cannot grasp this language, and I cannot mesh with this culture. When can we move somewhere else?"

So much for my resolve.

He takes my hand and squeezes it. He's quiet for a moment; his almond green eyes lock onto me as if to keep me from jumping off the ledge. "Let's take the 720 euros you would have spent for the class and put them toward a private instructor," he says. "The classroom setting isn't working for you."

I wipe a tear from eye. "That sounds like a good idea," I say.

This is why I love Marcus. His calm demeanor, his problem-solving skills, and his ability to ease my anguish are a marvel.

"And I will try to speak more German with you," he adds. "I

want to help you, my cute little thing. I want you to be happy. And I'll try to leave the office earlier."

Liberated from school, I take the train to Munich to attend a sporting goods trade show. I have plans to meet up with a German journalist named Niels who has offered to help me drum up some freelance work. I had hoped to see Bob there, a friend in Los Angeles who owns a snowboard company. When I called to inquire if he was coming, I told him I was living in Stuttgart. He laughed so hard I had to hold the phone away from my ear.

"You must be bored out of your mind!" he howled.

I considered his statement for a moment, mulling over Stuttgart's biggest selling points—that it's a one-and-a-half hour-drive to France, four to Italy. So I just said, "It's not that bad."

It's probably just as well he isn't coming.

Munich is about twice the size of Stuttgart, with a population of 1.3 million compared to Stuttgart's 590,000. Stuttgart may be closer to France, but Munich is a forty-five-minute drive to some of the best skiing and most scenic hiking in the Alps. It's also less than two hours to Italy. I sigh at the thought of all that red wine, pasta, and the fabulous shoes.

Munich is like a mini Paris. There's Maximilianstrasse with its Louis Vuitton and Chanel boutiques, and old-world department stores like Alois Dallmayr and Lodenfrey (where Marcus bought his wedding attire). The city's well-preserved civic buildings and art museums, spared from World War II bombings, run the length of entire blocks. Saint Michael's Church, a landmark with towering twin domes set against a backdrop of snow-capped mountains, can be seen from miles away. And there's the Rathaus-Glockenspiel on the Marienplatz.

I visited Marienplatz, this medieval town square, in 1983 (a mere 825 years after the square was built) with my grand-parents. They invited me on their autumn bus tour of Europe, traveling through the German parts—Austria, Liechtenstein, Switzerland, and Germany. In Munich, the forty octogenarians and I followed in line behind our guide and her flagpole to the glockenspiel. Sandwiched in with the other tourists packed onto Marienplatz, we waited on the hard, cold cobblestones for the clock to strike eleven. My grandmother in her wool beret, my grandfather in his gray fedora, and I stood with our faces tipped up toward the spire-filled sky. At eleven sharp we watched the thirty-two life-size mechanical figures—jousting knights, danc-ing men, and a bridal couple—spin and rotate around the clock tower on top of the red stone *Neues Rathaus* (that's New City Hall and in Germany anything built in 1908 is still considered new). We listened as the bells chimed for a full fifteen minutes, clanging out a melody like a supersize musical jewelry box. We snapped a few pictures. Then we got back on the bus.

Twenty years later, standing on the same cold cobblestones, I look up as the clock strikes eleven and the bells begin their chime, and for a brief, comforting moment, I imagine that my grandparents are standing next to me.

Munich, ranked as one of Europe's Most Livable Cities, is the capital of Bavaria, Germany's richest state. Bavaria excels at marketing itself. Every stereotype Americans have about Germany inevitably points to something Bavarian. Oktoberfest, Germany's most famous and largest beer festival, is Bavarian. The name Oktoberfest is trademarked, so Germany's second largest beer festival—held in Stuttgart, also in October—calls itself *Volksfest* (People's Festival) instead. During Oktoberfest more than six million people crowd into huge, temporary tents set up in Munich's *Theresienwiesen*, a giant meadow within the city limits.

Lederhosen, those signature brown (or khaki green) leather shorts and pants with suspenders? They are Bavarian. On Sundays in the mountain towns outside of Munich, men wear them with wool knee socks and hiking boots to the bar. They meet up with their friends for a *Stammtisch*, a regular meeting held at a reserved table where they talk soccer and politics over beer—while their wives are at church. When the ladies show up later, they are dressed in traditional *Trachten* clothing too, in their rather sexy *Dirndl* dresses.

The car and motorcycle company BMW—*Bayerische Motoren Werke*—is Bavarian, though non-German-speaking BMW drivers probably never make the connection even though it's right there in the name since *Bayerische* means Bavarian.

And when we joke that Germans drink beer and eat sausage for breakfast, well, it is true—in Bavaria. A Sunday specialty in beer gardens, *Weisswurst,* is white sausage, served with fresh-baked pretzels and Hefeweizen beer. Beer gardens are another well-marketed aspect of this area and not typical in other parts of the country; there are none to be found in some areas of the north. But ask an American and they think Germany is full of them.

Bavaria has charm. Munich has elegance. And Stuttgart has my husband.

Marcus actually suggested we rent an apartment in Munich, that I could live there and we would see each other on weekends. While I appreciated his attempt at a solution, my answer was an immediate no. "I didn't move to Germany to live alone," I told him. So Stuttgart is where we live. For better or for worse. For richer or for poorer. In sickness and in health. 'Till death do us part. *Death? I'll die if I have to stay more than two years in Stuttgart.*

On the subway ride to the Munich convention center I run into Tracy, a journalist I know from California. "You're living in Stuttgart, right?" she asks. "I went to school in Heidelberg for two years. That's a big university town one hour north of where you live. There's a U.S. military base there too. Lots of Americans." She talks loudly, oblivious to the other passengers crammed into the car, and doesn't pause long enough for me to tell her I've been to Heidelberg, that I think it's a darling town, and that it even has a good sushi bar. She rambles on. "After Heidelberg I went to Hamburg and I had a German boyfriend for a year. We only spoke German together. You can't speak English," she says. "You have to speak German."

"I never expected to come here and speak 100 percent German," I tell her, wondering how she knows exactly how much German I'm speaking and, even more so, why she is wearing those hideous purple overalls. "I certainly thought I would learn it much faster. I know it would help to practice at home, but my time with Marcus is so limited, we just speak English."

"No!" she argues. "When in Germany, we speak German. And

when Germans come to America, we speak English. You have to insist on speaking German. Whenever I speak to someone in German and they answer me back in English—because they all love to practice their English—I reply in German. They keep responding in English until they get that I'm not giving in."

I look around to see if anyone else is listening, longing to get drawn into someone—anyone—else's conversation.

"You know Niels, right?" she asks, her bug-like brown eyes narrowing.

"Yes, I met him during my last trip to Munich. Small world, isn't it?" I barely reply before she starts in again.

"Niels always speaks Eng . . ." The subway doors open. "Oh, we're here," she says. "You're going to the press conference, aren't you? I've got such a busy day. This is the first of about twelve appointments, plus I have dinner tonight with . . ."

I think about how few Americans I know—make that none—who are fluent in a second, let alone third or fourth, language. I know she's right: the bigger the effort, the bigger the payoff. But I'm not a twenty-year-old college student like she was when she took on the task, when the brain is still like a sponge and one doesn't have the accumulated worries, responsibilities, and ambitions of a forty-one-year-old. And while my *goal* is to be fluent in German, my most pressing need is to speak it well enough to get through a weekend with my in-laws.

We walk into the press conference together. After Tracy says hello to a few other journalists and PR people in the room, we spot Niels at the same time. "I'm not going to talk to him because he's going to speak English," she says.

"Well, I am," I reply. I go take a seat next to Niels.

Happily *and* luckily, that is the last I see of her.

Marcus and I take a Saturday afternoon drive out to Steinegg to see his parents. Joining them for *Kaffee und Kuchen* has become a routine, if you consider once a month routine. After the usual greetings at the front door, we take our seats around the dining room table. I have a regular spot now, between Wolfgang and Marcus, directly across from Andrea.

"*Kaffee, Bess?*" Andrea asks.

"*Ja, bitte,*" I reply.

I brace myself for the hours of German ahead, quick-paced conversation so impossible for me to follow I feel like a deaf-mute. From Marcus I know today's topics are about pensioners complaining that they're losing already-generous benefits, employees getting taxed on every cup of coffee provided by employers, and, as usual, the scuttlebutt over new speed limits being imposed.

As their guttural gab drones on, I run my fingers across the green tablecloth and study the chandelier's reflection on the silverware. I stroke the handle of my teacup. I count the number of coins mounted on the antique leather belt hanging above Wolfgang's head. Eight. Then I imagine questions that are never posed to me—"How was the trade show in Munich, Beth? Are you happy to be back after your trip to California and Costa Rica? We hear you're going to get a German tutor; have you found one yet?"

I practice translating my answers into German: "Munich is such a great city; I love spending time there. It's hard to come back because I miss my friends and family in the States, but thank you for asking. My new tutor? Yes, I hired my old teacher, Uwe, from Fokus and I'm going to have my first session with him next week."

"They want to know about Arnold Schwarzenegger's work as governor of California," Marcus says, interrupting my reverie.

"Sorry. What did you say?"

He repeats it.

"Oh, yes, I get asked this a lot since Arnold is Austrian. My mom says he's done a good job, especially by trying to bridge the two parties. She voted for him. And you know, she likes that Maria is Catholic."

Marcus translates. Andrea and Wolfgang stare at me, nodding, while he speaks. Then, like when the U-Bahn pulls away just as I'm reaching the platform, the conversation moves on without me.

In German, the word "you" has several forms: a formal way (*Sie*) and a familiar way (*Du*). Including the plural, dative, and accusative cases, the grand total comes to sixteen ways to say "you"—just as it does with the article "the." Using the proper form is one thing, but again, it must also be accompanied by the corresponding verb declination. Which is why the book *501 German Verbs* is essential to own; each verb has its own page of charts depicting its many possible conjugations.

Children are expected to address adults using the formal version *Sie*, as are strangers greeting other strangers. Employees normally say "*Sie*" to their bosses and, like Marcus, even co-workers at the same level often maintain this formality with each other.

"My dad has worked with people for thirty years and they still use *Sie* terms," Marcus tells me during our umpteenth discussion about the use of this little word. "It's effective in business, especially when you want to stay above the other guy."

"That's ridiculous," I reply. "At Microsoft, everyone calls Bill Gates 'Bill.' And that hasn't hurt his business any."

"When I'm doing business in the U.S. I use first names, but I like the ability to differentiate," he says.

"Well, I find it discriminating," I retort. "No wonder it's so hard to make friends in this country."

"When you grow up here, you get used to things like that. It's just part of our culture." I shrug my shoulders and agree to disagree.

Frau Koch brings out a fresh pot of coffee. She wears a white apron and holds the pot handle loosely to protect her red-painted fingernails. "*Frau Eisen, der zweite Pfirsichkuchen braucht noch ein paar Minuten*," she says to Marcus' mother, explaining that the second peach cake needs a few more minutes in the oven.

"*Danke, Frau Koch*," Andrea replies. "*Sie können gehen wenn das fertig ist*." And tells her—using the formal *Sie*—she can leave when it's done.

"You need to stay on *Sie* terms with Frau Koch," Marcus has instructed me more than once on how to address his parents' housekeeper. "She'll try to speak to you using *Du*. She always tries to get close," he says, as if being close is not a welcome thing.

Frau Koch is like a favorite aunt. Gifts from her fill our apartment—jars of her homemade jam and her hand-knit wool socks. She never misses sending us a birthday or holiday card. On the occasions I have encountered her in the kitchen peeling carrots and potatoes or polishing silver for Wolfgang and Andrea—or *Frau* and *Herr* Eisen, as she is required to call them after eight years of employment in their home—Frau Koch asks me, "How are you doing? Are you making some friends? Are you happy here?" And every time I see her she offers me encouragement, which I am badly in need of. "Your German is getting really good. It's really improving. I could never speak English as well as you speak German," she says.

"Thanks," I say, and not "Thank *you*," so as to avoid the *Sie* vs. *Du* issue.

The coffee cups are refilled; the family dialog continues. From what I can make out, Marcus explains what's new at the car company, Wolfgang gives an update on the Autobahn construction near their house, and Andrea offers her opinions, her disapproval, on how Marcus' cousins are raising their children (while avoiding any mention about us giving her grandchildren).

"Anybody got a good fart joke?" I want to ask.

Sipping my sixth cup of coffee out of the antique gold-trimmed china cup, dishes clank in the kitchen as Frau Koch unloads the dishwasher. I shift my butt in the chair. If only I could leave the table and go practice my German with her. She could correct my grammar and laugh her raspy, cigarette laugh as I relay my stories about Munich. I would ask for her jam recipe. I would ask what her first name is. And I would most definitely address her with "*Du*."

Instead, I stay seated in my straight-backed, silk-covered chair and pick at the remaining crumbs of my cake with the silver fork.

Marcus reaches his hand over and rubs my neck. "My parents have invited us to stay for *Abendbrot*," he whispers.

I anticipate Andrea's usual cold dinners of bologna salad—fine strips of bologna marinated in vinegar—served with tomato slices and buttered wheat bread. It is these meals that make me long to be married to an Italian.

I also know from experience that once dinner is over, Wolfgang will break out a few bottles of his homemade schnapps, wanting us to sample his pear, wild berry, forest herb, or whatever new infusion he is experimenting with. The German distilled spirit is served in small portions as a digestive, but it's potent and much too strong for me. I will take a tiny sip of each and offer to drive back to Stuttgart so Marcus can enjoy drinking with his dad.

Even the most casual of dinners with the Eisens will be, at the shortest, a three-hour affair. Nonetheless, I whisper back, "Oh, okay, sure."

I muster a smile for Marcus while inside my head I begin to hum the words, "You're so brave. You can do it. You're so brave . . ."

CHAPTER 8

Employment, Yoga, and Overcoming the Inner Pig Dog

L ENA, MY SWEDISH FRIEND FROM GERMAN CLASS, is twenty-four years old and lives with her boyfriend in a shared four-bedroom apartment. This kind of community living is common—called a *Wohngemeinschaft* or WG for short. The advantages of Lena's living situation are several, first of which being the apartment itself. It's in a gorgeous pre-war building with fifteen-foot-high ceilings, ornate molding on the thick, soundproof walls, dark wood wainscoting, a sunroom with floor-to-ceiling bay windows, and a central location in town with cafés and coffee bars nearby. With three roommates she has a built-in social network. Henry, Heike, and Verena go to their offices everyday—the car factory, the classroom, and the law firm, respectively—and return with bits of information about the latest night club opening, where to find the best African food, which sport shops are organizing ski trips to the Alps, the dates for this year's Bollywood Film Festival, and rumors that Starbucks is going to open on the Königstrasse. These are also the people who tell Lena, who then tells me, that Café Nescafe is hiring.

If I am sometimes envious of Lena's friends-and-family environs there is one distinct disadvantage: there is only one toilet.

I push play on the Bang and Olufsen, turning the volume up to a risky, potentially rule-breaking level, and change into khaki pants and a black shirt. As the angst-ridden singer of Linkin Park screams, *"I tried so hard and got so far,"* I apply a few brush-strokes of Dr. Hauschka bronzing powder to my cheeks . . . *"But in the end it doesn't even matter"*. . . dab a bit on my eyelids . . . *"I had to fall to lose it all"*. . . and coat my lips in my power-red lipstick . . . *"But in the end it doesn't even matter"*. . . before taking the tram downtown.

En route, I mull over my earlier phone conversation with Trish. "You have to face your fears," she said. "I know you'd rather work for a magazine, but why not just get a job at a coffeehouse? It would get you out of the house and you would be getting paid to practice your German."

"You're right," I said, adding a small protest, "but I'll barely be able to understand the customers."

She was ready with a quick comeback. "You only need to know the words for coffee and milk."

Café Nescafe sits across from *Volkshochschule* on Calwer Strasse, a pedestrian-only brick street of sidewalk cafés and designer boutiques. I arrive during a lull and the café's Greek owner, Theophanis, can spare a few minutes. First I tell him how I've been a regular customer during my classes at *Volkshochschule*. Then I stutter through my employment history—the abbreviated version—in my beginner's German. "I'm a writer and I've worked at coffeehouses since ancient times, back when Starbucks had one location."

I leave out the part about living on a Kenya coffee farm when I was twenty-four, where I picked and planted beans, pruned and fertilized the coffee trees, and learned about milling, sorting, classifying, cupping, and exporting. I don't explain how I came up with the idea to study coffee in Kenya while managing a coffee shop in Chicago, how I saved up money for Africa by holding three jobs, how I flew to London and met with a woman at the International Coffee Association who put me in touch with a Kenya Coffee Board representative who arranged for me to study coffee on his friend's farm outside of Nairobi. I don't bother to mention how I pursued this hands-on education in order to start my own coffee importing business, which I ran out of New York City for the next several years, or how I can identify origins of coffee based on their acidity or full-bodied characteristics and discern imperfections like the onion, grass, or potato taste of a fermented crop. What I also omit is the part about how *The New York Times* ran a story on my coffee, Grade AA Peaberry beans packed in a zebra-striped gift tin, and how that little piece of publicity led to marketing and public relations jobs with other coffee companies.

Even if I wanted to, I couldn't explain it in German.

Theophanis eyes me absentmindedly as my words tumble out in the wrong order. I finish my pitch, pause to get his answer, and prepare for rejection.

He asks, "Do you have a work permit?"

"*Ja, habe ich*," I answer. The tightness of my forced smile relaxes.

"Then bring it with you tomorrow. Can you be here at four?" he asks.

"*Ja*. No problem," I say.

I not only have a job, I have understood everything he said—in German. I will have the afternoon shift from four to nine p.m., Tuesday, Wednesday, and Friday. This means instead of sitting at home enduring the black hole of time until Marcus returns from work, I will be emptying ashtrays, rinsing out milk dispensers, restocking the refrigerator, sweeping coffee grounds off the floor, and asking strangers if they would like something *zu trinken*. I'm thrilled at the prospect. I am not in school; I am employed! I am finally going to have a life. Outside of the house.

"I don't know why, but I'm not exercising as much since I moved here," I tell Marcus.

In California, I was regularly running, biking, skating, and doing power yoga. Trish was like a personal trainer, calling me every day. Some days she would ask, "Want to meet for Vinnie's class at 4:15 or Shiva's class at six? Or how about both?" On other days she proposed, "Should we skate to Manhattan Beach or ride bikes up to Malibu?" And my brother, Miguel, would call most weekends. "We're going to catch some waves at San Onofre on Sunday. Want to meet us there?" In Seattle I had a logging road right outside my cabin door—free of cars and lined by Douglas firs, it was my own private, dirt path to sweat and solitude whose beckoning call I heeded daily, even when it was fifty degrees and raining, which was most of the time.

"It's because your *Innerer Schweinehund* is taking over," Marcus explains.

"My what?"

"Your Inner Pig Dog. That's what we call it when you procrastinate or feel too lazy to exercise."

"I need to get back into yoga," I tell him, "but finding a yoga class in this town is harder than running the L.A. Marathon."

When I complained to Trish about the dearth of studios listed in the Yellow Pages she asked ever so gently, "But have you tried any of them?"

"No."

"Maybe you'll discover something good in the process," she said.

"Maybe."

I call Yoga Zentrum. The woman I speak to tells me their next class is Wednesday evening. My job presents its first conflict and I haven't even started yet. I can't go to yoga; I have to go to work. "We also have a class on Thursday," she says.

I report for my first coffeehouse shift at 15:45—that's European time for 3:45 p.m. I am bright-eyed, eager, and scared shitless. A college student named Birgit is assigned to train me. She hands me a black apron and shows me how the machines work—the espresso machine, the milk foamer, the milkshake blender, the frozen coffee dispenser, the ice maker—and how to clean each one. The espresso machine, which I am aghast to learn, uses instant coffee powder (my coffee-discerning palate is rusty so I hadn't noticed) and is computerized with about twenty plastic moving parts inside. Each part has to be removed, soaked, and reassembled—all while customers are waiting. I fumble with the bits like an advanced 3D jigsaw puzzle, jamming them in the wrong places hoping they'll fit. "Don't force them," Birgit says, unconcerned about the line of people that has formed.

Birgit's next task for me is easier and thankfully less technical. She hands me a spray bottle of glass cleaner. I hop up on the back countertop, my butt pointing out toward the café's patrons as I wipe the shelves. I rip another paper towel off the roll and am struck by the irony: *This is exactly the work I resent doing at home!* At least I'm getting paid for it. I am one hour and two tasks into my training and I'm ready to collect my final paycheck. "Don't forget to wash the refrigerator doors and the bakery display case," Birgit says.

Next I am told to collect twenty cartons of long-life milk from the basement storage room. *What? The milk isn't fresh?*

"Take a crate with you, one that's already filled with empty bottles," she says. "Those will need to be sorted downstairs. We also need *Strohhalme, Orangensaft,* and *Zucker*." She sees my face, staring back at her blankly, so she switches back to English. "Straws, orange juice, and sugar," says boss woman.

As I learn the layout of the storage room, I discover that the croissants, blueberry muffins, and brownies I've enjoyed as a customer are . . . frozen.

Back upstairs, I am allowed to serve my first customer. A middle-aged woman stands in the same spot where I used to stand as a *Volkshochschule* student. I blurt out to her, *"Was möchten Sie trinken?"*

She's taken slightly off guard but she sees my smile and smiles back. *"Ich hätte gern ein latte macchiato, bitte."* Then she asks, "Are you American?"

"Yes," I answer. Under Birgit's watchful eye I place a tall glass (in Germany they serve lattes in glasses, not mugs) under the dispenser and push a button to make her instant-coffee drink.

"Don't forget the straw," Birgit hisses as I set the glass down in front of the woman.

Birgit hands me a round tray and tells me, *"Jetzt musst du aufräumen."* I know what *aufräumen* means. The word was in my textbook during Herr Keyser's summer class: Tidy up, clean up, straighten up, pick up, put away.

I carry out the remainder of my shift loading and unloading the dishwasher. After the café closes, after I've swept and dusted the entire seating area, including all of the leather couch cushions, it's 9:30 p.m. and I am allowed to go home. The job may not be fun, but mopping up milk beats memorizing irregular verbs.

Yoga Zentrum's large studio is all white with soft cotton curtains covering the windows. A single candle burns on a small altar in the front of the room. Of the fifteen people in the class, ten of them have gray hair and most of them have soft, fleshy bodies. Everyone but me is wearing baggy sweatpants and socks; I'm dressed for a workout in my sports bra, running tights, and bare feet. For the next hour we lie on the floor while the instructor, Gabrielle, reads out of a book. The only phrase I understand is "Let go." Before the class is over we have done exactly one Downward Facing Dog pose—a forward bend on all fours, a yoga practice standard intended to build strength and heat. We didn't hold it long enough for my pulse to increase even one beat.

My second day at Café Nescafe I'm supervised by Birgit again, but there is also another girl working. She has layered black hair with loose strands falling in her eyes and a stick-thin body accentuated by her bone-hugging jeans. She's wearing frosty eye shadow, heavy eyeliner, and a superiority complex. I introduce myself. *"Ich heisse Beth,"* I say. And I'd like to give you a makeover. I hold out my hand to shake hers. She offers me a few limp fingers.

As I pump her apathetic hand, she looks past me and says, *"Ich bin Irina."*

Irina is on cash register duty while I clean the frozen coffee dispenser. I start to lift the plastic vat off its metal base. "No, no, no!" Birgit stops me. "You have to take off the nozzle first and the blades inside." She steps in and does it for me.

I venture some small talk as Birgit unscrews the parts. "So, what are you studying?" I ask her.

"Physical therapy," she answers. She leans down into the machine, yanking on its innards. When the blades are freed—when her curiosity overpowers her German reserve—she asks me, "What brought you to Stuttgart?"

"I married a German."

"How old are you?" she asks, pulling the vat off its perch.

"I'm forty-one," I answer. "How old are you?"

"Twenty," she says, adding, "I thought you were younger."

"Thank you. How old is Irina?"

"Irina? She's nineteen. She's from Russia." She hands me the container. "Now you must wash these." Conversation over.

I start the dishwasher. Irina spins around and pushes the emergency stop button. "You use dee wrong soap," she says hurling Siberian switchblades at me from beneath her frosty-blue eyelids. She shoves a tray at me. "You go *aufräumen*. I fix dis." Birgit watches smugly, not saying anything.

As I move around the room collecting dirty dishes, Lena comes in the door. Dressed in a corduroy coat and fleece beret she flashes her vivacious, broad smile at me. "How's it going?" she's eager to know. I'm within earshot of my coworkers so I just scrunch my face and purse my lips. "Oh," she says and breaks into a welcome, helpful laugh.

"Do you want a latte?" I ask.

"Sure."

I walk behind the counter and make Lena's drink. I ignore Irina's shocked look. I turn to Birgit, stating firmly and resolutely as I untie my apron, "I'm going to take my ten-minute break now." With my eyes I tell her, "You can't tell me what to do, missy. I'm old enough to be your mother."

I go sit with Lena and, naturally, that is precisely when Theophanis comes in. He tells me, "When you're done with your break, I need you to clean the bathrooms. And make sure there's enough toilet paper."

"Jesus, should I salute him?" I say to Lena when he walks away. She smiles and sips her coffee through the straw.

"Hey, whatever happened with Uwe? Are you still getting tutored by him?" she asks.

"No. It only took two sessions to see it wasn't worth the money. He was never prepared, never gave me homework . . ."

"And he was always speaking English," she says, finishing my sentence.

"How'd you know?" I laugh and say, "My ten minutes are up. I have to go back to my 'Service with a smile.' That's the American way."

"Germany could certainly use some of that," she replies.

"Well, I'll never get to show them how service *should* be, or learn more German, if they only want me to be their cleaning lady."

"Maybe it'll get better," she says.

"Yeah, maybe."

Yoga studio No.2 is run by Herr Steinberg. Over the phone I tell him I'm looking for a fitness-type of yoga and he tells me his classes are movement intensive; he adds that he occasionally reads *Yoga Journal*. My expectations grow. If he reads this bible of American yoga magazines then he must know something about the way Californians like their yoga. Herr Steinberg, in white sweatpants and a gray beard, greets me quietly as I enter the foyer. For the next hour I, along with three other students, complete six Sun Salutation cycles. I don't even come close to breaking a sweat. I wait for Herr Steinberg after class. He walks very slowly and when he finally reaches me he says thoughtfully, "Perhaps you should try Yoga Stuttgart down the street. I think you may find what you are looking for there." He gives me directions. "It's just two blocks down. Look for the small sign in front." When I try to hand him a ten-euro note as class payment he waves my hand away and says, "No, no charge."

I find Yoga Stuttgart before going home. The entrance is locked so I peek in the windows. The room is cottage yellow with purple and blue yoga mats hanging along one wall. Votive candles burn in the windowsills. A pair of feet kicks past my Peeping Tom view as a muscular man positions himself into a headstand. I go back to the door and take a schedule. The studio offers daily classes of varying levels. I can't wait for Thursday.

On Tuesday neither Birgit nor Irina are there; I am on duty with Katrina. A former Milan runway model, she returned to Germany to finish school. With her strong cheekbones and her light blond hair woven into Rapunzel-long braids she looks way too wholesome to be flaunting Prada's latest fashions. "We always need to be busy," Katrina explains as she looks around for the spray bottle of glass cleaner. "That's how Theophanis likes it."

That's how he likes it? What are we, his German geishas?

"Has anyone shown you how to clean the milk foamer?" she asks.

Oh boy, here we go again. I will myself not to roll my eyes.

"No, not yet," I say sweetly. "But I'd love it if you could show me." I get another lesson in mechanical engineering as she demonstrates how to keep the nozzles from clogging, and how to check the air hoses and temperature gauges.

"My boyfriend is American," she says. "He's an art director. He's from Wisconsin."

"My mom is from Wisconsin," I say.

"What about you? What about your husband?"

I give her my standard answer. "He's German. I'm here because of him. We're here because of his job, his promotion. I'm working here so I can practice my German—and you're not helping me any."

She laughs. "Well then, from now on I'm only going to speak

German to you." I know a certain American from the Munich trade show who would be pleased to hear this.

Katrina lets me wait on customers, keeping her distance but coming to my rescue when my comprehension is lacking. At 9:25 p.m. when the last croissant crumb has been swept off the floor, Katrina and I put on our coats. We both say, "It was nice working with you. I look forward to seeing you tomorrow." And we mean it.

Yoga Stuttgart's foyer is lined with coat hooks and built-in shelves. There are racks of health magazines and brochures for upcoming yoga workshops. But any initial similarities to home end when I see my fellow yogis disrobing in front of each other, right in front of the main entrance door. The women pull off their sweaters and bras, wriggling out of their jeans to reveal G-string panties and bare buttocks before changing into in baggy T-shirts and Lycra tights. The men remove their jeans and socks, exposing tight black briefs and hairy legs before pulling on gym shorts.

I've gotten used to Germany's relaxedness about co-ed nudity—kind of. During weekend road trips Marcus and I stop at various mineral baths. After the first few visits, one finds that the naked bodies—sprawled on lounge chairs or crowded together in the saunas—become just bodies. With a little conditioning, pubic hair and penises become almost invisible. Even the tattooed nipples and intimate body piercings cease to shock after a time—with the exception of the guy in the Munich spa with the silver hoop dangling from his foreskin. I don't see any pierced genitalia at Yoga Stuttgart, but like at the mineral baths, the lack of dressing rooms will take some getting used to. I adopt their casual, unselfconscious attitude and slip out of my winter clothes and into my tank top and yoga pants.

The studio has two rooms: the candlelit yellow one I saw through the windows, which has hardwood floors, and another one, painted mauve with florescent overhead lighting and a linoleum floor. I follow the crowd of about twelve other students into the more inviting yellow room.

Our instructor, Christa, has short gray hair permed like Marcus' grandmother's and wire-rimmed glasses with thick lenses. Her bicycle-style shorts may show off her buff legs but her baggy scoop neck T-shirt doesn't hide her large belly and her even larger breasts, which protrude straight out like submarine torpedoes. She looks like Mother Superior dressed in the wrong clothes, as if she left the convent for the ashram twenty years ago, but hasn't quite shaken her roots.

Her cartoon-shaped body may defy the notion that she can teach yoga, oh, but she can and she does. She leads us through a full Vinyasa flow, working our way through Series A and B into lunges, Twisting Triangles, and backbends before coming to a rest in Savasana. I follow along perfectly, though my German yoga vocabulary is limited. I try not to laugh every time she says *Hund,* knowing that "dog" is short for Downward Facing Dog. I hear the word *Kiefer* several times and I wonder why she keeps talking about pine trees, but I ask Marcus later and he tells me it also means jaw. I hear *Oberschinken* and think it's odd to refer to thighs as "upper bacon," until I learn the word is actually *Oberschenkel*. I know all the poses regardless, but it's an ironic relief when she occasionally uses their Sanskrit names. Christa makes her way around the room. When she comes to adjust my arms during a tree pose she asks, "What's your name?"

"Beth."

"Where are you from?"

"*Amiland*," I answer, using the German nickname for the U.S. Then she moves on.

It's not the hold-poses-until-you-cry yoga of Vinnie's class, but I get a good workout and I know I will be coming back.

On Friday I'm back at Café Nescafe. I arrive at 3:59 for my 4 p.m. shift—why bother coming earlier than necessary? The only reason I don't quit is because of Katrina. She wants to know more about American men and I want to know more about Germans. We serve customers. We refill the espresso machine. And we agree that all men, no matter where they're from, are prone to leaving dirty dishes in the sink.

Marcus, who is scoring an A-plus in dishwashing lately, has accepted my new routine, but he hasn't said much about it. I don't need him to tell me he's impressed with my resourcefulness, though I would like him to. But then I remember the Swabian quote—that not saying anything is compliment enough.

In between my work and yoga schedule, we still manage to

sit down for dinners together, albeit never before ten p.m. It is during a proper German meal of pork cutlets and sauerkraut that Marcus tells me, "A new union law is being enforced. All employees must punch out by seven p.m."

"That's great news! You can come to yoga with me," I reply.

A week goes by and there's no mention of yoga, there's no coming home at seven o'clock. He simply gets up from his desk at 6:59, walks to the time clock mounted on the wall, punches out, then returns to his office for another two unpaid hours.

"You're not getting paid?" I roar. "It's a law. You say your manager will suffer consequences, yet you stay?"

"I'm not there alone," he says. "Hannes and Anton are there too."

"This means your extra hours aren't counted for comp time either."

"No, but I still get six weeks of vacation a year."

I let out an exaggerated, one could even say rude, sigh. "I don't care about the vacation. I just want to have dinner with you at an hour that's not past my bedtime."

After six consecutive yoga classes in the ugly mauve room, I find a growing sense of disappointment creeping in. Why aren't we in the yellow room? And why can't they at least turn off the florescent lights during Savasana? Christa instructs us to do Triangle pose from a kneeling position and Warrior Two with a rear foot braced against the wall. I wonder why, when she has a class full of experienced students, she is regressing to this introductory level. When she asks us to turn to do Triangle on the other side, I bend from a standing position while everyone else obediently stays on their knees. For Warrior Two, I move away from the wall so I can extend my arms out fully.

I have broken the first rule in Germany, which is: Rules must be followed. *All* of them.

We move down to the floor. I lie on my back, knees up and parted hip-width as if I'm about to have a gynecological exam. My feet are on the floor and pointing slightly out. Christa, however, thinks my feet should be pointing somewhere else. She leans over me, puts her hands on my knees, and digs her fingers into my kneecaps. Peering at me through her thick glasses she screeches, "*Sprichst du kein Deutsch?*" She hasn't just asked me if I don't speak German, she has more like *accused* me of it.

I nod. "*Ja, ich spreche ein bisschen.*" Yes, I speak a little.

"*Bist du Französin?*" she asks.

Am I French? What? No! Blood rushes into my cheeks. "*Ich bin Amerikanerin,*" I remind her.

Come on, lady, you know *I'm American.*

"Maybe you just don't understand my dialect," she continues, as she kicks my toes to point inward. *Kicks* them.

Maybe you're just getting Alzheimer's.

"*Ja, dein Dialekt ist schwer für mich,*" I answer. I don't know what is so funny about telling her that, yes, her dialect is hard for me, but the whole class erupts into laughter. She walks away. I say a few silent oms but nothing can block out the echo chamber of mocking laughter.

"I got reprimanded in yoga!" I blurt out the second the apartment door shuts behind me. Marcus steps out of the bathroom. "I am so sick of getting into trouble. And I hate my stupid coffeehouse job. I'm only working there because you work so late. I can't stand living here!" Tears suppressed from earlier—from when my misplaced feet made me the object of humiliation—explode to the surface. Marcus lets me cry, waiting, hoping that the sedative effect of tears will take hold. In between sobs, I detect his feeling of helplessness and exasperation, but when I eventually stop, when I've wiped the last globs of snot dripping from my nose, he's there with a tender hug.

"How about a glass of red wine and a hot bubble bath?" he offers.

"Okay," I whimper.

In the steaming waters of the bath I mull over what happened. Yoga, no matter in what country, is supposed to be a sanctuary. If I were in Santa Monica, Vinnie would have gently shifted my feet into the proper position without a word. Maybe the class would have laughed, but only at one of his well-timed jokes.

"Do you mind if I join you?" Marcus slips into the tub with me, interrupting me from wallowing further in thoughts of home. He takes my foot in his hand and massages it, rubbing the tension until it dissolves into a distant memory.

One week later I have a dream: I am taking Christa's yoga class and she has taken an inappropriately long break in the middle of the session. The class thus begins to fall apart, everyone is talking, straying from their mats and getting their belongings out of their lockers. When Christa finally comes back into the room I start yelling at her in English. "Where were you? You don't just walk out on a class! What kind of yoga teacher are you?" After I finish reprimanding her, others from the class add their complaints, also in English even though they are all Germans.

I wake up agitated. My God! I'm becoming just like them!

I scrap the yoga classes and buy a pair of new running shoes. I lace up the Nikes, beat my chest in a battle cry as I wind down the vineyard path to the Neckar River bike trail, and announce to my *Innerer Schweinehund*, "Look out, little piggy. You don't know who you're dealing with."

CHAPTER 9

Paris

Stuttgart slowly shakes off winter. Dampness clings to the thawing grapevines while new leaves struggle to emerge from their tight buds. With no foliage yet to block the view, the car factory's logo is still visible from our balcony, its white star spinning lazily against the gray sky.

Jun calls. "I'm taking Lucas to Paris for his spring holiday. Deutsche Bahn has a special offer; round trip tickets are less than a hundred euros," she says, adding, "on the high speed train."

"Wow, that *is* a good deal. Last time I checked that trip was double that."

"Why don't you come with us?" she asks. "We're going for four days, coming back on Saturday night. I've already booked a hotel, right by the Eiffel *Turm*," she says, using the German word for tower.

On Saturday morning Café Nescafe is having a mandatory

staff meeting. Birgit says if I miss it I'll probably lose my job. "Okay," I say quickly. "I'd love to come."

Paris. I know Paris. The first time I went there was to meet my sister for her twenty-fifth birthday, when I was almost twenty-three and spending a year in Switzerland. It was also in spring. I still have the pictures of her performing arabesques in front of every marble statue she encountered in the Jardin des Tuileries. To this day she imitates the Texas drawl of the American man in our hotel who greeted the day with a booming "Bone Jure," a pronunciation that would make even the most tolerant of French cringe.

I was in Paris again when I was thirty, spending two months in an intensive French course at the Alliance Française. I shared an apartment with a French girl, Celine, who would only speak to me in English. It was also then that I declined a would-be romance with the debonair grandson of the hot air balloon inventor. Alas, I took a different path, one that eventually led me to marrying a German instead.

My most recent visit to Paris was three years earlier, when my dad and I had a layover on our way to Niger. With only a few hours between flights, we squeezed in a walk to the Notre Dame Cathedral and lit candles inside. I bought him a beret, showed him the hotel where my sister and I stayed on Ile Saint Louis, and we ate Nutella-smeared crepes, all before heading to the shifting red sands of the Sahara Desert.

I don't have a burning desire to go to Paris when the weather is so cold and gray, but I welcome the chance to *parler français* instead of German. And anytime I get an invitation to get out of Stuttgart, well, I take it.

By coincidence, I've just finished reading *Almost French* by Sarah Turnbull, a memoir by an Australian woman living in Paris, married to a Frenchman. I devoured the story, hungry for clues of how to manage the cultural differences in my new country next door.

"Listen to this," I kept saying to Marcus, reading him passages from her book. "She got dirty looks for wearing sweatpants to the bakery . . . strangers keep telling her how she should care for her dog . . . she helped herself to champagne before it was offered by the party hosts who were late and got reprimanded. That sounds almost German."

If only she knew how easy she had it.

I attempt to track down the author to meet her for coffee. I try Paris Directory Assistance, then the Internet, and, finally, I call her publisher in New York. The receptionist puts me directly through to Sarah's editor.

"Yes?" says the editor, a Type A executive short on time.

My heart races. I drop a few of my journalism credentials—*Elle, Travel + Leisure, Shape*—so she doesn't hang up on me right away. "I'm going to be in Paris and I was hoping to meet with Sarah," I say.

"That's not possible," she says bluntly. "She and her husband moved to Tahiti. But I'm glad you liked the book." Click.

I immediately call Marcus at work. "You know that book I was reading? The one about the Australian in Paris? She moved to TAHITI!" I blare into the phone. And then I start laughing, almost maniacally, as if this affects me personally. "Tahiti! Did you hear me? That's tropical paradise. It makes perfect sense—it's closer to Australia and in Tahiti they speak French. They deliver baguettes directly to your house there; they have special mailboxes just for the bread." I ramble on so excitedly it takes me a moment to realize Marcus is not responding. I stop my gleeful tirade and say softly to him, "See? Even she didn't want to stay in Europe, and she was in *Paris*."

"I can't talk. I'm in a meeting," he says. His abruptness is not unexpected. I know he's in work mode. I also know I am pushing too hard for something he can't yet give me: a new home. I replace the receiver and write an email to Trish to share the story with her.

On Wednesday morning I arrive at the Stuttgart *Hauptbahnhof* with just enough time to buy a sandwich on pretzel bread from one of the several kiosk bakeries inside the station before the train leaves.

I spot Jun. Dressed in a knee-length black down jacket and black pants, she's pulling a small suitcase and dark-haired boy behind her. Lucas, Asian-looking but with the strong bones of a German, is already almost as tall as his mother. "This is Lucas. Lucas, this is my friend Beth," she says. He looks at me only for an instant before averting his eyes.

"It's very nice to meet you," I say, bending down to kiss him on each cheek. He jerks away as I try to touch the side of my face to his.

We settle into our seats on the high speed EuroCity express, a sleek, silver bullet train that will blast us to Paris in five hours at three hundred kilometers per hour. Jun pulls out of her tote bag sandwiches from home, a bottle of water for herself, and apple juice for Lucas who is already engrossed in his new *Asterix* comic book. I sit alone, directly behind Lucas whose body is sprawled crosswise from the armrest to the windowpane. "Have some juice, Lucas," Jun instructs him.

"I'm not thirsty," he replies, not looking up from his comic book.

"At least have one drink. You need to stay hydrated," says Jun.

"No, Mommy, I don't want any."

I get the feeling this is how it's going to go for the next four hours and forty-five minutes.

"Here, I brought this for you," I say to Jun, handing her *Almost French* over the seat.

"Oh, I'm looking forward to reading it, but I want to finish the *Stuttgarter Zeitung* first," she says, shaking out the local newspaper in front of her. "I like to read this paper; I learn so much German and I get the news at the same time."

"Well, you're a better person than I am," I say. "But I think you'll like the book more." Then I sit back in my seat to eat my pretzel sandwich, and thumb through my French dictionary.

Our train arrives before sundown at the Gare de Lyon. At the hotel check-in, the receptionist assigns us rooms next door to each other. Jun and Lucas' room has two beds, flower boxes outside the windows filled with blooming red geraniums, and a view of the Eiffel Tower. Mine has a single bed that fills 90 percent of the room, and looks out to a brick wall. A few minutes after I've set my bag down, there's a knock on my door. It's Lucas. "My mother wants to know if you want to go have dinner."

"Yes, I'm starving. Aren't you?"

"Not really," he answers and then runs away, back to his room.

We walk to a neighborhood bistro, pushing aside a heavy purple velvet curtain to enter. Jun and I share a carafe of red wine. I hold up my glass to clink with Lucas' Orangina. "To Lucas, whose school holiday made this trip possible." He fumbles with his straw and looks away, slumping down into the banquette.

Five minutes after we say goodnight I get a knock on my door. It's Lucas again. "My mother wants to know if you want to see the lights on the Eiffel Tower."

"Of course," I tell him, following him as he turns and runs.

The three of us lean out on the sooty windowsills and watch the show. Twenty thousand strobe lights sizzle up and down Paris' most famous icon, giving the impression that the steel tower is being electrocuted.

"Wow, that's very cool," says Lucas.

"*C'est magnifique*," I agree. "*Très, très jolie.*"

As we stare at the flickering lights in silence, it occurs to me that Germany doesn't have a world icon like the Eiffel Tower, a singular monument that represents the country. The closest thing, the one that attracts the most tourists, is the Neuschwanstein Castle in the town of Schwangau. Located in the Alps about an hour south of Munich on the Austrian border, King Ludwig II built this fairy-tale castle between 1870 and 1879. He had barely moved into his palace when he mysteriously drowned, just days after doctors certified him mad. The elaborate, costly monstrosity, whose construction nearly bankrupted Bavaria, is what Disneyland modeled its Magic Kingdom after.

But the castle has never achieved Eiffel Tower status. Sadly, Germany is better known for beer. And Hitler.

We eat breakfast in the hotel. The croissants are as flaky and melt-in-your-mouth as one would expect from a French pastry. We have croissants in Stuttgart, but the ones I've tried were tough and chewy—which led me to the search, and subsequent disappointing discovery, that there is not one French bakery in town. But right now I'm not complaining about a lack of buttery crumbs; I'm inhaling them. And I'm drinking my *café au lait* out of a white porcelain bowl. *Vivre la différence.*

Jun and Lucas are heading to the top of the Eiffel Tower; this morning I'm going to Salon Antoine, a hair salon where my friend Alayne had her curly locks styled by the proprietor himself. She emailed me a picture of her new look: spunky sportswoman transformed into French supermodel.

"Stunning," I told her.

"You should go get a haircut there next time you're in Paris," Alayne insisted.

The fact that Antoine had availability for "whatever time I wanted" should have been cause for suspicion, but this is the kind of knowledge that becomes apparent only in hindsight. I cross the Seine River, pass the chain stores on the Champs-Elysées, and turn onto Avenue George V, the posh *rue* lined with finely detailed, stone buildings and manicured gardens. I am so lost in my fantasy of what it would be like to live in one of these resplendent apartments, my eyes focused upward instead of where I'm walking on the sidewalk, that I almost step in dog poop.

Inside the Prince de Galles Hotel, I'm greeted at the salon's reception desk by a very pretty, very skinny young woman in a blue satin blouse with matching glitter eyeshadow. She leads me to a chair in the empty waiting area. "*Asseyez-vous*," she says.

I pick up a copy of *Paris Match* to catch up on the unflattering escapades of Princess Stephanie of Monaco. She has joined the circus and is pictured next to an RV with a cigarette hanging out of her mouth. Someone please get this poor girl some therapy.

Antoine comes out to greet me. "*Bonjour*," he says. "You're a friend of Alayne? Any friend of Alayne is a friend of mine." He extends his hand to me.

Trim, dark hair swept back, black shirt opened two buttons too many, and tan, he looks as if he stepped straight off a Saint Tropez yacht. He glides rather than walks. He croons rather than talks. He leads me to his chair and immediately begins lathering on the compliments. "You have stunning blue eyes. And what a beautiful, strong jaw you have."

Save the charm, buddy. I'm happily married.

"Thank you," I say politely. "*Merci*."

"I know just what we will do with this luscious hair of yours. Trust me."

If there's one thing I've learned in life it's that whenever someone, especially a hairdresser, says, "Trust me," it is almost always a red flag. I suffered from an experience in my early twenties in Italy. I met a sexy hairdresser who held his hands up to me, framing my face with his fingers so he could "picture" his hairstyle idea for me. Falling victim to his charm, I let him have his way—but only with my hair. By the time he was through, he had shaved my head down to less than one inch, leaving a little rat-tail running down the nape of my neck. I wore skirts for the rest of that summer for fear of being mistaken for a boy.

I should bolt from Antoine's chair immediately. But I'm in Paris. Paris, France! I'm in the hair salon of a five-star hotel just off the Champs-Elysées! And I want to look like a French super-model. So I trust him.

Trust is when you watch large clumps of your hair fall to the floor even though you're quite sure you said, "I want to keep it long, just add some layers." I take a deep breath and remind myself to stay open-minded. As he keeps snipping—more like hacking—I adopt a new mantra: *It's only hair. It will grow back. It's only hair. It will grow back.*

When he's done blow-drying me with his round brush, he swivels me around in the chair to face the mirror. "What do you think? It's bee-youuuu-tee-fullll," he says, admiring his work.

I swallow hard. Rod Stewart is looking back at me. My pony-tail has been replaced by an early eighties shag. These are layers all right—spiky layers that start at the top of my scalp instead of below my ears.

"Now we are going to give you some highlights, just a few to brighten your color."

I don't argue. I just nod, very slowly.

"Frahhnk, Frahhnk," he calls out across the salon. Frank, his short, bald Italian assistant, swooshes over to the chair. "Frahhnk is really an artist," Antoine tells me. "Frahhnk, please take care of this beautiful mademoiselle."

I've never colored my hair. When I surfed in Southern

California my hair was so perfectly streaked from the sun and salt water that stylists always asked, "Who does your highlights?" But since I've spent the last few years in Seattle and Stuttgart, I've lost my lightness—and not just with my hair.

When I am at last free to leave, Antoine meets me at the front desk. He hands me his business card, printed with a photo of him taken at least thirty years ago. And then he hands me the bill. The shock of the price is worse than the sight of my new haircut. With the unfavorable Euro exchange rate it's about four hundred dollars. I think I'm going to be sick.

"Let me take a picture of you," he insists. "We'll email it to your husband."

"No, really, please. You don't have to," I argue. But the skinny receptionist has already turned on the digital camera. She snaps a photo of me standing in between Antoine and Frank while my credit card gets approved.

I meet up with Jun and Lucas at Le Printemps department store near the Opera House. The store is so enormous that Jun and I have to use our cell phones to locate each other. She's on the third floor of the second building in the ladies' designer clothes department. I find her looking through a stack of folded pink and green Lacoste sweaters. "Oh, there you are," she says. "Well, let me see it." And she steps back to study my new do. "I really love it. It suits you."

I grunt.

"I need a haircut," she continues, "and I've been looking for someone who really knows hair. This guy seems to know how give a good cut."

I can't imagine why she would want to look like an aging rock star.

"Do you think I could get an appointment there tomorrow?" she asks.

"I guess so. He didn't seem very busy," I say. "But we can call and find out."

Standing between Jun, Lucas, and two mannequins in sequined cocktail dresses, I call the salon. Antoine answers. "*Bonsoir*! How are you loving your haircut?" he gushes.

"Oh, well, my friend loves it. And she wants to come in for a haircut tomorrow. Do you have any appointments available?"

"*Mais, oui*," he says.

"Great! Now let's get out of here," Jun says taking charge. "This place is just too crowded. Now what should we do for dinner? Let's go someplace fun."

"I know a place near the Bastille," I offer. "It's been ten years since I was there, but I remember it as being very lively, with good food and a local crowd." Then I turn to Lucas and say, "And they have the best chocolate mousse in all of Paris." I catch a glimpse of his smile before he turns away.

We make our way down to the metro station, pulling out our tourist maps to find the subway line to Place de la Bastille. The metro tunnels are alive with movement and noise—stiletto heels and business loafers click against the concrete, screeching brakes signal arriving trains. We push through the rush hour of body traffic at a determined pace. Blurry snapshots of color come toward us: a yellow silk scarf, the red lipstick of an African woman, an orange stocking cap pulled over brown dreadlocks, and countless navy blue overcoats. Street musicians line the hallways—Peruvian pipes, guitars, and portable keyboards—but it's the melody of an opera singer belting out a very off-key rendition of *La Bohème* that stands out amidst the blend of echoing underground sounds.

"Oh, she's terrible, isn't she?" I yell to Jun over the volume, laughing. "But isn't this great?"

"She better take some singing lessons if she wants to make it on stage," Jun yells back, pushing Lucas ahead of her. Either Jun is more concerned about keeping her son from getting trampled or she doesn't share my enthusiasm for this vibrant contrast to Germany.

Tucked behind the Place de la Bastille, a traffic-congested roundabout with a fat, towering column in the middle, is Café de l'Industrie. The café's adjoining dining rooms are tightly packed with art; antique oil paintings and Toulouse-Lautrec posters cover every inch of the walls. Sculptures and overgrown plants cram any floor space left between the many tables. Lamps with fringe shades give off a dim but warm light. A hostess says she has a place for us, though there is not an empty table visible. We follow her through a maze, a magical Bohemian menagerie, to a table along the edge of a wall from where we can observe the entire room of animated, wine-consuming, French-speaking patrons.

"Thanks for this idea," Jun says. "This is an ideal place."

"I'm relieved I didn't lead us astray. I wasn't sure it was even still here."

We order leek soup and *Boeuf Bourguignonne*. Lucas orders

entrecôte and french fries. "Lucas, you call them *pommes frites* here," Jun says. "The French don't call them french fries."

"I know, Mommy. Can I go to the toilet now, please?"

"Yes," she tells him. When he's out of sight she turns to me and sighs. "This is a hard year for us," she says.

"Is it because of the German language?" I ask, projecting my own difficulties.

"No, the problem is the kids at school tease him. Last week he came home and told me, 'Mommy, they asked what toilet I come out of.'"

"Why would they say that?" I ask, clueless.

"Because of his skin color. He doesn't have white skin!" she snaps.

I take diversity for granted. Even though we may look different—and, ahem, speak different languages—we are all still one species sharing one planet. I am aware that Germany is predominantly white (I would not dare use the word Aryan), but I have been shamefully ignorant as to how this might impact my Asian friends. Lucas', or Jun's, skin color never registered in my mind, except to think how smooth and beautiful it is. "Kids are always mean; it's a universal trait," I reply, trying to be helpful.

"What bothers me most is that they learn this from their parents," says Jun. "Also, this is the year they will determine if he goes to gymnasium next year or not. So there's a lot of pressure on him, on all of us."

The German school system determines a child's future at the age of ten. If Lucas is "chosen"—if his grades are good enough—he will go to gymnasium, a college prep school like American high school. Gymnasium is for the "smart" kids and puts them on a nine-year path toward university. If, by the age of ten, his German speaking abilities are not up to perfectionist standards, or if he's not terribly good at math, he will be sent to *Realschule*, a trade school that eventually qualifies him for clerical jobs. If he proves himself worthy during his six years at *Realschule*, he can still take an *Arbitur*, a college entrance exam, and still become a doctor or a lawyer—or an automotive industry executive. However, if he is deemed "slow," unmotivated, or lacking in any other respect—judged at ten years old, mind you—he will go to *Hauptschule* to learn mechanics or carpentry, where after five years, followed by a craftsmanship-apprenticeship program, he can qualify for blue collar jobs. Going to *Hauptschule* means you can kiss your college dreams goodbye. God forbid the kid is disruptive in class one day as this could make the difference between him becoming a CEO or a CEO's plumber. (Nothing against plumbers—we need them as much as, if not more than, CEOs—but it demonstrates the disparity.) Even if he does make it to university, the degree programs are usually seven years long so he will be in school until he's close to thirty.

"Gosh, Jun, I really feel for you. It's a very different system that seems unfair. But I'm really impressed with your positive attitude."

"Otto is happy with his job," she says. "But as soon as he can retire, which should be in about four or five years, then we're going to leave. We want to go back to Australia."

We scrape our bowls of *mousse au chocolat* clean and then take the metro back to the hotel. The subway is not as crowded now so there are seats for all three of us. A man with a guitar steps in the door just as it's about to close. *"Excusez moi,"* he says positioning himself in front of the handful of seated passengers. *"Je ne veux pas vous deranger."* He apologizes for his disruption and begins strumming the energetic Spanish rhythm of a Gipsy Kings song.

"Jun," I say, leaning over to whisper to her, "how come we never see anyone playing music on the trams in Stuttgart?"

"I'm sure there's some rule against it," she replies. "There's a rule for everything in Germany."

"Oh, yes," I laugh. "I know about The Rules."

"No vacuuming or laundry on Sundays," she says. "No honking at cars waiting too long at a stoplight, and no performing in public places."

"That's what I love about the French," I say. "They have their rules, but then they break them. They snub their noses and say, 'These rules, puh! They do not apply to us!' That's my style." It's true. I was raised to be an independent thinker, to question authority, and to follow my bliss—within reason. Manners and responsibility were still enforced by my parents. But whenever I encounter a rule, my subconscious immediately calculates its logic and, if in disagreement, devises a way around it. Clearly, Germany is not a good fit for someone like me.

Jun smiles. The train stops. The guitar player says, *"Merci,"* holds out his hat for contributions, then steps out of the car and into the night. Before the doors close, another musician steps in. His dark hair is messy and his ragged tweed overcoat is two sizes too big. He tows an amplifier on a luggage cart with a plastic cup for donations taped to its handle. With the flick of a switch, background orchestra music starts to play. He holds his clarinet to his lips and blows the notes of "Yesterday." His right foot taps to the beat of the Beatles and each rise of his scuffed-up leather shoe reveals the peeling layers of its rotting sole. He plays with his eyes closed, his body sways to the rhythm. Perhaps he is singing along inside his head: *Yesterday, all my troubles seemed so far away. Now it looks as though they're here to stay . . .*

The train rumbles along, its mechanical hum harmonizing with the clarinet and violin from the loudspeaker. Stirred by his melancholic music, the bittersweetness of his passion—and his need for new shoes—a lump forms in my throat. This is what I've been missing—freedom of expression, public display of creativity, and the unrestrained exposure of life in all its diversity of colors, shapes, styles, and imperfections. I am in a place where emotion is embraced, not tamped down by law and order—the kind of place I long to be. I turn my head away from Jun and Lucas and wipe away the lone tear that has escaped from the corner of my eye. When his song is over I place a five-euro note in his plastic cup and say, "*Merci.*"

Back at the hotel I am again invited to watch the lights on the Eiffel Tower, another sparkly, spectacular display of modern electricity. After the ten-minute show I go back to my room and call Marcus.

"I got that email today, the picture of you with two men," he says.

"Yes, that's Antoine and Frank at the salon. What did you think of my haircut? It's awful isn't it?"

"It's not really your style," he says, his diplomatic way of saying he agrees with me. "I have to go to sleep now," he says abruptly. "I have an early meeting tomorrow."

"I miss you, too," I say without masking my sarcasm.

"I didn't mean to . . ." he starts, then stops. "I miss you too."

I go to the salon with Jun and Lucas. I read more back issues of *Paris Match* while Lucas pores over more *Asterix*. In less than thirty minutes, Jun steps into the waiting room. Putting her hand to her ear, tucking in a loose strand of hair, she announces, "I'm really happy with this. This is exactly how I used to have my hair cut when we lived in Singapore."

I'm looking at Dorothy Hamill, the figure skater from the seventies. "It really suits you," I tell her. And it does. The short wedge hairstyle fits her petite frame and brings out her bright face, emphasizing her wide cheekbones and her full lips.

Antoine follows her out. "She looks just bee-youuuu-tee-fullll, doesn't she?" I smile at Jun. Then he looks at me, squints his eyes, and cocks his head. "Let me just fix your hair a little," he says. He doesn't approve of the bobby pins I've used to hold back my bangs-from-hell, so back in his chair I go for another rendezvous with his blow dryer.

Jun doesn't flinch when she gets her bill. I've prepared her for the sticker shock. "We must take your picture," Antoine fusses. The skinny assistant brings out the camera again so he can email another picture to another husband. The credit card machine makes its tick-ticking sound as it spits out the receipt.

We ask Antoine where we can go for a good chocolate éclair. "My son is the maître d' at Ladurée. You must go there."

Ladurée, the most Parisian of all Parisian patisseries, is just around the corner on the Champs-Elysées. Set slightly back from the busy boulevard, the entire front side of Ladurée is a sunroom filled with tables. Inside in its bakery section, rows of macaroon sandwich cookies in pastel shades are lined up next to creamy, flaky *mille-feuille* frosted with vanilla icing, and bright raspberry tarts, the berries lined up in perfect symmetry—all delicate art forms that look too precious to be edible.

"Is Louis here?" I ask the hostess.

"*Oui*," she says and picks up the telephone to call him.

Louis appears before us. The antithesis of Antoine, he is pale, tall, and bone-thin. He's dressed in a shiny gray pinstripe suit with wide lapels and a purple tie. We introduce ourselves, but he shows no enthusiasm when we tell him we are friends of his dad. "Let me get a table for you," he offers flatly.

"We'd like to sit by a window," I tell him as he starts to lead us away from the sunroom toward the back of the restaurant.

"Those tables are reserved for lunch guests," he says.

"But they're all empty," I argue. "We just want to eat a pastry. We'll be very quick and then we'll leave. Your lunch guests will never know we were here."

"No, madam. I cannot seat you there, but I have a place for you." He shows us to a table pushed under the stairs. If I knew Jun better I might grumble about our treatment; instead, I give her a helpless, apologetic look.

The éclairs are served on a silver tray. The coffee is served in individual silver pots with miniature silver spoons. We drink from the china cups and dab our mouths with starched cloth pink napkins. We may be stuck under the stairs, but the niceties of French elegance prevail.

"It's so wonderful to find someone in Europe who can cut my hair," says Jun, still gloating over her new do. "Though Paris is quite far to come every five weeks."

"Just say the word, Jun, and I'll come back with you," I say as I deposit another forkful of chocolate cream and puff pastry into my mouth.

After we've filled up on sugar and caffeine, we set out in separate directions for the afternoon. Jun is taking Lucas to the Louvre. I am going to chase the ghost of Sarah Turnbull.

I can't be called a stalker because the author doesn't live here anymore, but because in her book she describes places in Paris I've never heard of, my curiosity is stirred. Besides, I've been to the Louvre—and to the Musée Rodin, the Musée d'Orsay, and Musée du Jeu de Paume—several times. I want so see something new.

From the Châtelet–Les Halles metro stop, I climb the stairs to daylight and spot a metal archway marking Rue Montorgueil's starting point. Its charm is instantly apparent. Closed to motorized traffic, the narrow cobblestone street is lined with fruit and vegetable stalls whose colors liven up the otherwise gray afternoon. There are butcher shops with chickens and sides of lamb hanging in the windows, beneath cheerful orange and blue awnings. There are coffeehouses and art boutiques interspersed in between. The street is swarming with grand dames, the stereotype of the quintessential Frenchwoman—elderly, aristocratic looking, and somewhat haughty. I fix my gaze on one who wears a long wool coat that reveals only her nylon stocking-covered ankles and medium-heeled pumps. She picks out pears and apples, inspects an eggplant, and waits in line to pay for her Cornish hen. She carries her growing load of shopping bags in the effortless way that says she's done this a thousand times. She leads her miniature poodle on a rhinestone-encrusted leash; the dog is wearing its winter coat too, a Burberry plaid one. I observe this scene, this woman (and the others like her) with a Mona Lisa smile and think, "You don't see this at the Louvre."

I stop for a cappuccino at the Centre Ville Café, where Sarah Turnbull spent her mornings writing. I wish she were here so I could ask her, "Did your apartment have a dishwasher? Does your husband cook? Have you ever spent any time in Germany? Do you miss living in Europe? How has your move affected your marriage?"

Venturing deeper into the neighborhood, I follow a series of small side streets that lead me to a lingerie store. *Well, when in Paris . . .* I go inside the tiny, sparse-but-elegant boutique where there is exactly one style of bra to choose from—a push-up. It comes in four colors—white, pink, light blue, and black. In the dressing room I scrutinize my haircut in the mirror before looking at the bra, black, padded, and uplifting. I am ripe for retail therapy, so without asking the price I tell the sales clerk, "I'll take it." The cost of my mental healing is seventy dollars, which is sixty dollars more than the last bra I bought at Target. I hesitate before leaving the store when I see the matching lace panties. "I could surprise Marcus by wearing these under my *Lederhosen*," I muse, but I've already tucked my credit card back into my wallet.

We end our last evening in Paris with the Eiffel Tower light show. I go back to my room and call Marcus. "Remember, my love, our train gets in at 4:45 p.m."

"Yes, I know," he says. "I'll be there to pick you up."

The EuroCity Express pulls into Stuttgart's *Hauptbahnhof*. The train station, with its dim lights, feels dark, almost disquieting. I search the platform. "He said he would be here," I tell Jun.

"We need to get home," she says. "We'll have to meet him some other time."

Lucas, as if on cue, as if he can sense my disappointment, says, "I forgot. I have something for you." He reaches into the pocket of his baggy jeans and hands me an Eiffel Tower keychain. "They gave this to me when we went to the top. You can have it."

"Thank you, Lucas," I say. "I know just what I'm going to do with this. I'm going to get a motor scooter and this is what I'll use for my key." He smiles and this time he holds my gaze.

I watch the two of them, mother and son, walk toward the escalator that leads to the tram. When they've disappeared from sight I go outside to wait for Marcus. Just as I've ordered a cappuccino at a coffee bar, he shows up.

"Welcome home, my love," he says, and pays for my drink. He doesn't comment on my hair.

A few days after I'm back, I go to Café Nescafe to check in. Two new girls are working behind the counter and my name appears nowhere on the schedule. Theophanis hands me a used envelope filled with cash, payment for my entire four weeks of employment, and says, "This is for you." And that is the subtle way in which my employment at the coffeehouse comes to an end.

In the evening, I pour myself a glass of wine and stand in front of the bathroom mirror. I take off my shirt and see that my breasts have, once again, fallen completely out of my new push-up bra. I push my flesh back down into the demi-cups for the fourth time today and say aloud, "I'm going to do this." Taking Marcus' barber scissors in my hand, I reach around my face and make my first cut. Snip. Snip. I watch my blond locks fall to the brown tile bathroom floor. I continue cutting with growing determination, stopping only once for a sip of wine. I make my way around my head, twisting to reach the back, until I've cut off the entire bottom layer of the shag. There's nothing I can do about the short bangs except wait for them to grow out, but with the longest of the layers gone at least I don't look like I'm about to step onstage and sing "Maggie Mae."

I call Alayne to see if she got the salon picture I emailed her. "See what they did to me?" I ask.

"I love it," she says.

"Well, it doesn't look like that anymore," I tell her. "I don't understand, Alayne. The haircut he gave you looked so good."

"He didn't *cut* my hair, sweetie," she replies. "He only blew it dry."

"Oh."

I hang up and go look in the bathroom mirror again. I think back to the lights of the Eiffel Tower, the flaky croissants for breakfast, the musicians in the Métro, the crowded warmth and rich food of Café de l'Industrie, the old ladies with their dogs on Rue Montorgueil, the secret thrill of my overzealous push-up bra, the keychain gift from Lucas. As I run through the list I decide that if I had this trip to do over again, I wouldn't do one thing differently.

I slide a sparkly daisy bobby pin into my bangs to corral them. I stand back and say to my reflection, "Dahling, you look bee-youuuu-tee-fullll."

Except next time I would skip the haircut.

When Marcus comes home I'm still in the bathroom sweeping hair off the floor. "You look really cute," he says.

"You mean my hair?" I swing my head from side to side to show him my new bob. It looks better, doesn't it?"

"No," he says, swooping in to give me a hug. "I mean *you* look really cute." His compliment surprises me—I'm not dressed very nicely in my baggy fatigues and a T-shirt. Maybe it's the bra.

He pulls away from me to inspect my hair. "You did a good job cutting it. It definitely looks better. I really like it." He runs his fingers through my bangs. I close my eyes savoring his tender touch, his unhurried attention, his arrival at home before eight p.m. His hand keeps moving—down my back, around to the front, and up my shirt where he finds an unleashed breast.

"Ooh la la," I whisper in his ear. "Ooh la la."

CHAPTER 10

Stuttgart by
Motor Scooter

I N MARCH, A FEW WEEKS AFTER PARIS, MARCUS, who might be feeling a tinge of guilt over his preoccupation with work—or over the new Ducati motorcycle he has just bought—comes home from work one night and says, "I called Thomas today." There is only one Thomas in our lives, Thomas Wein, who owns a motorcycle dealership in the city of Pforzheim. Marcus went to elementary school with him and bought from Thomas the Suzuki Bandit on which our courtship began. "He said he has a used scooter for sale. It's ten years old, but it runs well. I think we should go look at it this weekend."

"Yes, please," I say. "I live for the day when I don't have to wait for the tram."

On Saturday morning we suit up in our protective motorcycle gear—I'm still wearing Marcus' hand-me-down padded pants. I take my place on the back of the Ducati and hang on as Marcus accelerates, leaving Stuttgart behind.

I lean to the left, then right, then left again as the motorbike angles sharply into each curve during the forty-minute ride east. Marcus reaches back and rubs my thigh with his gloved hand. I return the silent message by tapping his stomach.

Situated on the northern edge of the Black Forest, Pforzheim is surrounded by trees and rivers. It is said to have once been one of the most beautiful cities in Germany, but that was before the bombs were dropped. During World War II, British squadrons obliterated the city center, because Pforzheim's jewelry and watch-making industry was thought to be making "precision instruments" to aid the German forces. Marcus restates this more matter-of-factly: "They were making bomb fuses." After the rubble was cleared away, the city became yet another victim of postwar reconstruction—new buildings erected as quickly as possible to house the few people lucky enough to survive. The resulting 1950s architecture is functional but aesthetically void, with the flat-roofed train station being one of the most prominent eyesores. The good news is that the jewelry industry has recovered enough to sustain the local economy, aided by people arriving by the busload from all over Europe to take gold and silversmith classes.

Thomas is in his blue coveralls, his hands caked with black grease; he is tightening the chain of a shiny black bike. "Hey, Thomas," Marcus says, pointing to the bike. "That's the new V-Strom 1000, isn't it? I read about that in the last issue of *Motorrad*. It looks like a sweet ride. If they'd make it with ABS brakes I'd buy one."

I take a breath. I hope this isn't going to take all day.

Luckily, Thomas doesn't have time for shop talk. "Let me show you the scooter," he says, not bothering to wipe off his hands. An outdoor courtyard is filled three rows deep with bikes in various states of disrepair. "Here it is," he says. The little machine is black with fuchsia trim, including the wheel rims, and rust free. "It's been adjusted," he continues, meaning that a few illegal holes have been drilled into the muffler, allowing for an extra ten or fifteen kilometers per hour of speed.

Since the formation of the European Union, individual countries have been required to adopt new laws to get in synch with one another—laws for driver licenses, food packaging, pollution controls, and store opening hours, to name a few. When harmonizing the laws, they look to the country with the least common denominator. In the case of motor scooter speed limits it was Italy. While France, Spain, and Germany had speed limits of fifty-five kilometers per hour, Italy's limit was set at forty-five in order to avoid a helmet requirement. Therefore, every other E.U. country was forced to adopt the lower speed so Italians could still feel the wind in their hair. Forty-five kilometers per hour in miles is twenty-eight. I can ride a bicycle faster than that. Even Germany, where high-speed driving is considered a right, not a privilege, couldn't win this fight.

"Go ahead and take it for a ride," Thomas instructs.

I strap on my helmet—because Germany has a helmet law no matter what your speed—and drive around the block three times. The wind rushes in my face and my smile stretches.

Marcus doesn't have to ask if I want it; he just gets on his motorcycle and drives straight to the bank to get cash from the *Geldautomat*. He takes out enough euros to pay Thomas in full, the scooter's cost being just slightly more than my Paris haircut and French push-up bra combined.

I follow behind the Ducati, holding Marcus back with my top speed of seventy kilometers per hour (an illegal forty-three miles per hour), returning to Stuttgart on the back roads. I'm not sure why Marcus has veered off course, until I see the BMW Motorcycles sign. Ah, another Saturday, another motorcycle shop. By the time I pull into the parking lot he is already off his bike and removing his helmet. "What are we going to do here?" I ask.

"We're going to get you some new motorcycle pants," he says. "This is where I got mine. I think it's time you have your own."

I look down at my lower half, bulging in black leather pants five sizes too big. "These are fine," I say. "Pants are so expensive. I can make do with these. They're perfectly comfortable." I lose the battle; he's already heading inside the store.

We're combing through the rack of women's gear when a salesman approaches. "What size are you looking for?" he asks.

"Thirty-six," I answer, still searching the rack.

He looks me up and down, furrows his brow, and says, "Let's start with size forty. Let me go find you a pair in the back."

As soon as he walks away I take a size thirty-six into the dressing room and try them on. "They fit perfectly," I tell Marcus.

"You look so sexy in those," he says.

"Wow, these *are* really nice," I say, rubbing my hands up and down the thick suede leather. "I didn't realize what it would feel like to have motorcycle pants that fit right."

The salesman returns with the larger size. His mouth drops opens at the sight of me. "Oh, well," he starts awkwardly, "I have to admit, when I saw you in your other pants I would have thought you were a bigger size."

"Let me show you the new enduro bike that I was telling you about," Marcus says. "It's this one here, silver with the red leather seat. It has . . ."

"I *knew* you didn't come here just to get me pants." We both laugh. It's a day of lightness and adventure. I love to spend this kind of time with my man; we need more of this.

When we finally get back to Stuttgart I go straight to my desk drawer and take out Lucas' Eiffel Tower key chain, sliding my Suzuki 50cc key onto it.

"The scooter will be great for driving to work," Marcus says with a teasing grin. "I'll be able to drive straight to the factory gate."

"Don't even think about it," I reply. I throw my arms around his neck and kiss him on the lips.

With each passing day the cherry tree outside our kitchen window erupts with more white blossoms. Temperatures inch up. Like a bird freed from its cage, I go exploring. I pack up my laptop in my backpack and kick-start the engine of my little Suzuki.

Bad Cannstatt's city center is only a mile down from our vineyard perch, but since Marcus resumed taking his own suits to the dry cleaners, I rarely go there. While considered a stepsister to Stuttgart, Bad Cannstatt maintains its dignity with several claims: it has the largest source of Europe's mineral water outside of Budapest. It is where Gottlieb Daimler invented the automobile in 1886. (The internal-combustion engine, for which he is also credited, was simultaneously invented by Otto Benz in another part of Germany.) Daimler also invented the motorcycle. (His garden-shed workshop is now a modest museum.) And it boasts the oldest building still standing within the Stuttgart city limits—the *Klösterle*, a "small monastery" built in 1463. Built in the *Fachwerk* style—thick wood beam "compartments" filled with straw and covered in stucco—it represents what Germany's houses looked like in the Medieval Ages.

The *Klösterle*, tilting like the Tower of Pisa, is now a restaurant. Contemporary buildings surround it outside, but inside it remains in its original state with warped wood floors, rows of rough timbers holding up the ceiling, and thick wood tables with built-in benches. It feels as if robed knights will show up any minute, tying their horses to the tree before going inside to slam back a few steins of beer. This is where we bring our out-of-town guests to dine on Swabian specialties, like *Kutteln* (that ubiquitous pickled cow's stomach) and *Schmalz*, a greasy paste made from the boiled fat of pigs or geese.

"You actually *like* this stuff?" I ask Marcus when he spreads the *Schmalz* on his bread.

"Good *Schmalz* is a cultural achievement," he says, "like the art of making fine wine."

"Oh, brother." I turn my head so I don't have to watch him ingest the greasy substance.

Also on the menu is *Rostbraten*, roasted pork loin served with *Spätzle* egg noodles, another of Marcus' favorite dishes. "Want a bite?" he asks.

One taste tells me enough to know I couldn't finish a whole serving. "Wow. With food this salty it's no wonder Germans love beer."

I pass the *Klösterle* and ride further into Bad Cannstatt toward the city hall, a glass and steel structure presiding over the market square. A big farmers market is held here, though not today. The square is dotted with people filling plastic bottles with water from a weathered copper fountain, one of many in the area that still spurts mineral water from deep underground. I pass more *Fachwerk* houses, relics of the 1500s, which now house bars and gift boutiques. I weave through the back streets, left then right, and notice a cobblestone alley called Küblergasse—*Gasse* for lane as opposed to *Strasse* for street. Faded Himalayan prayer flags hang between the houses and two torches burn outside a stone barn-like building. These adornments, curiously out of place, pull me toward them like a beckoning finger.

I turn off my engine and wheel my scooter further into this car-free zone. When it comes to scooter parking there are—miraculously—no rules! As long as you're not blocking anyone's way you can park anywhere. I stop in front of a photography studio, its large windows displaying fuzzy, airbrushed portraits of brides and grooms, and lift my scooter onto its kickstand.

A few more doors down, past a tea store, a bead shop, and a tailor's boutique, I find that the torches and prayer flags mark the entrance to a coffeehouse called Café Chico. I step out of the ancient alley and enter a modern environment of exposed brick, steel beams, orange and green walls, and sleek track lighting. An overstuffed white sofa sits in one corner. Through the speakers Sade sings, "Your love is king, I crown you in my heart." I recognize the music and its familiarity feels like an invitation. A waitress smiles warmly at me. I venture further in. A tiny handwritten sign sits on the bar reads, "Please look in the refrigerator to see today's homemade pastry selections." I look. It's filled with quiche, cheesecake, and apple strudel whose layered apple slices and raisins inside a roll of flaky dough look particularly delicious. I sit on the white sofa and a young woman with a long blond braid takes my drink order. *"Ein latte macchiato, bitte,"* I tell her as I lean back in the cushions to work on the freelance project I've just scored, writing conference materials for a company back in Seattle. Welcome to my new office.

Three hours, two lattes, and one apple strudel slice later, I head back outside into the dusk, the cobblestone alley now glowing with light from the shop windows. I'm ready to head home, and am looking forward to an evening with Marcus.

When I reach my scooter, I find a note taped to the speedometer. It's a receipt from the photography studio. Written on it in red marker it says in German, "This is not a parking place. Do not park here again or next time we will call the police." I shut my eyes, willing myself not to let this spoil my day. I calmly pull the two pieces of cellophane tape off my scooter and wad the note up into a ball, stuffing it in my pocket. I unlock the seat and pull out my helmet from underneath. Just as I am buckling the chinstrap, a stout woman steps out from the photo studio and rushes toward me like Rottweiler on a drug bust. In German she barks, "Don't park your scooter here again . . . blah, blah, blah!"

I ignore her, proud that I am learning to steel myself against these random yet frequent confrontations. I continue preparing for my ride home, zipping up my jacket and tightening the straps of my backpack. But she's not done. My reprimand has not been thorough enough. She snarls, "Blah, blah, blah . . . call the police."

Finally, I crack. I yap back at her in English, unconcerned if she understands me or not. "I already got your note. You don't have to come chasing after me. Anyway, it's not illegal for me to park here and I was careful not to block your entrance or anyone's path."

She surprises me by replying in very clear English. "This is a business, not a parking place," she says. "Next time, park at the end of the street with the other bikes." She watches me with her arms folded across her chest until I turn the corner.

Back home, I smooth out the wrinkles of the "Don't park here" note until it lies flat and leave it on my desk. Marcus reads it, its glaring red ink impossible to miss, but he doesn't say anything. I don't say anything either. I'm not ignoring the advice in *100 Ways to Stay Together* to "communicate, communicate, communicate." No, my communication—albeit nonverbal—is clear: "This isn't working out for me here. We need to think about moving." To which I already know his response based on my previous pleas: "I can't leave my job yet." Before I go to bed I wad up the note again and give it a final burial under the banana peels and coffee grounds in the trash can.

Stuttgart's Bohnenviertel, or Bean Quarter, is named for the fifteenth-century peasants who grew beans in this downtown neighborhood. Some of its narrow streets, lined with peaked-roof buildings from the 1700s, possess a glimmer of residual charm, but a few of its blocks are designated as the *Rotlicht* district. Prostitution is legal in Germany, but unlike Amsterdam's Red Light district with its marijuana cafés, drugs are strictly *verboten*. Life in the Bohnenviertel, with its eclectic mix of sex shops, bakeries, X-rated movie theaters, and Italian espresso bars, is colorful but hardly a risk. Statistically, Stuttgart is one of the safest cities in Germany.

Rita's Garden is an Indian restaurant tucked in between a bank and a hair salon, and though it's in the Bohnenviertel, it's several blocks away from the nearest red light.

I ride my scooter there to meet Lena for lunch.

"Anna is joining us," Lena says when I enter the restaurant. Indeed, Anna is already there, beaming her smile at me.

"It's good to see you again," I say to Anna, who is another student from Fokus. Cherubic with curly dark hair and freckled black skin, she too married a German—also an auto executive—whom she met in her home country of South Africa. These Germans do get around.

I order the curry chicken lunch special, ignoring the *Scharf—*

German for spicy—warning symbol. When the waiter is out of earshot, I say, "That's the first time I've heard German spoken with an Indian accent. It sounds cute."

"I remember the first time I heard an American speaking fluent German," says Lena.

"It wasn't me, was it?" I ask, winking.

"No." She smiles and continues. "Americans enunciate every word, and pronounce the Rs hard."

I nod. "Yes, makes that much easier to understand, doesn't it?" Lena nods. I turn to Anna and ask, "How is the teaching going?" She has a job teaching business English.

"It's good," she says. "But it has its challenges too. My current class is a group of bank lawyers. Just this morning I had them read their homework assignments aloud and when I asked one of the guys to define a term from his paper he got very testy. 'As . . . I . . . already . . . said . . .,'" she mimics his condescending tone. Lena and I laugh at her imitation of an arrogant German. "And today they made a big fuss about a coconut smell and opened up all the windows in the conference room. I told them, 'It's my hand cream.' So I guess you could say we're still trying to get to know each other."

"That's a very generous way of putting it," I tell her. "I wish I had your patience, and your compassion. Take last week for example . . ." I relay my latest mishap, and my subsequent outburst, about the note taped to my motor scooter.

"Noooooo, I can't believe it!" Lena says, her brown eyes widening, her laugh deepening. "Tell Anna the story about taking your wedding dress to the dry cleaners."

"No, I don't want to relive that one again. You must have a good story for us, Lena. Or doesn't this kind of thing ever happen to you?"

"Of course it happens. All the time. Just yesterday my supervisor bitched at me," she says, referring to the hotel where she works as a breakfast waitress. "She told me I was being too friendly to the customers and that I was taking too long to pour their orange juice."

"What did you say back to her?" I ask.

"Nothing, I just smiled, but inside I was swearing at the old witch. Later, I waited on a table of rock stars. Have you ever heard of the band Alice Cooper? They gave me free tickets to their concert tomorrow night. I'm taking Martin."

"That's so typical of you," I say. "Your stories always have a silver lining."

Our curry arrives and I take my first bite. I swallow quickly so the food doesn't have time to burn my throat.

Noticing my red face and watering eyes, Lena says, "Let's order you some plain yogurt. And here, take my rice. It will help."

"Lena tells me you want to move back to the U.S.," Anna says.

"Um, actually, yes, I do," I reply, trying not to sound too quick to answer, and not wanting to offend her since she plans to make Germany her permanent home. "But that has always been the plan. We said we'd stay here two years. It's been almost one so far, but I wouldn't mind going back already."

"You should stay, Beth. You'll get used to it."

The art of adjusting to a new culture is getting used to things being different than your own. I know this, and I have been doing this, from the nudity in the mineral baths to laying my bottles down on the grocery store conveyor belt. But I still can't seem to settle in. If Anna weren't so sweet and softhearted I would give her a forceful reply: "I don't want to get used to it!"

There is much I admire about this culture. The people are educated, hard working, and family-oriented. They are practical—not materialistic, not flashy or superficial. They are direct, and even though it often comes across as harsh, they give straightforward answers instead of ambiguous ones. They are stewards of the land, with a deep appreciation for nature. They are strong-bodied and strong-willed, traits that helped the early Germanic tribes win the Battle of the Teutoburg Forest against the Romans, a defeat that contributed to the end of the Roman Empire's expansion. The Germans, outnumbered and insufficiently armed, ambushed the Roman troops, surprising them by jumping out from behind the trees, wielding axes and screaming, with bare-breasted women fighting alongside the men. If they had lost, Germany would have become part of Italy. (*Oh, the thought of it!*) But they triumphed—at least in that fight two thousand years earlier, and luckily not in certain later ones—and their culture continued to develop. Throughout history German culture has influenced the world with incomparable contributions from its scientists, intellects, philosophers, artists, musicians, poets—and supermodels. Einstein, Beethoven, Bach, Brahms, Mozart, Nietzsche, Goethe, Rainer Maria Rilke, Herman Hesse, Gutenberg (inventor of the printing press), Kepler the astronomer, Busch and Coors (if only they knew how much the Americans have watered down their beers), Levi Strauss,

Anne Frank, architect Mies van der Rohe, Hugo Boss, Heidi Klum . . . the list of powerhouses is mind-blowingly long.

I have been a direct recipient of this influence, as the most pivotal book I read in college—besides Edward Abbey's *Desert Solitaire*—was Goethe's *Faust*. Faust is a successful but discontent scholar striving for knowledge, hungry to understand the meaning of life. He feels alienated from others and no matter how much he learns and accomplishes, he realizes he will never be satisfied. Upon reading this, I felt understood for the first time in my life. Would I sell my soul to Mephistopheles to know the feeling of ultimate satisfaction? No, but it helped me understand that a certain amount of discontent is a fair price for being curious, questioning, interested, and alive.

I apply this dissatisfied-but-determined approach to Germany, still striving to learn and to understand. But will I ever get used to it? I don't think so, and I'm not going to make a Faustian Pact to find out. So I simply reply, "Thank you, Anna. I appreciate your encouragement," as I scoop up another spoonful of cooling yogurt to douse the flames in my esophagus.

There's a voicemail from Marcus waiting for me when I get home. "Do you want to meet me and some of my coworkers at the *Frühlingsfest* this evening?" he asks in his seductive British lilt.

As a wine drinker, I'm not a big fan of the German beer tent scene and thus not that enthusiastic about going to this springtime version of Oktoberfest, but how can I resist that sexy voice?

And I will take any opportunity I can get to spend time with my hard-working husband. I call him back and say, "Sure. What time should I meet you, and where?"

At 7:30—19:30 in German time—I ride my scooter down from the vineyard to the Neckar River and head in the direction of the Mercedes-Benz factory. Halfway down this road—paved over many times since the days Mr. Daimler test-drove his motorized inventions on it—is a fairground called the Cannstatter Wasen (pronounced "vah-zen"). Like Munich's Theresienwiesen, the meadow where Oktoberfest is held, the *Wasen's* space is similarly enormous with room for the temporary city of beer tents, food booths, carnival games and rides, and a giant Ferris wheel. I park at the entrance, make fleeting eye contact with the security guards at the gate, and breeze through since there is no entrance fee. "Meet me at the Fruit Pillar," Marcus had said. On the phone I had no idea what he was talking about, but it's instantly obvious—a fifty-foot tall stalk of fiberglass apples, carrots, onions, cauliflower, and celery looms in the middle of the fairgrounds. The *Wasen* festivals started out as a farmers market and the Fruit Pillar (or Veggie Tower, as I see it) commemorates the roots of this gathering place.

Marcus and I find each other in spite of the swarm of people angling for space. He gives me a big hug and says, "Hello, love of my life! We're over in the Schwabenbräu tent. Follow me."

I hold onto his hand as he pulls me through the crowd. We enter a beer tent the size of an airplane hangar. Ten-foot-tall loudspeakers next to the stage blare out the rock band's electric guitar melody of "Smoke on the Water." We make our way through the rows of long, wooden beer tables, folding tables with matching benches that are a fixture at all German festivals. In the middle of the noisy madness we find our group, the truck production-design department of Germany's largest automotive company. I get introduced to Jens, Begonia, Manuel, Anita, Simon, and Simon's girlfriend Frederica. I already know Hannes—and Anton, who is reportedly only staying for one beer before going home to his twins. From the looks of the table, cluttered with beer mugs, puddles of spilled beer, and empty plates streaked with grease, brine, and breadcrumbs, it appears I'm late to the party. After the introductions are made, they return to their conversations. I squeeze in on a bench between Marcus and Frederica, a tall blonde in a starched white blouse, pearls, and gray dress pants. Marcus immediately starts talking about work with Begonia on the other side of the table, so I turn to Frederica. As an opener I ask, "So, what do you do?"

"I'm a law student in Munich," she replies. "I have two more years left. I commute to Stuttgart every . . ."

Her response comes to a quick halt as the band begins a new song. It's a German pop tune that prompts an instinctive response from the audience. "Come on! Get up here!" Jens instructs everyone. Jens has jumped up on the wooden bench and is already shaking his hips to the beat. One by one, the suit-clad men and women follow his lead, arms waving, heads bobbing, until only Hannes, Marcus, and I are left sitting. Not surprisingly, Frederica stays seated too. She strikes me as someone who would rather be sipping a Cosmopolitan at a hip bar and listening to chill-out music. I get it.

Our beer waitress arrives; she holds six liter-size beer mugs in her left hand and six in her right. While we English speakers call them mugs, in Germany they're called *Mass*, short for *Masskrug—die Masskrug* (feminine noun). But *Mass—das Mass* (neuter noun)—also refers to "measure," as regulation states each glass must hold exactly one liter—the equivalent of almost three bottles of beer, and with a higher alcohol content. Sometimes *Mass* is spelled *Maß*, using the Eszett letter. Unique to the German alphabet, it looks like a capital B but sounds like an S. Language reform is making its usage less common, replacing it with a double S, making it easier to type. And don't call the glass beer mug a stein when in Germany. *Stein* means stone or rock. The ornamental stoneware tankards with the hinged lids that we call steins and buy for souvenirs? Those are for decorative purposes, not for use as beverage containers.

Each liquid-filled *Mass* weighs five pounds, so our waitress is carrying thirty pounds—in each hand! It's such a marvel, and a feat, that there are actually beer mug weightlifting competitions during Oktoberfest. With this kind of brawn, it's no wonder the German women were instrumental in fighting back the Romans. She reaches between the pinstripe pant legs and leather wing tips on the bench to set down a few of the mugs. Beer foam hovers on the rim but she's done this a few times and doesn't spill a drop.

As the song continues, the bench wobbles to the rhythm of the adults bouncing on it. I clutch my beer glass with both hands. The people at neighboring tables have climbed up on their benches too. A waiter delivers our dinner, setting down two plates of bratwurst curled around a bed of sauerkraut and two slices of brown bread; the mild fare is welcome after my fiery Asian lunch.

"I heard you got a scooter," Hannes shouts across the table. "Now you're going to have to learn where all the speed cameras are."

I get his sardonic joke. "My scooter is faster than you think, Hannes. But don't worry, Marcus points out the cameras every time we pass one."

"Did you hear the story about the guy on the motorcycle whose girlfriend on the back flashed the camera?" he asks.

"If it's the same one that Marcus told me, then yes. But tell me again. I want to hear your version."

Leaning forward, holding his tie away from the spilled beer, he says, "This guy was on his Harley-Davidson and he saw a speed camera so he turned around to drive past it again. He was speeding on purpose and his girlfriend lifted her shirt to flash her bare breasts at the camera. He didn't think he'd get caught because motorcycles don't have a front license plate to identify them, but because there are so few Harleys in Germany they were able to track him down."

"Yep, that's the same story I heard. I love to hear about Germans breaking the rules. How much was his ticket in the end?"

"I don't know. I just remember he was fighting it in court and it made the national news."

"Well, cheers, Hannes," I say, lifting my liter of beer. "Here's to your new assignment in Japan."

"*Prost*," he says, taking a much bigger gulp than me.

"*Prost*," I reply. We slam our mugs together. If it were the year, say, 1433, there would be a real purpose to toasting with this much force; a hard hit splashes beer into each other's mugs to prove neither is trying to poison the other.

Hannes lets out a satisfied sigh; I suppress a burp.

The members of the truck department don't return to the ground for the rest of the evening. They stay on the benches, arms hooked, singing along to the music, ordering more beer, and getting drunker with each liter. "It's going to be an unproductive day in the office tomorrow," I say to Marcus. He nods.

"Come on, Beth. Get up here," Jens insists without relenting.

"Yes, come on. Stand up and dance with us," Manuel joins in. "You too, Marcus."

We stand up, balancing on the crowded bench. From the elevated height we can survey the tent, jam-packed with bodies, and get a view of the band on stage—four aging men in cowboy hats and black leather vests that pull tight around their beer bellies. Marcus isn't the party type either, so as soon as we empty our mugs we excuse ourselves from the festivities. Anton stays for another beer.

"That was an interesting evening," I say to Marcus on the way out.

"Now you know what one of Germany's big beer festivals is really like," he responds. "Did you have a good time?"

"I did. Really. It was unlike anything I've ever experienced." I hand him my extra helmet and tell him, "Now get on, because I'm about to show you an even better time." He slides onto the scooter behind me and grabs my waist. I rev the engine and yell to the sky, "Woo-hoo!" as we motor off into the balmy spring night.

CHAPTER 11

Berlin

JUNE COMES AND GOES, AND BY THE END OF JULY I'm still wearing wool turtlenecks and a raincoat. Last summer we endured the heat wave—thousands of people died from the high temperatures and our normally breezy apartment became so hot we had to move the mattress onto the balcony. This summer the flannel sheets remain on the bed.

I put on my scarf and gloves and motor downtown on my scooter to *Volkshochschule*. It is my last day of *Deutsch Intensiv IV*. (It's Level Four, albeit a much shorter version of the course I tried to sign up for in the winter.)

The four grammar-filled weeks in the classroom have passed unremarkably, except for the daily competition between two know-it-all students anxious to answer the teacher's questions.

The mousy Serbian girl to my right shouts into my ear, *"Ich weiss! Ich weiss die Antwort!"* (I know the answer!), interrupting

Frau Herman every few minutes in a voice that is shriller than a dental drill. I plug my ears—and not discreetly—but she never gets the hint.

In a now-predictable pattern, the equally loud, chubby Greek girl to my left interrupts the Serbian girl. *"Nein, du hast nicht recht,"* she says, telling her she's wrong.

Their pissing matches escalate until Frau Herman says, "Okay, let's move on to the next lesson. Listen to the discussion, then we'll have a quiz to see what you have understood." She presses play on the tape recorder so someone else can talk for a change.

Anyone browsing through my copy of *Passwort Deutsch 4* can see how this course has gone for me. Every other word is circled in my blue ink followed by an equal sign and the corresponding English translation. *Asylbewerber* = asylum seeker. *Staatsangehörigkeit* = citizenship. *Entstehung* = development. *Arbeitsbedingungen* = working conditions. I should be circling and translating words to describe myself, like *ungrateful, privileged,* and *self-absorbed*, as the majority of my fellow students are migrants. Their circumstances are far more difficult than mine, unimaginable even, and yet they are handling their adjustment to Germany with a far better attitude than me, and with much more grace.

Mark Twain proves I am not alone in my battle to learn German. In *A Tramp Abroad*, he writes (though I am abbreviating here), "A gifted person ought to learn English in thirty hours, French in thirty days, and German in thirty years. The latter tongue ought to be trimmed down and repaired. If it is to remain as it is, it ought to be gently and reverently set aside among the dead languages, for only the dead have time to learn it."

If the mustaches doodled over every face in my textbook are any kind of prediction, I have reached my saturation point. It's time for an extended break from my German studies. Mercifully, this last class will be over in two hours. I take the last coffee break in the Treffpunkt Café like I've taken all my others this summer—alone.

Course complete, Marcus takes a Friday off work so we can enjoy a three-day weekend road trip. "I want to go to Berlin," I tell him.

"That's a good idea. I've never been there."

"You've never been to Berlin?" I ask, incredulous.

"No."

"I can't believe you didn't even have a school field trip there. It's your country's capital."

"We did have a field trip to the capital, but the capital wasn't Berlin then; it was Bonn."

"Oh."

"Bonn was made the capital of West Germany in 1949. It was moved in 1999, then . . ."

"Okay, okay."

One deterrent to traveling by car in Europe is that the highways are so clogged it makes L.A. driving look easy. Germans even have a variety of compound nouns to describe the different kinds of traffic. There's *Reissverschlussverkehr*—zipper traffic—where multiple lanes merge into one. Signs are posted as a reminder for cars to politely alternate when entering the single lane, as they come together like a zipper. There's *Geisterfahrer*, someone who drives into oncoming traffic. Strangely—and horrifyingly—the Autobahn traffic report announces these rather frequently. And the most amusing: *Urlaubszurückverkehr*, a compound noun for "returning from vacation traffic." Our current traffic, however, is just a normal *Stau*. That's one German word that actually sounds like what it means: stall.

Four hours into our drive to Berlin I comment to Marcus, stating the obvious, "It's going to take us longer than six hours to get there. Your cities are so close together, you can never get away from the congestion. And all this construction . . . it never ends."

"That what it's like when you have eighty million people living in a country the size of Montana."

"Well, it's obvious that cruise control was not invented here," I reply.

Marcus turns up the stereo volume. As *Nirvana Unplugged* plays, I keep myself busy noting all the *Ausfahrt* signs. When my dad stayed in Germany after our wedding, he asked, "Why are there so many towns called *Ausfahrt*?" I smile to myself as I remember telling him that it's the word for exit.

Sometime after midnight, nine hours after leaving Stuttgart, we are introduced to Berlin via its version of Times Square: Potsdamer Platz. Here, the Sony Plaza and IMAX 3D Theater create the biggest concentration of neon Germany has ever known. This and the searchlight sending solid beams of light into the night sky, give a glittery first impression of the former communist municipality. But its radiant glow, as we will discover when we view the city's darker historical sites, is a lot like Hollywood; it's only superficial.

We drive past the *Gendarmenmarkt,* the square flanked by French and German cathedrals and a concert hall where Hitler attended the symphony. (Though the grandiose porticos appear to be sixteenth-century originals, they have been rebuilt out of their own World War II rubble). Hearing the music of a lone violin player echoing off the stately buildings, we park and get out of the car. We sit on a bench and listen to him play Vivaldi's *Four Seasons*, the beauty of the music overpowering any thoughts about *Der Führer* having once stood here.

We drop a few euros into the violin case, noting that Berlin's street performing rules must be more lax than Stuttgart's, and drive to our hotel in the Kurfürstendamm, a shopping district with a disproportionate concentration of American establishments like McDonald's, Dunkin' Donuts, Niketown, and Hard Rock Café.

Though it's 2:30 a.m., we're so invigorated by the big city, we go out for a beer. The waiter sets our full mugs down, walks to the next table to collect a check, and comes right back. "I need to take your glasses," he says.

"You just served us," Marcus argues. "We haven't even taken a drink yet."

"*Nein.* We're closing."

"Let us finish," Marcus rallies back.

"I'm taking your glasses."

Berlin may be alive with energy, but it's still Germany.

"I was hoping to have a Berliner for breakfast," I tell Marcus, having searched the buffet for the puffy jam- or cream-filled do-nuts known in America as a Bismarck.

"Those are called *Pfannkuchen* here," he says, smearing Nutel-la on his bread roll.

"Pancakes?"

"Yes. And here they call pancakes *Eierkuchen*.

"Egg cakes. Hmmm." I take a sip of orange juice. "Okay, but I still want to eat a Berliner—I mean, *Pfannkuchen*—while we're here."

Berlin is flat, giving us a good opportunity to tour the city on inline skates. Leaving the hotel along Kurfürstendamm we first pass the Gedächtniskirche (Memorial Church), one of many (many, many, many) tokens of the war. The church tower, left standing in its bombed-out state, has a new ultra-modern church made of blue glass built around the crumbled stone.

"It's beautiful and well done, but it's disturbing," I say to Marcus.

"It's supposed to be disturbing. It's supposed to remind peo-ple about the ruins of war."

"To keep them from starting wars again," I add, still gazing up at it. "Then someone needs to bring our U.S. politicians here."

We skate past the *Tiergarten*, cutting through the expansive green Berlin Zoo, in Berlin's version of Central Park. By avoid-ing the park's gravel paths we take a wrong turn, which leads us to the Scandinavian Complex. We stop to look at the sleek wooden lodges and eavesdrop on a tour guide. "The buildings are each built in the style of their country, and all the materials used came from Scandinavia. Now over here, there was one architectural error made." The guide points up to a window. "The conference room in the Swedish embassy looks directly into the Finnish embassy's sauna." Her flock laughs. We skate on.

From there we skate around the Grosse Stern—the big star—an intersection of five major streets designed to create a visual axis of the city. We veer off onto the broad, tree-lined Boulevard 17 Juni (the date commemorates the first of the anti-communist uprisings), until we reach Berlin's most celebrated symbol—the Brandenburg Gate. (You don't have to go to Berlin to see it, because it appears on the back of German one-euro coins. Though like Abraham Lincoln on the penny, you forget it's there.)

The Brandenburg Gate is an imposing rectangular structure of archways supported by twelve columns capped with a horse-drawn chariot. Holding the reins of the four horses is a woman with wings and an olive wreath around her head. She is also holding an iron cross with an eagle perched on it. It is no coincidence that it looks like it belongs in Greece as it was modeled after the gateway leading to the Acropolis.

Because Marcus cannot skate and talk at the same time, we sit down on a bench. "You do want to know about the history, don't you?" he asks.

"Sure." I loosen my buckles and prepare for a lengthy monologue. I know how he gets going when it comes to his favorite subject. No, not motorcycles. History. He talks . . . I take off my skates . . . he talks . . . .a warm breeze soothes my feet . . . he keeps talking . . . a few pigeons fly by. I nod a few times to show I'm paying attention.

ly, the story—Marcus' version of it—goes like this:

sian Kings from Swabia (the southwestern region of Ger-
that includes Stuttgart) came from a strong and somewhat
aggressive family. When they inherited a castle near Berlin they
thought, "It's nice here. Let's get a little more of this land for ourselves." With the help of a strong military they did, and thus the
kingdom of Prussia grew, along with the number of grand buildings they built in Berlin. Kaiser Wilhelm II (the last emperor of
Germany and King of Prussia, before the monarchy was dissolved)
had many of the buildings designed in the styles of France, Holland, and Russia in order to attract talented workers from these
countries and make them feel at home. This is what gives Berlin
its aesthetic of international variety of pre-war architecture.

After World War I, when Germany went from being a collection of kingdoms to a country with a central government, Kaiser
Wilhelm II was asked to abdicate, which he did in 1918. (He had
ruled since 1888.) Wilhelm influenced Hitler, who shared the
Prussian King's desire to acquire the surrounding land, so in 1939,
the fascist dictator invaded Poland. That, of course, started World
War II, which we know ended badly for Germany and for Hitler.

Hitler, his lover, and his closest comrades committed sui-
cide in his Berlin bunker as the Russians were closing in. Allied
forces bombed the bunker and later used its debris to build a
monument to the Soviets, just down the road from the Brandenburg Gate, to remember the troops they lost when seizing the
city from the Nazis.

This "victory" was followed by the Communist years (1945
to 1989), which included the Berlin airlift in 1948. The Soviets

tried to cut off supplies to West Berlin, but American and British Forces saved the city with an eleven-month-long airlift supplying food, fuel, and more to its diehard inhabitants.

Then came the building of the divisive Berlin Wall in 1961, constructed after one too many uprisings. It was needed to keep the people in "for their own good," communists claimed. President John F. Kennedy arrived on the scene in 1963, and gave his famous speech in front of the Brandenburg Gate stating, "All free men, wherever they may live, are citizens of Berlin. And therefore, as a free man, I take pride in the words *'Ich bin ein Berliner.'*" Years later, in 1987, President Ronald Reagan visited West Berlin and in his speech, standing with this same gate visible in the background, he too uttered a legendary line. He said, "Mr. Gorbachev, tear down this wall." And Gorbachev did. The wall finally came down in 1989, the borders were re-opened between the East and West, and the country was reunified.

With the reunification of Germany came gentrification of Berlin's run down buildings (good news), relocation of the country's capital (good or bad news, depending on how you look at it) and 20 percent unemployment in eastern German areas outside of Berlin (definitely bad news). To this day, Germans in the West pay a Reunification Tax, subsidizing the restoration of a deprived East. In spite of generous incentives for businesses to relocate to the poorer areas—a logical way to provide an infusion of jobs and income—there are few takers.

"Did you get all that?" he asks, lesson over.

"Yes, I think so."

Who needs a guide book when you're married to a history

major? (Marcus' engineering degree came later, after the history studies.) And as a bonus, my feet got a tan. I put my skates back on. "Can we go through the gate now?"

Built in 1791 as a symbol of peace, used by Nazis as a symbol of power, now a symbol of unity, we skate under the grand stone monument that is the Brandenburg Gate. We roll on our wheeled boots through the middle arch where in the days of the monarchy only the Royal family was allowed to pass. Everyone else was required to travel through the narrower arches flanking the main one. Reaching the other side, we stand on what used to be communist land. And yet, what is the first thing we see as we enter the sweeping Pariser Platz? Starbucks Coffee. We skate past it, crossing the square filled with rickshaws for hire, toward the Hotel Adlon, a luxury hotel-turned World War II military hospital-turned rubble pile-turned luxury hotel. Its celebrity clientele has included Charlie Chaplin, Marlene Dietrich, Brad Pitt, and Angelina Jolie. It's the hotel where Michael Jackson created an international uproar by dangling his baby over the edge of their balcony.

We change out of our skates into sandals and walk over to the entrance of the hotel. "May I help you?" asks the doorman/bouncer, buttoned up in his ascot.

"We're here for *Kaffee und Kuchen*," Marcus says.

He looks us up and down, eyeing our inline skates in our hands. Casual as we appear, he deems us worthy and waves us inside to the marble lobby. Under the jewel-dripping chandeliers, we sink into one of the soft velvet sofas next to the other good Germans honoring the punctual three p.m. coffee and cake ritual, but willing to pay more than double the Starbucks prices. "Screw the coffee," I say. "Let's have champagne!"

"Let's have both!" Marcus replies. "This is a day to let the soul dangle." *Die Seele baumeln lassen* is one of the first (and best) German expressions Marcus taught me, and just imagining a soul suspended in air, as if on a tree swing, has an instant calming effect.

After the waiter in his white tuxedo jacket loads our table with crystal glasses and china cups, he wheels over a cart full of creamy cakes. For a delicious, leisurely, soul-dangling hour, we are not reminded about world wars, death, or dictators. Marcus leans over and kisses my cheek. I rest my hand on his leg. Being together in this relaxed state, I feel a surge of something that's been eluding me lately: happiness.

When we extract ourselves from the sofas, we skate a lap around the Reichstag, Germany's capitol building.

"This is another Prussian legacy," Marcus starts. I look around for a bench to sit down, just in case. "It was refurbished by a British architect who gutted the insides to create a more open space and added a glass dome on top to lighten things up, literally and figuratively."

"For someone who's never been to this city, you sure know a lot about its buildings." Inside the dome, visitors are winding their way up the spiral staircase. "Do you want to go in?"

Noting that the line of people waiting to get in is Disneyland-long, he shakes his head no and starts skating again.

We travel one block and stop in front of the Chancellor's Residence, Germany's version of the White House, though its straight lines of stark metal and glass bear no resemblance to America's classical presidential palace. "The modern design is deliberate. It represents a contrast to the old ways," Marcus explains. "The Chancellor lives on top, in a penthouse."

Moving along, we see a bronze plaque embedded in the sidewalk. It reads, "Here stood the Berlin Wall from 1962 to 1989."

"This is it! This is the wall!" I blurt out. More accurately, this is the foundation where the concrete barrier used to be. All that remains is its representation, a cement sidewalk that cuts through an otherwise all-cobblestone plaza. We skate along, following the paved line. I straddle its width, rolling a skate on either side, and then I begin zigzagging across it. "East or West?" I ask Marcus as I alternate sides. He laughs and follows my lead, but I think about what I've just said and immediately regret my insensitivity. Over a hundred people lost their lives trying to climb over this wall; it's not a joke. "I'm sorry," I say. "That wasn't funny."

After several more miles of sightseeing on skates—along the tree-lined boulevard called Unter den Linden, past the ornate Berliner Dom (cathedral) with its bulbous green domes, to Hackescher Markt, an industrial-chic hub of cafés, shops, and welcoming courtyards filled with umbrella tables and prayer flags—Marcus notes: "You need to eat." Smart man. He knows how to avert my hypoglycemic-like bouts of fatigue and irritability. "Sushi?" he asks as we pass a Japanese restaurant.

Hot sake takes hold, relaxing my body along with my tongue. "I'm having such a good time. This city is so fascinating. Its history is so dark, but it's countered by all this modern light and new life." I wave my arm to point out the white walls, designer lighting, and hipster wait staff in the sushi bar. "There's so much going on here. Why can't we live in Berlin?" I slur in my happy buzz.

Marcus just smiles and refills my sake glass. "I'm glad you're having a good time," he says. "I am too."

The Berlin suburb of Zeuten, southeast of the city, is the last stop on the S-Bahn. We have our car, so we drive, and Marcus recaps his family's story on the way. "My grandparents lived in Berlin for two years, in Zeuten. My Opa Harry was a talented engineer. His skills were valued so the communist government asked him to work for them. He didn't mind the work—it was in the Ministry of Industrial Development—but then the *Stasi* . . ."

"Wait. Who are the *Stasi* again?" I interrupt.

"Secret Police. They were the most important element of Communist Germany. The Secret Police tried to enroll my grandfather as an informer. They put increasing pressure on him and he realized that if he didn't give in to their demands he would face consequences. He knew he had to get out of there so he put Oma Inge and my mom—she was twelve at the time—he put them on the tram and went to West Berlin. You could still go shopping there for the day."

"But they weren't really going shopping," I interrupt again.

"No. And they couldn't tell anyone they were leaving. My mom got in big trouble later when she told her parents that she left a letter in the mailbox to say goodbye to her friend across the street. It could have been used as evidence against them. When they got to West Berlin they drove directly to the West German embassy and they were given asylum."

"Then what?"

"The Americans offered Harry a job in the U.S."

"What?! You mean you could have been *American*?"

"They decided to move to Bremen, because Harry had cousins living there."

"And that's where your parents met, and had you . . ." I say, jumping ahead in the story.

But Marcus isn't finished. "They were some of the lucky ones. They left every single belonging behind—my mom had to leave all her dolls, clothes, and books—but they escaped with their lives."

"That must have been terrifying." I think about how traumatic Andrea's childhood must have been and quietly add, "Maybe that explains why she collects teddy bears and doesn't like to travel." A quote by Ian Maclaren runs through my head: "Be kind, for everyone you meet is fighting a hard battle." Andrea has had a harder battle than I ever knew. I vow to have more compassion toward her.

Zeuten is a suburb one might expect to find in, say, Iowa. Single family houses, sizeable and spacious, have big yards—back, front, and side yards!—and are painted bright colors. We drive past a barn-red house with royal blue shutters reminiscent of Sweden, and a yellow house so rich in its hue that it would fit right in on the Italian Riviera. Only the street signs indicate we are still in Germany.

We drive up and down the quiet, tree-lined blocks and eventually find Harry and Inge's old house. Tan with windows trimmed in white, a pitched roof, and a wrought-iron gate painted forest green, it looks homey—making it all the more heartbreaking to know its residents had no choice but to flee.

We park the car and get out. There's no one around; the only sound is the rustling of leaves in the trees. Marcus turns on his digital camera.

"It's immaculate. So elegant," I whisper. "It looks very inviting." He nods.

It became a syndrome for residents who fled the *Deutsche Demokratic Republik* (DDR) to return later, to see where they had once lived. Some attempted to reclaim their property, but the government quickly passed laws to forbid this. We don't know who lives here now; we only know they don't want to be disturbed.

"How do you feel?" I ask interrupting Marcus' silence.

"It's powerful to be here and imagine how their lives were, and how they left," he says. And then he's quiet again.

"Has Inge ever been back?" I ask gently.

"Yes, my parents drove her here a few years ago. After Harry died. But she doesn't get nostalgic. You know how positive she is; she's happy in Bremen."

I take the camera from him and snap a few pictures of him in front of the house.

We drive a few blocks from Marcus' grandparents' old house to Zeutensee. Surrounded by sandy soil, tall pines, and old oak trees, Zeutensee is one of several fresh-water lakes in the area. The lake is the reason the streets were so quiet. The whole of the town seems to be here. The public beach/park area is packed. Local residents are windsurfing, swimming, and throwing sticks for their dogs. We stand on the grass, amidst blanket-to-blanket picnicking families. We change into our swimsuits (in front of everyone, because that's how it's done in Germany) and head straight into the lake.

"I needed this," Marcus says resurfacing from the cooling water.

"I know." I float on my back, listening to the background noise, the barking dogs and the squealing laughter of happy children. The sounds and the fresh water make me think I'm back at Lake Rathbun in Iowa, where I swam during my child-hood summers, days so free of cares we didn't wear sunscreen or seatbelts. But back in Iowa we didn't have Nazis or *Stasi*, and the greatest hardship my parents and grandparents ever suffered was walking to school in the snow. The thoughts of Marcus' family's struggle and the ghosts of wars past weigh so heavily, I dive deep down below the surface to swim away from them. But the sorrows follow me down, propelling me to go even deeper. In the quiet, amniotic darkness, questions brought on by the day fill my mind: Why do humans feel the need to control others? How are they capable of such evil and cruelty? And how is forgiveness possible after such unforgive-able atrocities?

When I can't hold my breath any longer, I come up for air and hear the laughter and animated chatter of the other swimmers. Their sounds answer one of my questions: Forgiveness is not just possible, it's essential. I see examples all around Germany, how forgiveness is what it takes to carry on, to move forward, to rebuild (as they've done with the bombed-out buildings), and to have family picnics at the lake. To forgive is to love, and Zeutensee is one big lovefest.

"I'm over here!" Marcus waves as he sees me looking for him. I swim over and attach myself to him like a barnacle, clinging as if the *Gestapo* were about to take him away. But we are safe—Germany is safe—and that is something to be grateful for.

There is a Sunday evening traffic jam heading into Berlin, but there's no traffic going our direction. "That should make you happy we're going to Stuttgart," Marcus teases me from the passenger seat.

"Very funny," I say keeping my eyes focused on the road.

Halfway home, we see blue police lights flashing ahead. I pull over to let an ambulance pass. We inch along until we see the reason for the emergency vehicles. A car is turned on its side, smashed flat against the meridian. A semi-truck is butted up against it, blocking three lanes. The ambulance driver who has just arrived on the scene is running through the piles of broken glass and jumping over metal pieces toward what is left of the vehicle.

"Oh . . . my . . . God, Marcus!" I say as we move past.

"Yes, that's bad," he replies.

"That car probably passed us ten minutes ago."

"Do you want me to drive?" he asks, seeing my grip tighten on the steering wheel.

I shake my head and squeeze even tighter. A speeding silver

Mercedes flies by us. "And look, no one is even slowing down!" I gripe. "Don't they teach defensive driving in *Fahrschule*?"

"Yes, they mention it," he says.

German Autobahn driving isn't always a Formula One race. Sometimes there is a limit posted of about seventy-five miles per hour, but the rule is when there's no signage there's no limit. And since we're driving in a no-sign section, we continue to get passed by cars careening along at one hundred twenty-five miles per hour and higher.

I'm so tense driving at a snail's pace of sixty, I should take him up on his offer to drive.

"Percentage-wise, the death toll from car accidents is lower in Germany than in the States," Marcus informs me in some backward attempt at calming me down.

"I don't believe that for one minute!" I snap. I check out the figures later on the International Road Traffic and Accident Data Base (IRTAD) and find out he's right. The credit, it is surmised, goes to the demanding curriculum of German driving schools (courses which cost about two thousand euros to complete), German cars engineered for safety, and tough regulations for the cars allowed on the roads, along with random checkpoints to curb drinking and driving. They'll even stop you to measure the depth of your tire treads!

Closer to Stuttgart we pass another accident scene. Even more sobering this time, a motorcycle is lying on its side, its metal parts strewn around. The ambulances are gone, but the police are still taking measurements. We drive past in silence, but we are surely thinking the same thing: No motorcycle driver could have survived this.

By the time we are in bed the illuminated numbers on our bedside clock read 12:24 a.m. "Hey, wait!" I say to Marcus as he turns off the light. "We forgot the Traveling Buddha." I get up and walk to his side of the bed to where our Happy Buddha statue sits. In our post-travel ritual, I place my fingers on the chubby belly of this sandstone figure, a smiling Chinese man with a knapsack slung over his shoulder. "Thank you for our safe trip," I say, rubbing his tummy.

Marcus joins his fingers with mine and adds, "And please look after those people who were in the accidents tonight, and their families."

And all those people who were victims of the Nazis, the Stasi, and the wars, I add silently.

I crawl back into bed. "Marcus?"

"Yes?"

"If we go anywhere next weekend, let's go by train." We lie in silence for a few minutes and then I say to the slumbering body next to me, "I never did get to eat a Berliner."

CHAPTER 12

A High School Reunion
and an Anniversary

OVER THE NEXT FEW WEEKS, MY INBOX FILLS UP with emails from high school friends asking, "Howie, are you coming to our twenty-fifth reunion?" I stare vacantly at my desk, contemplating the idea of going back to Davenport, Iowa—a place I couldn't leave fast enough when I was seventeen. I notice a layer of dust has formed on my huge yellow German dictionary. I take it as a sign that, yes, I should go.

I check the Internet every day for tickets.

"I can't go," I protest to my friend Margaret in a phone call. "Summer airline prices have gone up to three thousand dollars a ticket."

"I'm going to ask Stem," Margaret replies, referring to our classmate Kathy Stemlar, the one with the perfect pleats in her plaid skirt. "She still works for an airline; she can get you a companion ticket. You only have to pay the tax."

The mid-August Chicago afternoon is hot and muggy, the air so thick with humidity that the sky is a milky haze, as if veiled by a gauze curtain. I step outside of O'Hare's baggage claim and inhale deeply. No cigarette smoke. But the distinct pungent scent of fertilizer confirms that I am back on midwestern soil. I turn on my American cell phone—the one thing I didn't give up for my move to Germany—and just as my parents in Southern California answer my call, a delivery truck rolls by. "Hi Mom and Dad. You're not going to believe what I'm looking at right now." A logo emblazoned on the side of the truck reads: *Franziskaner Bier, Bavaria's Favorite Hefeweizen Beer, Made in Munich, Germany.* "Jesus, I can't get away from the place!" My dad laughs his infectious belly laugh, even my mom giggles.

"Ah, Boo," my dad says. "Have fun in Iowa."

The class reunion is a dressy affair held on a Saturday night at the Outing Club, a plantation-style social club with white columns and tennis courts. The club's atmosphere begs the question, "Where are the slaves?" but according to Mr. Ambrose's American Civilization class, Iowa wasn't part of the confederacy and instead was an integral part of the Underground Railroad.

Fifty out of a class of one hundred former Assumption High "Knights" show up. Including spouses, there are ninety or so partygoers. I check in at the registration table to pick up my nametag. The tags, displaying maiden names, as well as our senior-year photos, are lined up alphabetically. I scan through the rows—Baumeister, Deggendor, Heim, Himler, Hintermeister, Kaufman, Krueger, Leininger, Froeschle, Freund, Schloemer, Schmid, Weigand. THEY ARE ALL GERMAN! I have been surrounded by Germans all these years! Even the name of our neighboring town, Bettendorf, is German. Had I studied German instead of Spanish in high school, I might have recognized this before. But I was too busy leading cheers and going to keg parties to know I was raised right smack in the middle of America's German Belt.

Those paying closer attention to their American heritage might already know that in the 1700s and 1800s Germans left their economically troubled country in search of jobs in the Promised Land of America. They arrived by the thousands on steam ships and filtered out across the country's fertile lands, where most of them took up farming. Thus, the attraction to Iowa, which ranks the sixth most populous of German settled states. (The top five are also midwestern states: North and South Dakota, Nebraska, Wisconsin, and Minnesota.) Most of the German settlers were Protestants—Lutheran, mainly—but many were Catholics, proven by Assumption High School's student roster. They procreated (what else to do during those cold winters?) and procreated some more. According to a recent U.S. Census Bureau survey, forty-six million Americans claim German ancestry, making Germans—surprisingly not Latinos, African Americans, or Asians—America's largest ancestry group. That's more than 14 percent of the entire U.S. population!

I shake my head at the late realization. I find my own tag with my English-Welsh name, remembering that besides being one-quarter Norwegian, I am also one-quarter Austrian, which is almost the same as being one-quarter German.

I slap the label on my strapless dress, and start milling around the large dining room.

When word gets around (to all these Germans) that I'm living in Germany, anyone who's got any connection to the country seeks me out. A girl named Diane approaches. I have to look at her nametag to refresh my memory. *You're Diane?!* No longer a scrawny teenager with stringy hair (and I thought my senior year picture was bad), she's a striking, shapely blond wearing an elegant white cocktail dress and sexy sandals. "So I hear you live in Germany," she says. "I lived in Kaiserslautern for four years."

"Oh, yeah, I've heard of K-town. Then you must have been in the military," I say.

"I was a civilian in the military," she replies coolly.

"So you didn't have to do boot camp or combat training?"

"I was a *civilian*," she repeats.

"Did you like living there? Was it hard to settle in? Were the people nice to you?" I bombard her with questions hoping she might unlock Germany's secret to happiness.

"It was great. I loved it," she tells me. "I made such nice friends. I hung out with a lot of Germans and we would always go out to a beer garden after work. I wish I could go back. I'd love to live there again." She takes a sip of her wine, her pinky finger extends as she tips back the glass. Just when I think that's the end of the conversation, she asks, "Where do you live?"

"Stuttgart," I say.

"I went to Stuttgart quite a few times. I love Stuttgart," she says.

"Really? I'm having such a hard time there. I'm looking forward to the day we can move somewhere else," I tell her.

"Why?" she asks with a disapproving look. "Stuttgart is such a fun city. The people are so friendly. I would love to go back."

"Yeah, you said that already." My stomach tightens.

Would my life be different, easier, *better*, if, like Diane, I had moved there for a job instead of a man? Would I feel more integrated, make friends faster if I were there for work—or if we had kids? I had seen expats with school kids assimilate so quickly because of the built-in community of parents. But I don't have a job or kids—I have Marcus. I just wish I could love his country as much as I love him.

This conversation with Miss Wild-About-Germany is a black fly in my Chardonnay. I don't want it to muddle my evening so I say, "Well, gosh, Diane, I hope you can get back there someday. It was nice talking to you. I'm going to go get some of that fresh shrimp now before they run out." I can feel the knives hitting my back as I turn away.

Sean O'Donnell is there, my chauvinist "husband" from our Christian Marriage class. We say a cordial hello as we pass by, but we haven't had anything to do with each other since we our class ended. My best friend, Nan, fills me in on his stats: married for fifteen years, has five kids, owns a big home on Chicago's North Shore, is making a killing in real estate development, and is a generous contributor to his Catholic church. I imagine her telling him mine: she got married at forty . . . to a German, no children, lives in a small one-bedroom rental, barely pulls a five-figure income, and as far as her religion, she falls somewhere between pagan and Buddhist. Hopefully, she would add, "And she's a Democrat," to really piss him off. But she doesn't talk to him about me and he doesn't ask. He's too busy leading the evening's entertainment, a game of Trivial Pursuit.

Everyone is asked to take a seat, so I join Margaret, Nan, and Kathy Stemlar, and their husbands, at their table. They ask, "Hey, Howard, where's your man?"

"In Germany. He had to work."

Sean growls into the microphone. The feedback from the speakers screeches in our ears. He asks questions pertaining to our 1980 graduating year like "Who ran against Carter and became president?"

The table next to mine yells out, "Reagan!" The room erupts with cheering and applause.

Who are these people and when did they become so conservative? A trivia question of my own enters my mind: *Would I rather be living in Germany or here with a bunch of Republicans?*

Germany! (Though to Reagan's credit, he got Gorbachev to tear down the Berlin Wall.)

Sean announces awards during the evening. Though I assumed I would win the Who Traveled Furthest to Get Here award, it does not go to me. For two reunions in a row now it goes to Jim Johnson, a short, blond marketing executive with an American car company. Five years ago he was living in China; he's since moved to Taiwan. He steps up to the mic to accept his trophy: a plain white T-shirt with AHS in small letters on the chest. (No great loss for me on the prize.) He bows his head and says, "I am so grateful to Jesus Christ our Lord for letting me be here today. God bless you all." He pushes his wire rim glasses up on his nose and walks back to his table. I decide against asking him for help finding Marcus a job with his company.

What has happened to these people and when did they get so religious? Another trivia question pops into my head: *Would I rather be living in Germany or here with a bunch of born-again Christians?*

Germany!

Kathy Stemlar leans over and says, "Hey Howard, let's go to the bar and get a glass of wine."

"Hell, yes!" I say. We cut out of there faster than the way we used to skip class to go to McDonald's, leaving our classmates to their political and religious fervor.

I take a swig of my Sauvignon Blanc and say, "Stem, thanks so much for making it possible for me to be here. I thank the Almighty Lord God our Savior for friends like you."

"Oh, shut up!" she says, getting the joke, her trademark cheek dimples deepening as she smiles. "I didn't have to do anything. You're the one who had to sit on a plane for eight hours."

"I know this is going to seem random," I say, "but I always remember your uniform having perfect pleats."

"You are so funny. I don't remember that at all."

"I always wondered how you got your skirt to look so good," I go on. "No matter how long I held down the iron I could never get my pleats to lay flat like yours."

"Oh, I think my mom took it to the dry cleaners."

"Oh."

Chef Andreas sets down two glasses of Alpirsbacher beer on our table. "Welcome back, you two. Happy anniversary. I can't believe a whole year has gone by."

"Thank you, Andreas," Marcus says. "And thank you for this." He hands him our gift certificate that reads *Dinner for Two, Compliments of Hotel Löwen-Post, Good Only on Date: September 20.*

I reach across the table to hold Marcus' hands. "Did you ever worry that we wouldn't make it to see this day?" I ask.

He looks at me for a thoughtful moment before answering. "No, but I think it's hard for you to be married." I rear back in my seat, my brow furrows. He continues. "Don't worry, I knew that about you before I married you. You're independent and I love that about you. But you also want things a certain way and you don't like to deviate."

"What do you mean?" I'm curious as to his answer, as I've always considered myself to be flexible. One has to be when raised in a family of five kids.

"Like making the bed. You always make the bed right away in the morning, but I would rather hang the duvet on the balcony to air out."

"The balcony is filthy," I reply. "And I don't like the bottom sheet to be exposed all day when our place gets so dusty. I know everyone does that here, hanging their duvets outside to air and then leaving them folded back on the bed, but I base my bed-making standards on the Four Seasons Hotel. And they keep their bottom sheets covered." I pause, contemplating what else to say until realizing there's an easier answer. "You're right. I don't like doing it the German way."

He's right. Marriage is hard for me. I'm still adjusting.

I take a breath and continue. "I think marriage is hard for you too." He squeezes my hands tighter. "I mean, wouldn't you rather be left alone to do your job without me hassling you to come home earlier all the time?" He cocks his head, not quite nodding but almost. "Wasn't life easier when you could go out for a drink after work without having to check in with me—and when you could leave your dishes in the sink?"

"I've been good about doing the dishes."

"You have. You've been great."

He leans forward, holding my gaze. "I like being married, and I intend to spend the rest of my life with you," he says. His words send a rush of hot blood into my heart. Tears spring from my eyes. He gives my hands a final squeeze before letting go to take a drink of his beer. He brings his glass toward mine to clink. "To the most beautiful woman. *Zum Wohl*, my love."

I look back into his warm green eyes. I study his features, strong but soft at the edges, his wavy hair thick but receding slightly, his shadow beard that he has recently grown, his commanding-yet-sensitive presence. "To the sexiest man alive." I clink back. "*Zum Wohl.*"

If only Chef Andreas could pack up this romantic evening *zum mitnehmen* so we could continue savoring this delicious time back in our daily life in Stuttgart. Too bad life doesn't fit in a doggie bag.

CHAPTER 13

The American Therapist

"I GOT THE PROMOTION," MARCUS TELLS ME HALF-way through dinner.

I choke on an arugula leaf. "You're just telling me now? Why didn't you call me as soon as you got the news? This is huge! Congratulations!"

"It won't be official for another four months," he says. "There's a probation period."

"A what?!" I put my knife and fork down a little too hard. "That whole panel approval process wasn't excessive enough?"

A few days earlier, he appeared in front of a panel of six higher-level executives for what is called an assessment center. The six suits grilled him with questions like "What makes you think you're qualified to do this job?" They then discussed Marcus amongst themselves and made him sweat it out for another ten hours before deigning him with their approval.

"It's a company policy. It's because this is a jump up to the executive level where they can't fire you. They want to make sure you're not going to just take the promotion and then slack off."

"Slack off? You've already more than proven yourself." I shake my head. "If you were in the States your boss would just offer you the position, effective immediately, and take you out for a steak dinner to celebrate. What about the company car?" I ask.

"I won't get that for eight or nine months."

"Fuuuhhhhhck. God forbid that this company allows you to achieve something and feel good about it. They promote you and keep you oppressed at the same time. That's great. That's just really special."

"There's one more thing I need to tell you," he says. He pauses, his eyes lock on me, his jaw tightens. I know this look and it doesn't mean good news. I brace myself. "I have to commit to this position for two years."

The blood pumps so hard in my ears I can't hear anything but its whooshing sound. The room starts to close in on me. All this time I've been holding onto The Big Promotion as our ticket out of here. Work toward it, support him in every way, get it, then we'll be gone. Instead, our two-year commitment to living in Germany has been extended to four. I have to remind myself to breathe. And to hide any sharp objects.

"Oh, I see," I murmur. Inside my head, the collective voices of Trish, my sister, and my mom say, *BE NICE TO HIM, BETH! Right now you need to be nice!* I adhere to their wisdom. "Well, I'm sorry for not sounding more excited," I continue. "I really am happy for you." I raise my wine glass to his beer glass.

"Here's to your success, my love. Congratulations." I slug back my cabernet, emptying my glass. Without wasting any time, I refill it.

Over the next few weeks his "good news" has a sobering effect, because I can see where this is going. In the regular course of ambitious corporate life one promotion leads to another, thus, it's likely that before the next two years are up Marcus will climb up another rung and need to commit to even more time at company headquarters.

I put in an emergency phone call to Trish. "I am so depressed," I say, my nose stuffed up from crying. "I'm going to be stuck here forever."

"No, you won't."

"I'm going to pack my bags and come back to California."

"Can you find someone to talk to there?" she asks. "Can you find a therapist?"

When I hang up I have a new mission. Just as I did for the yoga classes, I consult the Yellow Pages, but decide against picking a name randomly. I have another idea.

EUCOM, the European Command Center for America's Armed Forces, sits in the Stuttgart suburb of Vaihingen. It shares property with Patch Barracks, one of four U.S. Army bases surrounding Stuttgart. When I arrived in Germany I expected to see camo-uniformed soldiers mingling on Stuttgart's streets. But the only evidence of the area's ten thousand-plus

U.S. military personnel is an occasional military convoy on the Autobahn, the handful of oversized Chevys or Fords (obvious as American for their huge size compared to Europe's compact, even miniature, vehicles), and Vaihingen's tiny English-language cinema. Each of the American bases harbors American banks and ATMs that dispense U.S. dollars, post offices that issue American stamps, and grocery stores stocked with Doritos, Oreos, and Skippy peanut butter. While I've previously avoided any military affiliation, maybe, just this once, I could seek refuge in their insulated world. Surely they have psychologists on base, if not to help people adjust to the foreign culture, then at least for marriage counseling. I call Patch Barracks. "You're a civilian?" the operator says. "We can't help you." Click.

Situated in the heart of downtown Stuttgart is the non-profit *Deutsch-Amerikanisches Zentrum* whose mission is to promote cultural and political relations between Germany and America. They will know of an English-speaking shrink. I dial the number. No, they don't know of anyone, but the woman I speak with on the phone, Annette, picks up on my quivering voice. "Would you like to meet for lunch next week?" she asks in a sympathetic tone.

Why yes, I would, because what I need more than a therapist are friends in this city.

I have never been this hard up for friends in my life. I'm told by various pioneering expatriate American women in Germany who have come before me, "It takes longer to make friends here. It took me seven years to become friends with one woman. But once you make a friend, it's a friend for life."

Puh-leez! Some of my closest and longest lasting friendships were formed in mere seconds. Like Maggie Galloway whom I met in a hotel restroom in a Nairobi, Kenya. She needed a coin for the pay toilet and I needed help with my broken bra strap.

"Thanks," I said as I tucked the repaired strap back under my sleeveless blouse.

"Thank you, too!" she chirped as she dashed back outside to meet her tour group waiting in a van. "Look me up if you're ever in Chicago!"

I did look her up when I returned to the U.S. and we've been close friends ever since. My connection with Maggie, and my many other instant-bonding experiences like it, makes my fifteen-minute Crater Lake encounter with Marcus seem long. But seven years to make a friend for life? Who's got that kind of time?

I meet Annette at the Grand Café Planie the following Monday. A gentle beauty with long brown hair and doe-like eyes, she greets me warmly. "The mushroom ravioli is very good here," she says.

"Thanks for wanting to have lunch, Annette. You are one of the few German women who has reached out to me."

"I know what you mean," she replies. "But I was born in America and I spent a year in Boston, so I'm probably more open than most."

"I've tried to make plans with other German women, but one of them needed three weeks just to schedule coffee. Another one invited me to her dinner party, but how can anyone plan two months ahead for dinner?"

Annette smiles gently. "People are like that here," she says.

"Maybe they're just set in their ways." When our ravioli plates are cleared and our espresso cups empty, Annette stands up to leave. "I'm sorry, I have to get back. My boss will be wondering about me."

I walk her back upstairs to her office in the historic courtyard building called Charlottenplatz. Occupying a full city-center block, its cheerful yellow color and red-tiled roof make it my favorite building in Stuttgart.

Next door to Annette's office is an English-language school run by Dr. and Frau Taubitz, an elderly couple whom I want to adopt as grandparents. They offered me an English-teaching job during my third month in Stuttgart. I gave it a try, filling in as a substitute for three days. My students, all two of them, were fifteen-year-old Thai girls in tight jeans who stared at me blankly as I stood at the blackboard, winging it with no lesson plan. I drew chalk stick figures to demonstrate the vocabulary for body parts. I chattered on, incoherent to the girls, pointing out the head, hair, eyes, ears, and nose. It wasn't until I drew the lips with my tube of pink lipstick that the girls finally cracked a smile. At the end of the session the lipstick wouldn't erase off and as far as I know it's still adorning the chalkboard in Classroom No. 2. I haven't seen the Taubitzes in at least six months so after I say goodbye to Annette, who is now thirty minutes overtime on her strictly regulated one-hour lunch break, I pop into their office.

Frau Taubitz sits behind her desk in the reception area, her magenta-colored hair is tucked behind her ears, her reading spectacles hang around her neck, and the *Stuttgart Zeitung* newspaper is laid out in front of her. Dr. Taubitz, who is

American, sits across from her in the black leather guest chair. He is wearing his uniform of a knitted vest over a white shirt and tie, and Birkenstock sandals with black socks. His gray hair is combed back neatly and his large wire-rimmed glasses sit on the bridge of his pointy nose.

"How are you adjusting to life in Germany?" they inquire.

"Oh, well . . . um, well, it's . . . you know . . . it's . . ." They look at me expectantly. I look down at the floor and give them the straight answer. "Not very well."

"*Ja*, it's terrible, the German mentality is so different," says Frau Taubitz, her voice raspy, her English accent thicker than the walls of this medieval fortress. "And I'm from this region of Germany. I moved away for twenty-five years; we lived in Arizona, then in Spain. I've had a hard time adjusting since I returned. Germans are not so open like the Americans. We only came back because we had two small children and wanted to be closer to my parents. My husband started a business, the children got settled into school, and then it got harder to leave. The next thing you know twenty years passed."

I don't say it out loud, but the thought rattles my brain: *Twenty years. Yes, this is exactly what I am afraid of.*

"Here, this was published just one month ago." Dr. Taubitz, who has vacated the guest chair for me, hands me a book. "I think you will find it helpful."

I begin to read *German-American Contacts in Southern Germany* in the ravenous way my dog Gidget used to eat beef jerky, and start combing the text for anything that might look fruitful in my quest for happiness here.

"You can keep it. Just take it with you," Dr. Taubitz says.

"Thank you," I reply without looking up. I continue thumbing through the 300-page bilingual lifeline until I come to the last pages. There, in the back of the book under "*Sonstiges*"—which I learn means "miscellaneous"—is a lone entry for Psychotherapy.

"You never sent me that recipe for *Kaiserschmarrn*," Frau Taubitz says, lifting me out of my book obsession. "I have never heard of *Kaiserschmarrn* made with mascarpone cheese. I'm still very curious to try it."

I close the book and respond to her mention of this Austrian dish, a chopped up pancake otherwise known as "Emperor's Mess." "You're going to love it. Out of all the *Kaiserschmarrn* I've had, this recipe makes the fluffiest eggs. And it's made with lemon zest. You sprinkle it with powdered sugar and serve it with applesauce. It's sooooo good. I promise, I'll send it to you."

It's growing dark by the time I return home from lunch. I go straight to the phone and call Phyllis Brenner, bearer of an M.F.T. degree from the University of Washington. Fixer of problems. Adjuster of attitudes. And resident of Freiburg, a two-hour drive from Stuttgart. Her answering machine picks up and plays her recorded message in German, English, Spanish, and Portuguese. If everyone would speak German as clearly as Phyllis I would be fluent by now. I leave her a message.

She calls back while Marcus and I are out for dinner and gets our answering machine. Marcus plays her message when we get home. Her voice is low and restrained. Marcus asks, "Who is that depressed woman?"

"Oh, just some American whose name I got from a contact list."

I dismiss her subdued speech to discretion and professionalism. After three messages, we finally connect and arrange to meet.

I load up Marcus' Volkswagen with my commuter coffee mug, a bag of trail mix, a stack of CDs, and a map. Everything is helpful for my journey, except for the map. I drive south on Autobahn 81. After an hour I am convinced I have missed my exit to go west. I look for a place to pull over so I can check the map. I exit the Autobahn onto a secondary highway, but the shoulder is blocked with reflective posts to keep cars like mine from stopping. *Why would a perfectly paved shoulder be blocked?* With no other choice, I keep driving. After detouring eight miles in the wrong direction, I now have sixteen minutes less to make my appointment on time and sixteen minutes more for my blood pressure to elevate. Still unable to stop or turnaround, my fuse has been lit and it's racing toward my inner nitroglycerin. I can't stop the ticking bomb that is *me* from exploding. "I HATE LIVING HERE!" I scream with the full force of my lung capacity. "I HATE IT! I HATE IT! I HATE IT!" I continue wailing in an impressive display of primal rage. I begin sobbing so hard I scare myself. I have to take action. Immediately. I either disobey the roadblocks or end up in a ditch with my face plastered against a shattered windshield. I downshift three times, ease the car in between two red-and-white-striped posts, and turn off the engine.

It's a damn lucky thing I am going directly to a therapist's office. If I can ever find it.

I study all the squiggly colored lines on the map, tears forming puddles on the paper. After ten minutes of microscopic examination I still have no idea where I am. A car pulls up behind me. It is not the police, which is lucky because I changed purses this morning and left the required car registration papers in my other handbag. I lock my doors. A middle-aged, blond-haired, mustached man gets out of the car and knocks on my window.

You probably want to reprimand me for stopping where it's not allowed. Forget it. I won't give you the satisfaction. I pretend to ignore him but he won't go away.

"*Kanne ich Ihnen helfen?*" he asks.

Oh, he only wants to help.

I relent and roll down the window. I say to him in English. "I need to go to . . ." I gasp for air. *What is the name of the town? Come on, for God's sake, Beth, pull yourself together!* ". . . Freiburg." I wipe my nose on the back of my hand.

He looks at me with gentle eyes and nods his head. "Follow me," he says. "I vill lead you to zee highway."

It's a miracle I can drive, I've been crying so hard. My emotional state may seem extreme under these relatively benign circumstances, but this is not about *getting* lost. This is about *being* lost.

When we reach the highway I wave goodbye to my escort and head east across the southern edge of the Black Forest. For the next thirty mountainous minutes I'm almost convinced I'm driving through Northern California. The pine forests are thick, undeveloped, and, most notably, unpopulated. This rare glimpse of wilderness shakes me out of my self-pity; the natural beauty of this sub-alpine scenery is so soothing I forget that I was bawling mere minutes ago.

This scenic route leads me directly into downtown Freiburg.

I am only fifteen minutes late, including the time it takes to park the car and make an emergency stop in the drugstore for tampons. I walk the remaining two blocks briskly, the gusty wind refreshing my tear-stained face.

Phyllis is fifty-something with weathered olive skin and dark eyes. Her shoulder-length hair is dyed in the unnatural dark magenta color that so many German women favor, a color better suited for, say, sofa upholstery or curtains. A skunk-like streak of gray running through her bangs, however, makes a rather creative statement, especially by don't-call-attention-to-yourself German standards. Her burgundy corduroy blazer matches her hair.

Our session begins with me reading a page-and-a-half-long synopsis of the issues I am here to work on, an assignment she had given me when we spoke by phone. "My main issue," I read to her, "is not only about my struggle to adapt to living in Germany but also, more generally, about living in a society where a woman is expected to give up so much of herself when she enters a relationship with a man. I mean, geez, even the United Nations declares that an equal marriage is a basic human right. With the combination of these two things, being in Germany and being married, I'm feeling completely out of balance. I need help sorting myself out."

I look up from my notebook and add, "I've made a lot of sacrifices to be here, to become a wife. My previously full and adventurous life has been reduced to learning German and buying groceries. I love my husband, but I expect more out of marriage than this." I let out a big sigh. "I want to be more productive, and more positive."

She stares at me. I wait, but she says nothing. What is she thinking? I haven't revealed some irresolvable psychotic secret. My problem is that my life is easy. Too easy. I have everything I need: food, shelter, sex, health insurance, and down pillows. I have everything I ever wanted: a loving companion, an international lifestyle, and a checking account in the black. (Of course, I would still like to have thinner thighs.) I continue to wait for her response.

Her prolonged silence forces me to change the subject. "Would you like to know about my family history?"

"Yes, good idea," she says. "Just hold on. Let me go get a notebook."

I sit there alone and study the rows of books lining the walls, German titles about herbs and biology. The wooden shelves sag from their weight.

When Phyllis returns, she fumbles to find a pen and then draws a diagram of my family tree. She fills in the names of my four siblings—one sister and three brothers, all close in age—and my parents, who are still married after five decades. She draws a circle around my sister, one of my brothers, and my parents to indicate they live near each other, in California.

Yeah? So? What does this have to do with anything? I restrain any facial expressions that might convey my annoyance.

I change the subject again. To something within her grasp. "Can we talk about why life in Germany is so difficult for me?"

"Yes, good idea." She relaxes a little and sits back in her chair.

"I'm no stranger to foreign lands," I begin. "I've lived and traveled abroad most of my adult life to places far more inaccessible than Germany. I lived in Kenya, I spent a winter in Thailand, three months in Mexico, half a year in Jamaica, I even lived in France and Switzerland for a year. From my first visits to Germany, I had the impression it would be easier to adapt. I figured since it was Western Europe, and with more and more globalization, it wouldn't feel so different from the American way of life. I had so much fun visiting, before I moved here. And Marcus has some very nice friends. But they are all busy with their careers and kids." I stop for a second to make sure she's following. "It would help if I could just find a good yoga class."

"There must be some good teachers in Stuttgart," she says. "There must be fifty to a hundred in this town alone."

Deducting that since Stuttgart only has six teachers and a population twice that of Freiburg, I dismiss her estimate as delusional and continue without wasting time telling her about the German yoga classes I've already tried. "I am very athletic. I need a certain level of . . ."

She interrupts me excitedly. "That's it! Write this down in big letters. FITNESS CLUB."

My heart sinks. "I don't go to fitness clubs," I tell her. "I don't like exercising on machines."

"But you need to release the endorphins," she says.

"I know plenty about endorphins, Phyllis. I've done three triathlons, a marathon, and I completed the Eco-Challenge, which was a ten-day adventure race. I ski, I mountain bike, I surf. And in Stuttgart, I inline skate, but mostly I run," I explain. "But it gets lonely to run by myself."

"Loneliness . . ." she repeats and writes down the word purposefully on her notepad, though I can only wonder for what purpose. She then tells me, "You should look for clubs, organizations."

"How do you think I found you?" I ask, waving the *German-American Contacts* book at her. "I've exhausted all of my networking techniques," I say. "And if there is one talent I have, it's networking, meeting people, connecting with people, and then connecting those people with other people. Have you ever read the book *The Tipping Point*? That's me. I'm a connector. In Seattle, I established a journalist's networking group that went from twelve to 120 people in six months. But that is just not happening here. Even my husband is impressed with how much effort I make and how many things I'm trying."

I want to hear something new, something I haven't thought of. I want to know if I'm overlooking some deeper issues that are keeping me from being happy here. Surely there must be something wrong with me. Maybe I'm a latent xenophobe, less capable of acclimating outside my own country than I had presupposed. Maybe I'm too independent and restless to ever be happily married. Maybe my feminist tendencies have caused me to focus so much on my perceived injustices of our society's structure that I'm unable to have a healthy relationship with a male partner at all. Maybe I'm too demanding of people—of my husband—and expect too much from others, from *myself*, and from life. Maybe, in spite of desperately not wanting to be, I'm just a glass-half-empty kind of person. Whatever my problem is, I'm willing to face it and fix it. But since I am not getting any insight into this—and after forty-five minutes I no longer expect to—I want the session to be over.

"You light up when you talk about your professional life," she says. "You perk up considerably. I can feel the change in your energy. So you need to focus on that."

She is right. The only time I am not complaining in her presence is when I am talking about my work, about building relationships with magazine editors, about the story ideas I want to pitch, about how I could do international PR for sports companies. But this is no revelation. "Well, Phyllis, I wouldn't be sitting here if I could get my career going from this blasted country."

"I would tell you to move back to the U.S.," she replies, "at least spend more time there, get a job there, and just travel back and forth to see Marcus, but if you want to have a baby, you really need to be together."

"TELL ME SOMETHING I DON'T ALREADY KNOW!" I want to scream. I collect myself enough to explain, "I've considered this scenario a million times, but we spent the first year and a half of our relationship doing the 7,000-mile, trans-Atlantic commute, which is an expensive and exhausting way of life considering airline tickets, long distance phone calls, and a nine-hour time difference. There's no way I'm going back to this complicated existence."

"You really need to work at having a baby like a project," she goes on, oblivious to anything I've said, oblivious to whether or not I'm even a good candidate for motherhood given my current state of mind.

"I had my fertility tested and all my hormone levels are normal, but even my gynecologist said, 'You won't get pregnant if you're not happy.' One friend said 'You have to be warm in the belly, and living somewhere where you feel safe.'" I don't tell her—I don't tell anyone, not even Marcus—about my real fear: *If I have a baby in Germany, we may be here forever.* It's a terror amplified by my mother's story of a family friend living in Poland who lost custody of her kids when she and her Polish husband divorced. "It broke her," my mom warned. "And she never recovered."

During our courtship, when Marcus and I talked about where we might live, I told him, "I'll be happy anywhere as long as we're together, even if it's in Tuscaloosa." I meant it as a joke, because his company has a factory in this small Alabama town. It's a town that wouldn't even make my Top Ten Thousand Places I Want to Live list. But right now, Tuscaloosa sounds like paradise.

Phyllis moves on to her next piece of redundant advice. "You need to learn the language," she says. "Sign up for a German class. Plus, you'll meet people there."

Now I'm steaming! Does she really think I'm that stupid? Does she really think that after living here for sixteen months that I've never attempted to learn the language?

"You said that learning German was your goal when you agreed to living in Germany," she reminds me. "And like it or not, Germany and the German language is always going to be a part of your life from now on. I imagine your children will be bi-lingual, and they should be. Marcus will want to speak German with them, and they will have their German grandparents. And you won't feel so isolated if you learn the language."

I can't believe I am actually paying money to hear this. I think of all the other more beneficial things I could have paid for with the cash I am about to hand over to her, like a train ticket to Prague, a new pair of Italian boots—or another intensive German course. Now I remember why I didn't seek out therapy before.

She looks at her watch, so I look at mine too. The digital read-out on my Timex Expedition tells me we have exactly six minutes left of our ninety-minute session. In the end, I am surprised at how fast the time has gone by. I'm tired from crying. I'm tired from repeating my same old story, from hearing myself sound so negative. Worst of all, I feel even more discouraged than when I arrived.

"Let me give you an assignment," she says.

Oh, good, maybe something constructive will come out of this session.

"Write down your *Lebensentwürfe*," she tells me. "I can't remember the English word." She searches the ceiling. "Oh, I am trying to think of it."

Please God, don't let me live in Germany for so long that I forget how to speak my own language.

"Life plan," she says at last. "Write a three-year life plan."

Three years, it seems she has determined, is how long I will agree to live in Germany because of Marcus' career. Um, excuse me. I agreed to two years, and at this point I am certain I will not survive one more day. If I even make it that long.

When the session ends at exactly 3:30, we do something unorthodox; we cross the professional line and go out for coffee. We arranged this beforehand, and I had agreed, mostly because, well, I need friends.

"I want to know what's new in Seattle," she says. I think she wants to hear about Seattle because she has lived there before and is simply interested in how things have changed. I can tell her how Highway 520 is experiencing growing traffic jams. How the King Dome football stadium was demolished and replaced by state-of-the-art, open-roof digs for the Seahawks and Mariners. How Starbucks, Microsoft, and Amazon have influenced the local culture—and the 520 traffic. But noooo, nostalgia is not her objective at all.

"I am closing my practice here and moving to Seattle," she tells me over a bitter cappuccino at a touristy Münsterplatz café. I practically spit out my coffee. I want to start crying again, not because I'm sad she would be leaving, but sad that *she* would be leaving and not me!

"I want to know what the mood is like there, and how people feel about therapy. Do they seek out therapy? Would I be able to build up a good practice there?" she asks excitedly. She was not even close to being this attentive during our session. "I've lived here twelve years and I've been depressed the whole time I've been here."

I cannot believe I am hearing this!

I spend the next hour coaching her on how to rebuild her life in Seattle. I explain how to get started, how to do an Internet search to find contacts. "Are you living so far in the Dark Ages you haven't heard of Google?" I want to ask her. Seattle is not my favorite city—only because I don't do well in the rainy climate—but to hear me talk you'd think it was the world's most promising place for success. I pump her up with my enthusiasm.

"You can do it," I tell her in my rah-rah "Go, Phyllis" speech. But I become detached from myself as I speak, my words separate from my inner thoughts: *How did I end up in a café in Freiburg, Germany sitting with this person who calls herself a psychologist for whom I've just driven two and a half stressful hours to see and paid seventy-five euros cash to get help for my challenged state-of-mind?* The reality is astounding: I am acting as *her* therapist; she should be paying *me*!

I am so hungry for company of any English-speaking kind that I don't gulp down the rest of my coffee and excuse myself immediately. Instead, I let her take me on a walking tour of the town center, but I can't really look around because I am too focused on following her, and she doesn't know where she is going. "I don't have a very good sense of direction," she admits, though she's lived here nearly one quarter of her life.

We visit the city's historic church, the Freiburger Münster. At least I am getting a little bit of enlightenment. Unfortunately, it's not spiritual, but architectural. This Gothic cathedral, a national landmark of spires, stone, and stained glass, was built between 1120 and 1330, and miraculously survived the war.

We pass the Merchant House, an ochre-colored beauty with a façade covered in decorative paintings and a Coat of Arms, which, in the sixteenth century, served as a customs and finance office. "You don't see stunning buildings like this in Seattle," I tell her. "Or in Stuttgart."

"Yeah, everyone tells me Stuttgart is the pits," she replies. So much for her respecting my goal to be more positive.

She meanders into a women's clothing store. I dumbly follow

her. She buys two T-shirts, like the one she is wearing. We have gone way, way beyond the patient-therapist boundary now. Coffee is one thing, visiting the church another. But shopping for clothes? I am so completely uncomfortable I feel like I need a long shower.

Finally, we reach the parking garage where I left my car four hours earlier. As we say goodbye, she adds, "You should come back for another appointment in two weeks."

I say, "Sure," though I know I'll never see her again.

I feed eight euros into the self-service cashier machine, but it takes me longer to find my car than the ten-minute grace period allows. When I reach the gate, the slot in the automated exit booth rejects my ticket and there are two cars already lined up behind me. I fear I may catapult into another crying jag, but I contain myself. I push the "Info" button on the exit machine and a voice comes over the loudspeaker.

"Do you speak English?" I ask the voice.

"*Nein,*" she answers.

"My ticket is not working," I say to her in English anyway.

To my great surprise—and relief—she doesn't argue with me. She pushes a button from her remote office and the parking garage barrier rises, allowing me to be on my way.

I take a different route home. I stick strictly to the Autobahn, taking no scenic mountain shortcuts, risking no repeats of the morning's route-finding fiasco. The night is moonless and dark; my eyes are puffy and tired. I make a pact with myself to ignore the cars flying past at death-defying speeds in the left lane and fight any impulse to pass the lumbering trucks in front of me. I stay put in the right lane, moving along steadily at the glacial (by German standards) pace of sixty-two miles per hour. "You speed demons in your BMWs are not going to bother me," I announce and turn up the volume to my *Windham Hill's 25 Years of Classical Guitar* CD. "Slow and steady wins the race, you bastards."

Once I get home—yes, *home*—I employ a much more effective and affordable kind of therapy: a glass of Merlot, a hot bath with Dr. Hauschka lavender oil, and a good night's sleep snuggling with the man I love under our down comforter. I make a plan to call Annette for lunch again and commit to visiting the Taubitzes every few weeks. And I carry my suitcases back down to the basement storage room since I won't be packing them. Yet.

CHAPTER 14

To Los Angeles and Back

"**M**ARCUS, WHAT DOES *WELPE* MEAN?" I ASK, scanning the classifieds for pets in the free weekly newspaper, the *Stuttgarter Wochenblatt*.

He's looking through his closet for a shirt and answers absentmindedly. "Puppy," he says.

A smile sweeps across my face. "Oh, really?" It's been two years since Gidget died and while I know nothing can ever replace her, I'm longing to have a dog again.

He sees what I'm thinking and tries to correct himself with a witty comeback. "No, actually it means very old dog in terrible health." But he knows it's too late. I'm already dialing the number in the ad.

I had been to the local dog pound five times—each visit a heart-wrenching episode—but the dogs were far too big for our apartment. "If we get a dog small enough to fit in the cabin,"

I persuade Marcus, "it can fly everywhere with us." Marcus doesn't need much persuasion though as he grew up with a dog—a beagle named Billy—and from the way he talks about his childhood pet, he loves dogs as much as I do. Our landlord is another story.

"I have to ask Herr Schindler for permission," he says. I groan, my glimmer of joy killed.

My joy returns tenfold a week later—after Marcus has a formal discussion with Herr Schindler over a bottle of French wine—when we become the proud new parents of a Jack Russell-Yorkshire Terrier puppy.

When we bring home the puppy in the evening, I get under the covers with him. "Look, Marcus, he's trying to nurse on the sheets. He must miss his mom." I hold him close to share my body heat, smelling his delicious puppy breath, and examine him closer, admiring his black button-nose, his blond eyebrows, his intelligent brown eyes. I lift his floppy ear to study his tattoo, required by European law. (It's either that or a microchip as a way to identify canines traveling between countries.) "Hey, Marcus, I thought we picked out Number 67. This one is Number 68." Marcus scoots under the covers with me, careful not to disturb the miniature ball of black and brown fur.

"So Number 68, what are we going to call you?" Marcus asks, kissing the puppy on the head.

"How about naming him after one of those cowboys in that German TV Western you grew up with?" I ask. "*Winnetou*, right? And what was the Indian's name?"

"*Klikipetra*. There was also Old Shatterhand."

"Those names are long," I reply. "How about Felix? Since that means happiness."

"Let's wait a few days to figure it out." He turns off the light and we go to sleep—with the dog in between us.

Like having a baby to save your marriage, getting a dog can make a difficult situation worse. Our division of dog-care is not the issue. Marcus adores our new family member. He is a great dog dad and voluntarily takes the early morning and late night shifts, walking Number 68 over to the neighborhood soccer field to *pinkeln* (pee) and play fetch. There aren't many people around when they go out. Even Herr Schindler isn't up yet, though, to our surprise, he actually likes dogs.

I walk the puppy twice during the day. To the vineyard. When people are out sweeping their sidewalks. On our third day together, we leave the apartment and walk along the quieter backside of our row of houses instead of the street. We reach the end of the block where a woman is sweeping her proprietary square of concrete. (It's not just a stereotype that Swabians are obsessed with clean walkways—it's the truth. But remember the rule: No sweeping on Sundays!) Dressed in a gray tweed coat, thick stockings, and orthopedic shoes, she watches us as we approach. She stops sweeping and leans against her broom.

I feel an attack coming. But then I look down at Number 68. The size of my shoe, he's so bouncy and cute he could put a smile on the face of anyone, even the dourest of old ladies.

"Don't let your *Hund* pee here," she grumbles.

Except for this one.

"If one *Hund* pees here, den all dee *Hunde* pee here. I try to keep zis corner clean and if everyone lets their *Hund* . . ."

As she rambles on I intentionally give her a dazed, dumfounded look, pretending not to understand a word she's saying. I pull my jacket tighter around my neck and walk faster. Her barking follows us until we turn the corner.

No, Number 68, regardless of his limitless unconditional love, his ability to make me laugh, and how he fills my days, isn't helping my German matters any.

My calls to Trish become calls to my mother. "Mom, I'm losing my patience. We've lived here for two years now, he got his promotion, and there's no sign that we're ever going to move."

She doesn't give me some expected devout Catholic line like, "He's your husband; you have to honor your vows." Instead she surprises me by saying, "You don't have to stay. I worry about you. I've never seen your confidence get so low."

I slump back against the sofa. "I know."

"I've known Sigrid for forty years," she goes on, "and all the time I've known her she has always been talking about how wonderful Germany is and how much better they do things there. Frankly, we all got tired of hearing about it. We always wanted to tell her to just move back. But lately she's been telling me how much she loves being in America and how she wouldn't want to live in Germany again."

"How is that going to help me get Marcus to move?"

"I don't know," she says. "I just wanted to share that with you."

"Oh, okay. Well, thanks."

My arguments with Marcus increase, though they can't really be called arguments since it's only me who's doing the fighting. I'm taking out my frustrations on Marcus and using him as my punching bag. But he's the heavy kind that doesn't move no matter how hard you hit.

"I hate that you always work so late! I hate feeling like I'm only in this world to support your career. I get that you can't leave your job, but can't you come home earlier?" I shout the way people do when speaking to a foreigner, as if talking louder will make them understand. But he is as impossible to crack as his "awful German language." (Thank you, Mark Twain.)

"I hear you," he says after enduring another boxing session. "Things will eventually change."

But nothing changes. Except for me. I'm becoming more and more unhinged. My tears flow too easily and too often. One morning Marcus leaves for work and I start to cry. Over what, I don't even know. Maybe just the prospect of facing another day alone. I am sobbing so hard the puppy hides under the bed. I lift my head from the bathroom floor when I hear a key in the door.

"I heard you crying from outside. Are you okay?" Marcus puts his arms around me and holds me.

No. No, I'm not.

I subscribe to the belief that we are responsible for our own happiness. And since I've tried everything I can think of in Germany, including getting a dog, I develop what's known as *Torschlusspanik*—an economical German word for "fear that time is running out and life is passing me by." So I start looking further afield. As in 7,000 miles further. I search for jobs on the Internet.

When the weekend comes, while we're sitting on the sofa with our second latte of the morning, I broach the subject. "I'm submitting my résumé for a job in L.A.," I tell Marcus. His face turns white, his almond-shaped eyes constrict into slivers. "I should have told you I was looking," I continue. "Let me read you the job description: 'Magazine looking for a writer/editor with knowledge of fitness and beauty.' I don't know a thing about beauty, but I can certainly handle the fitness part."

I wait for his response, expecting a defensive speech about how he's working so hard to provide for us—for me. Finally, he says, "I think you should go for it."

I set my printout down and look him in the eye. "Thank you, my love. Your support means a lot to me." We don't talk for a while, so I change the subject to diffuse the tension I've caused from my ambush. I pick up Number 68, letting him nibble on my fingers with his baby teeth. "What are we going to name this sweet little thing?"

What do you call a little dog with a big attitude? We've tried Bandit, Chief, and Sweet Potato, to name a few, but nothing has stuck for this Jack Russell disguised as a Yorkshire terrier.

"How about Jack?" he asks.

"I like it. It suits him."

I hand Marcus the puppy who squirms, then bites his nose. "It definitely does." He cradles Jack in his arms and strokes his ears. He is so tender with the puppy. And even at my worst he is tender with me. I want this marriage to work. Why, oh why, can I not just be happy here?

"Hey," I say to him in my most soothing voice. "I know it will add another challenge for us if I get this job, but I believe we're going to be okay." His shoulders relax and he welcomes me as I lean in to kiss him. Jack joins in, licking our cheeks.

It's September 20, our second anniversary (since we count our Black Forest wedding as our official date). Instead of celebrating with champagne and sex with my husband, I am standing alone on a beach in Marina del Rey, California.

I got the job.

There is only one word that can describe being back in California: relief. The waves roll onto the sand, one after another, leaving behind a foamy trail as they get sucked back out to the sea. Jack races back and forth along the water's edge, chasing a sandpiper whose chirp only taunts him more. The sun shimmers on the Pacific waters, roughed up by the steady northerly breeze. I stop to take another sip of my coffee. It's seven a.m. and the police haven't begun patrolling yet, haven't written their first $200- ticket of the day. I look up and down the beach and count my fellow lawbreakers. There's a Great Dane, several Labradors, a Golden Retriever, and a white Maltese, all with their ball-throwing owners on yet another perfectly glorious Southern California morning.

With Jack tugging on the back of my flip-flop the whole way, we walk the one block back to our apartment, a one-room ground-floor studio, directly below my parents' two-bedroom unit. Nothing has changed since I used the place as a staging area when packing for my Germany move—the bathroom wallpaper is still peeling, the carpet still smells musty, and the huge walk-in closet is still a dream come true.

"Do you want some eggs for breakfast? Here, at least have some toast. We'll make sure Jack gets a few walks," my mom says, as she's said every day since I arrived three weeks ago. "I'll have your dad take him to the beach this afternoon. Now don't you need to get going? You don't want to be late for work."

My one-hour commute follows the scenic route north from Marina del Rey. In my dad's borrowed Volkswagen Beetle, I drive along Pacific Coast Highway, taking one last glimpse of the surfer-dotted ocean before making the turn into a deep, red rock canyon. I wind the car through a sage-scented landscape that looks more like Hawaii than the desert, until I drop down to the valley on the other, less picturesque side of L.A. I stop at Starbucks even though the line of customers is long and I've already had coffee, to prolong my time outside of my windowless gray cubicle.

"Did you edit this beauty piece?" my boss asks, waving a story at me as she approaches my desk. Several years younger than me, she's overweight with red hair, an overbite, and an addiction to Diet Coke. *And she's the editor of a health magazine?*

"Yes, I did," I reply, my voice unsteady.

"There are many problems with it. One, when you apply concealer you use your ring finger, which uses less pressure, not your index finger like it says here."

A few possible replies come to mind. I could say, "I've been using my index finger for years and it works just fine for me." Or I could say, "How would you know? You don't even wear make-up, and, trust me, you need it." Better yet, I could hold up my middle finger and say, "How about using this one?" But I just wag my head and say, "Okay, I'll take another look at it."

I ask Melanie and Kate, the junior editors in the cubicle next to mine, if they want to go to lunch. "I can't," Melanie says. "I'm on a deadline for my aromatherapy story."

"When is it due?" I ask.

"Three months from now."

I bite the inside of my cheek. I look at Kate. "Do you want to grab a sandwich from Whole Foods? I'll drive."

"No thanks. I always bring my own lunch," Kate replies, exchanging a conspiratorial look with Melanie.

I go outside the building and call Trish from my cell phone. "I don't mean to be paranoid, but yesterday when I walked into the break room their water cooler conversation screeched to a halt. I know they were talking about me."

"They're jealous," she says. "They probably wanted your job and didn't get it."

"I'm not sure. There's been a lot of turnover in my position, and no one has ever told me why."

"I'm sure it's nothing. Just ignore them," she says. "Oh, I got a babysitter for Friday. I can meet you for yoga and dinner."

"Sounds good." I hang up and go back to my desk.

I spend the next few hours wrestling with commas and fragmented sentences in a story about ten exercises to ward off osteoporosis. "You must do weight bearing exercise at least two hours a day. You must wear weights around your ankles. You must jump and run, not walk."

Yeah? You must kiss my ass. I didn't remember Americans having rules. Rule No. 5: You must look like a Barbie doll even after going through menopause. *Especially* after going through menopause.

My next break comes at three o'clock, the time of Marcus' daily call. I take my cell phone outside to the parking lot. "How's your day going?" he asks.

"Oh, fine. But I miss you," I tell him.

"I miss you too," he says. "I'm going to take some vacation time. I booked a ticket to L.A. for Thanksgiving, so I'll see you in a few weeks."

"That's excellent news!"

"It's after midnight so I need to go to bed now. I'll talk to you tomorrow. I love you."

"I love you too."

He goes to sleep; I go back to my cubicle.

I stop at the grocery store on my way home from work to buy bananas, milk, and toothpaste. Ordinary, basic, plain old toothpaste. I stand in the toiletry aisle lost in a dizzying daze as I read through the brand names and labels. Whitening, advanced whitening, tartar control, tartar control *and* whitening, baking soda, cavity fighting, extra fluoride, sensitive. I can comprehend the labels, since they're in English and not German, but it takes me twice as long to find what I'm looking for. The same thing happens in the milk aisle. At least four brands offer fat-free, one-percent, two-percent, whole, lactose-free, and acidophilus—with each variety also available in organic. *HELP!* It was so much easier in Germany. At Aldi, and most other stores, there is one brand name, two varieties (fat-free or whole), and one quick decision (whole). Done.

While surveying the deli section, I come across Black Forest ham. I glance around at my fellow shoppers, mostly women in sweat pants. I want to tell them, "They really do make this ham in the Black Forest and it can only be called Black Forest ham if it's made with certain herbs and smoked with special wood." I pick up a hunk of holey *Emmentaler* cheese. "*Tal* means valley in German, and *Emmen* is a river in Switzerland," I want to explain to the soccer moms loading up on Kraft slices about how the stuff we call Swiss cheese comes from the Emmen River valley. "My friend Eve took me hiking there once." But I keep my enthusiasm to myself.

I get to the checkout counter.

"Paper or plastic?" the woman asks.

I pull out my own canvas tote bags and answer, "Neither, I brought my own."

The clerk wads up the plastic bag she was prepared to use and throws it in the wastebasket. She starts to pack my groceries, but I press my body in between her and my food items. "No, that's okay. I can do it myself."

She shrugs her shoulders as if to say, "Lady, you're crazy."

I'm not crazy; I'm just . . . Oh my God, I'm German!

On Friday night I meet Trish for Vinnie's class at the yoga studio. "Hi!" I beam, and lean in to kiss her on the cheek. I lean in again to kiss her a second time, on her other cheek.

"You're so German," she teases.

"I know! Just be glad we're not in Switzerland where they kiss you three times."

After yoga, we go to a new restaurant in Santa Monica. A man in a black sport coat and black pants valet parks our car. A well-sculpted slender woman, draped in black from her halter top to her mini skirt down to her platform sandals, shows us to a table. A waiter in a black shirt comes to take our order. "Welcome ladies. Let me tell you about our dinner specials," he recites, projecting his voice as if auditioning for a movie role.

Trish asks, "Can you substitute vegetables for the duck in the duck breast risotto?"

He flashes his perfect, bleached white teeth back at her. "Yes, no problem. I'll be right back with your wine." He strolls off, his buff body moving confidently across the bustling room.

"That would never happen in Germany," I tell Trish. "Waiters practically ignore you. You have to work to get their attention. And forget about asking for special orders."

"Maybe people need to tip better to give them more incentive," Trish offers.

"Yeah, but you don't really tip there because waiters in Europe get a higher base wage. You might leave a little change to round out the price of the bill, but you don't tip the 15 to 20 percent we're expected to give here. Also, in Europe waiting tables is a career, but in L.A. it's an interim thing while trying to be an actor or sell a screenplay." Our waiter returns with our wine—something red and expensive from Napa Valley—smiling like he's in front of a camera as he pours it, and silently moves off again.

Trish lifts her glass. "It's great to have you back."

"Thank you," I say, holding my glass to hers. "It's great to be back. Cheers."

Our food is delivered quickly. On my plate is a lone fish filet encrusted in hazelnuts, and nothing more. No side dish, no garnish, nothing. This is what I get for thirty-two dollars? I am still chewing when Mr. Hollywood drops the check on our table. Trish looks at the check, looks up at me, and breaks into a grin. "I guess he wants to get his next table seated."

This would never happen in Germany either. Apart from Autobahn driving, life is not rushed—a more leisurely pace is valued, especially when it comes to restaurant dining. Chalk up some points for Deutschland where they let you linger over your dinner for as long as you like.

We flag him down again. "Oh, I am so very sorry, ladies. I didn't realize you wanted dessert. My apologies. I highly recommend the warm chocolate pudding cake."

"Perfect," Trish answers. "We'll take it."

The waiter's friendliness is as real as the color of his teeth, but, I tell Trish, "I don't care if he's sincere or not. At least he's nice to us."

The line of cars is two deep in front of Virgin Atlantic's baggage claim. Taxi horns honk against the deafening sound of turbo jet engines. The traffic cops shout at drivers to keep moving. "Dad, will you circle around again? I'll go in and see if I can find him."

Just then I spot Marcus in his wool stocking cap and heavy hiking boots, carrying his giant red backpack. But the giveaway to his disguise is his pants. "Hi gorgeous! Welcome to L.A.! Out of the twelve million people here, I'll bet you are the only person wearing *Lederhosen*."

He grabs me, squeezing me tightly, his rolled up *Die Zeit* newspaper poking me in the side. His skin is pale compared to my bronzed California complexion, his stubble is a few days old, and his sideburns have grown longer in the six weeks since I last saw him. "My love!" he says. "I'm here!"

He pulls my face to his. As his tongue probes deeper in my mouth I hear a cop shout, "You have to move your car now, sir."

I push Marcus away. "We'll have to continue this later or that cop will give my dad a ticket. That's him waiting."

During our time in California, Marcus and I settle into an easy routine. In the mornings we walk Jack on the beach together. "Look! He's digging all the way to Australia," Marcus says as Jack tries to bury a tennis ball.

"That's so funny," I say, dodging Jack's flinging sand. "We say 'digging to China.' I never thought about how Australia would be opposite of Europe."

Marcus drives me to work each morning. He then fills his vacation days browsing for books at Barnes & Noble, catching up on his economics or business management reading. He shops at REI for outdoor gear, and relaxes at a local espresso bar. And, several times a day, he checks in with me at the office. "How's my wife doing?"

"Ehh. These two chicky-poos I work with went to my boss today to complain about me."

"Those girls you were telling me about? What was their problem this time?"

"I'm responsible for editing this whole section of the magazine and they aren't turning in their work on time. First, they don't respect our deadlines. Then, they act like fifth-graders, running into my boss' office and tattling on me—for wanting them to work efficiently. But enough of that. How are my husband and dog?"

"Oh, we're very good. I like this role reversal. I could get used to this."

"Ha! That's what I've been trying to tell you. Quit your job and move here already. I can support you while you're looking for work or going to law school."

Marcus had wanted to become a lawyer. But like most German parents, his didn't want him to be a lawyer—or a doctor. No, in Germany, the pinnacle of achievement is becoming an engineer. "You'll be guaranteed a good job," they insisted, unaware there would be a glut of engineers by the time Marcus earned his degree. He acquiesced to their wishes, though he postponed his graduation for four years—much to Wolfgang and Andrea's dismay—by accepting a computer science fellowship in London, and exploring a different track (though technically it was still part of his engineering studies). It was, in part, this bit of his background that had given me the confidence to marry him. *This German doesn't always follow the rules. He has a maverick side, just like me.*

Nowadays his parents couldn't be happier with his executive status. And while I know that Marcus, too, is satisfied with his career progression, I can't stop myself from jabbering on about my idea—especially when the subject is about him moving to my country. "It always makes me sad to think you were never encouraged to follow your own dreams," I say. "Now you have your chance." That America has a glut of lawyers somehow gets left out of my proposition.

"Do you feel like going to yoga tonight?" he asks, dodging the subject. "Erich Schiffman has a class at seven. I bought his book years ago and the one thing I want to do while I'm here is take his class."

"Yes, just bring my mat when you pick me up," I reply. "Okay, I better go or my boss will report me to H.R. or something. I can't wait to see you."

"Me too. I love you."

"I love you too," I say. And I really do, madly and deeply, though I'm aware that this feeling comes much easier when I'm on my home turf.

I stuff my cell phone back in my pocket and sneak back to my desk, hoping no one noticed I was gone.

Two weeks and one gluttonous Thanksgiving turkey dinner later, Marcus returns to Stuttgart. Living the single life again, I fill my evenings with yoga, going to movies with my dad, and taking Jack for walks.

My friend, Colleen, had read my Tarot cards a year before I married Marcus. "You will marry him," she predicted. "The marriage will work, but it will be hard." Because she was right, I consulted her again before risking my relationship for this job on another continent. Well, whom else could I ask? She said, "Go to L.A. and let the beach soothe your soul."

I embrace Colleen's suggestion and take long beach walks with Jack at night, when the police turn their focus to drug dealers instead of unleashed dogs. The ocean, even in the blackness of night, never rests. I walk out to greet it, the water's foamy edge illuminated by a distant row of street lamps. Every single element—the roar of breaking waves, the salty breeze in my face, the empty miles of sand stretching out in front of me, and an exuberant puppy running with abandon—proves Colleen right again. My anger softens and my stress from the past two years subsides like the outgoing tide. I banish the memory of all my difficulties, frustrations, and German grammar lessons to sea.

Christmas approaches and to keep the time between our visits to a minimum, I hope to spend the holiday with Marcus. This means returning to Germany. But only for a week or two. First, I have to ask my boss for permission to go. I wait until the end of the day, when Melanie and Kate are gone, before venturing into her office. "May I take some time off?" I ask. "To visit my husband."

She looks up from her computer and eyes me curiously. "Let me think about it," she says. I can almost see the cogs turning in her brain.

I wait until the end of the next day to approach her again. "Did you have a chance to think about it?" I ask.

"Yes. You can go."

That was easy. Too easy.

It's a Friday at 4:45 p.m., three days before Christmas. I am marking up a "Liven Up Your Life With Lip Gloss" story in red ink when my desk phone rings. It's Amy from H.R. "Can you come to my office?" she asks.

"Now?"

"Yes."

This can't be good.

Thirty minutes later I am behind the wheel of my dad's Beetle. Beside me on the passenger seat sits a box of my personal items, packed up from my cubicle under the supervision of a security officer. The words ring in my ears the entire drive back to Marina del Rey. "Your employment is terminated effective immediately." I replay the conversation over and over.

"Come on, Amy. She can't say I'm not doing a good job just because of one story about make-up. I've contributed a lot in many other ways. I brought in new story ideas and new writers." For once I can appreciate Marcus' job security, how employees in his company can't be fired. At least not for misguided beauty tips. But my pleas are of no use. My boss needs an editor who knows the difference between mineral-pigmented herbal day cream and organic-tinted botanical moisturizer. Someone who knows that amaranth is a highly nutritious leafy vegetable and not a liqueur. Someone who knows how to pronounce the word vegan. (It probably didn't help that I said "vay-gawn" on my first day of the job. I blame my newly ingrained language skills for pronouncing the vowels the German way.)

"I'm sorry," she said. "Here is a check for two weeks' pay. Now I have to walk you back to your desk. You can collect your things, then we'll escort you out of the building."

I have to wait until ten p.m. (seven in the morning German time) to call Marcus. "Good news, my love. I can come to Germany."

"That's brilliant!" he replies with his favorite British word.

"And I can stay longer than two weeks. A lot longer."

Alayne, my friend from Seattle—the same one who referred me to the Parisian hairdresser—calls the next day. "Hi sweetie. I wondered if you would be interested in doing a big editing project for me. It will take about six months, but you can work from anywhere as long as you have an Internet connection."

I think of Lena, how her Germany stories always have a silver lining. I can't wait to tell her this one.

As the plane circles down for a landing, I look down to see that Stuttgart's usually green fields and red rooftops are covered in white, and the snow is still falling.

I hand my passport to the customs official. "Do you need to see my dog's *Heimtier-Ausweis* too?" I hold Jack's passport-like identification booklet in front of him, opening it up to the page with Jack's picture. He shakes his head no, and though he makes an effort to maintain his stern expression, I detect a smile in his eyes.

I push my cart past customs, Jack perched proudly on top of my duffel bags, until we reach the exit. Marcus pushes his way through the crowd. "Welcome back, love of my life!" He leans in and kisses me until another tongue tries to join us—Jack's. He bounces up and down, licking Marcus' face while wagging his tail at Autobahn speed.

"*Someone* remembers you," I say, pulling my body away and smiling at their reunion. I glance around at the airport crowd; everyone is in dark coats. Cigarette smoke fills my nostrils. Men outnumber the women ten to one and they all seem to have mustaches. A German voice booms over the loudspeaker announcing a departing flight. I nip the imminent panic in the bud. *You'll be fine,* I tell myself. *It will be different this time.*

We walk outside and let Jack stretch his legs for a few minutes on the lawn next to the parking lot. He runs figure eights, stopping only to scoop up the snow until his face is covered in the cold, white powder.

Marcus unlocks the door to a navy blue Mercedes station wagon, not the familiar old VW Golf. "You got your new car!" I squeal. He opens the door. "It smells so new."

"Here's the best part," he says. He pulls out a Shell credit card and waves it at me. "All the gas is paid for." This is no small perk considering gas is four times as expensive in Europe as it is in the U.S.

Marcus makes a nest out of his wool coat in the back seat for Jack. He then reaches in the back and brings out a long-stemmed red rose. "This is for you." I bury my nose in the red petals and take a long sniff. "And here, I thought you might want something to drink." He passes me a travel mug filled with a steaming Chai tea latte.

Yes, it will be different this time.

After being away from it for nearly three months, I'm back in our Bad Cannstatt apartment. I wonder what's different and what's the same as I instinctively take inventory: the red, L-shaped sofa with the crewel pillows I had made by the Turkish tailor piled on it; the glass dining room table with the silver candlesticks; my dark wood desk with my supersize German dictionary still sitting on top; the city panorama dominated by the power plant's steaming smokestack. It all looks exactly how I left it. Except for the heaping pile of Christmas presents covering the living room floor. Marcus sees me looking at them and says, "Those are for you."

I open the gifts in this order: two wool hats in different Norwegian patterns, two pair of Norwegian wool mittens, (two different sizes in case one didn't fit—bonus points for thoughtfulness), an incense burner in the shape of an elephant (he's paid attention to my small but meaningful elephant collection), handmade soap (you can't go wrong giving a girl bath products), a coffee grinder (no more begging the local bakery to grind our beans), and the grand finale: a motorcycle jacket with protective pads. The chivalrous gesture of the motorcycle gear is not lost on me—he wants to protect me. I zip up the tight-fitting coat of mesh and armor and spin around for him. "It fits perfectly. I love it." Jack gets a present, too—a doggie bed, which is also a perfect fit. He jumps right in, instinctively knowing it's his.

The snow continues to fall steadily outside. Surrounded by crumpled wrapping paper, Marcus and I cuddle under a blanket and watch Jack roll around in his new bed. Our puppy stops and looks up at us with his beaming brown eyes. I swear he's smiling, as if to say, "Hey, you guys, I'm so glad we're all back together."

I smile back at him and say, "Yes, my little dumpling, I'm happy, too."

CHAPTER 15

Schadenfreude

THE REST OF THE WINTER PASSES WITHOUT INCIDENT. Buried in my editing project for Alayne, I don't have time to venture out for more than dog walks and groceries at Aldi, but I do ride my scooter Café Chico in Bad Cannstatt every few weeks for a cup of coffee—making sure to park down the block with all the other scooters.

Just before Jack's first birthday, I take the train to Bern, Switzerland to visit Uschi and her sister, Eve, for a week. In my absence, Marcus invites the guys from work over to watch a big European championship soccer game on TV. A couple of his more enterprising coworkers chip in a few euros each and buy a little barbeque grill from a gas station, so they can have bratwurst to go with their beer. By the time Germany beats Holland, a dozen brats and three times as many beers have been polished off. The grill gets left behind as a token of gratitude. I don't believe that "Must perform random acts of generosity" is one of the German Rules—hell, it's not even a commandment—but every so often this kind of thing happens. I'm the grateful one, though, because it is through this squatty, flimsy metal cooker I discover that Marcus possesses a valuable skill.

Every morning now I get the same question. "Do you want to barbeque tonight?" he asks as he tightens his tie.

"Sure," I answer, smiling at him over the top of my coffee cup.

"Do you want pork chops, steak, or salmon?"

"Salmon."

"How about surf and turf?" he asks. He thinks this combo is such a clever idea, and tells the story (again and again) of how he discovered it during a business trip to North Carolina.

"Whatever you want, honeybunch," I tease. He kisses me and disappears out the door.

"You forgot your briefcase," I yell after him.

I smile as I close the door behind him for the second time, and sit down at my desk to work.

I never dreamed I could be this content in Germany.

I go to Aldi that afternoon with my shopping list filled out with the things we'll need: a frozen filet of Atlantic wild salmon, aluminum foil, and a bag of charcoal briquettes.

When I come back into the apartment building I pass Herr Schindler on the front steps. *Grüss Gott,* I say, greeting him first. I hoist the bag of charcoal higher under my arm as I reach for my key.

"*Grüss Gott,*" he grumbles. I keep walking. As my foot hits the first landing of the staircase, he turns around and squints at me. "Frau Eisen, are you going to grill? Grilling is bad for my building. The smoke leaves black marks on the paint."

"Well, Herr Schindler," I reply without missing a beat, "a man's gotta eat." And I continue up the stairs. I count my quick retort as huge progress in my ability to live among the Germans. For once, I was not drawn into combat; I was not reduced to tears. "Ha!" I think. "I can do this."

After several grilled-meat evenings in a row, Herr Schindler catches Marcus on his way into the building. "Herr Eisen," he says, "the neighbors are going to think my house is turning into an American quarters."

"What makes you say that, Herr Schindler?" Marcus asks.

"All that barbequing," he snorts.

Marcus relays their exchange to me when he gets upstairs.

"American quarters?" I reply. "That's ridiculous. Has this guy got nothing better to think about? I mean, please, who doesn't love the smell of a barbeque? If anything, our only crime is making the neighbors salivate."

We heed the warning and eat pasta for a week, until Marcus can't hold out any longer. Succumbing to his craving for marinated pork chops and ignoring Herr Schindler, he lights the grill out on the balcony. He's scrunching the cordless phone between his shoulder and ear while fanning the flames as Andrea, on the other end of the line, carries on about how his cousin got his girlfriend pregnant. "It's a pity," she says. "And she already has a baby from a previous boyfriend." Marcus' body tenses up. From the kitchen, I can see him jerking around in quick, panicky movements. But it's not because of his mom. The flames have turned into a plume of smoke and he's afraid the neighbors will complain.

One gentleman did ring our buzzer a few barbeques earlier. The wind was blowing west that night, causing the smoke to travel around the corner over to Einstein Street. The man kindly inquired, "I was just wondering if I should call the fire department." He didn't, however, mention anything about the neighborhood resembling America.

BAM! BAM! BAM! The knock is readily identifiable by now. "Herr Eisen?" Herr Schindler says as Marcus opens the door. "I'd like to have a word with you."

"I'm on the phone," Marcus says, pointing to the cordless in his hand. "I'll be with you in a minute." He shuts the door and Herr Schindler stomps back downstairs.

"Sorry, *Mutti*, I have to go. *Tschüss*." Marcus sets the phone down on the counter.

I stop slicing tomatoes, raise my eyebrows, and say, "I figured this was coming."

Marcus returns fifteen minutes later and delivers the report. "He says that Stuttgart passed a city law. You can only grill in residential areas three times a year."

"Three times a year? But we grill three times a week! This is the most outrageous thing I've heard yet!" I laugh like a rabid hyena, practically foaming at the mouth.

"Let's not let it ruin our evening," he insists as gently as a German is capable.

But I can't let it go. "How can you live like this? Grilling should be a *right* not a privilege, just like you consider driving without speed limits a right."

"I know, I know." He walks over to put his arms around me.

"Grilling is my salvation from cooking! That grumpy old bastard can't take that away from me."

Marcus finishes cooking the steaks and we begin our meal in silence. "The law says three days a year, *or* a maximum of six hours," he ventures. "I figure the actual grilling time is twenty minutes so that puts us up to eighteen times a year. And I can ask Herr Schindler permission for anything beyond that."

"Whatever." I get up from the table and take my empty plate to the sink. After Herr Schindler's sucker punch it will take more than Marcus' clever calculations to regain my breath.

In August, the rain sets in. Baden-Württemberg's vineyards and cabbage fields become so saturated, farmers fear for their crops. Floods in the Alps make international headlines. The rain is so relentless we buy Jack a raincoat.

"It's too bad you picked this month to visit," I tell Miguel who is spending ten days with us. "But then this is my third summer here and not one of them has had great weather."

"It doesn't matter. I've been getting the sense you're not going to be here much longer, so I wanted to come right away," he says. "I didn't want to miss out on a free stay with my big sis."

"Very funny," I reply. "But you have a point."

Miguel is two years younger than I am. He's a fellow seasoned traveler with his own trophy list of destinations that includes Thailand, Egypt, former Yugoslavia, Italy, England, Kenya, Peru, and China. Plus he owns a home in Costa Rica (unfortunately, purchased *after* our honeymoon). But he's never been to Germany. (Funny how this country so often fails to show up on even the savviest of traveler's itineraries.) Back in his Orange County, California home he runs a non-profit organization painting murals with school kids to teach them a positive alternative to graffiti. He's also become a bit of a real estate mogul, buying crappy, rundown houses that no one else would touch (because of things like twenty flea-ridden cats living—and urinating—inside). He scrubs them to the bone (the houses, not the cats) until they shine (and smell good), and turns a nice profit.

He is outgoing, open-minded, and someone who sees the good in all people. Which is why I'm surprised at his running commentary during his first two days in Stuttgart. "Wow, some of these people seem so grumpy. I'm surprised by the hardened looks on people's faces. All I see is dark-colored clothing."

Unless I've planted some preconceived notions in his mind.

But his commentary doesn't last—because we leave for France.

We begin a marathon week of travel kicked off by driving to Paris. It's a place he's always wanted to go, so we take the forty-eight-hour Speed Tour. Instead of *Let's Go* we make up our own guide: *Let's Go Fast*.

He hits the Louvre with his digital camera while I run laps around the Jardin de Luxembourg in my jogging tights. He takes the elevator up the Eiffel Tower while I shop for shoes. (I buy a pair of bright pink ballet flats, which, unbeknownst to me, are the trend *du jour* in the U.S.) He comes back with a picture of himself standing in front of the Mona Lisa. I come back with a box of freshly baked croissants and éclairs.

"*C'est très bon*," he surmises, talking with his mouthful of vanilla crème. "*Je suis très heureux d'être en France.*"

"*Moi aussi*," I chime back. "*Et absolument, je préfère parler français*. You seem to remember a fair amount of French yourself. God, I hate speaking German; I suck at it. French was never as hard to learn." I look in the pastry box to see what delicacy to try next.

"Come off it. Your German is damn impressive," he insists.

"That's only because I'm trying to show off for you."

After Paris, we stop in Stuttgart for a change of clothes and pick up Marcus for the three-hour drive to Munich. The rain falls in horizontal sheets. The BMWs and Mercedes passing us whip a blinding spray onto our windshield. "Osterwald Garten is our favorite place for a traditional Bavarian Sunday brunch," Marcus tells Miguel. "The drive will be worth it. Plus you'll get to see waiters wearing *Lederhosen*."

He's right. We wolf down *Weisswurst, Kaiserschmarrn*, and soft pretzels, and drink Hefeweizen before noon—all served by a wait staff in leather shorts.

We show him how to peel back the translucent skin of the sausage to get to the white meat. "Just think, Miguel," I say, "this is only one out of more than fifteen hundred types of German sausage."

"*Das ist sehr gut*," he replies, over articulating but correctly saying it's very good.

"Oh God, now you're going to learn German too?" I groan.

Marcus laughs. "We need to get you a pair of *Lederhosen*," he says, and picks up his beer to toast with his adventurous brother-in-law.

In spite of the floods, we stick to our plan and head south to the Austrian Alps for four days of backpacking. We hike the European way—hut to hut—with light loads in our backpacks, as dinners, beds, blankets, and toilets are provided in the mountain chalets. We climb up trails meant for mountain goats, weathering the rain, cold, and patches of snow, and are rewarded by having the normally crowded huts to ourselves.

On our way back to Stuttgart we stop in Steinegg to pick up Jack from his babysitters—Oma Andrea and Opa Wolfgang. But we can't just take the dog and leave. Like everything involving German elders, we have to honor the formality. And thus, we take our places around the dining room table for *Abendbrot*, with Miguel at the usually vacant chair opposite Wolfgang.

Andrea passes Miguel a plate of sliced liverwurst and asks, "Michael, *möchtest du etwas*?"

He helps himself to more. "*Danke*," he replies. And that's the extent of his verbal contribution for the rest of the evening.

She passes a plate of cheese and tomato slices to me. "Bess?" she asks, pointing to the plate.

"*Danke*," I reply. And that's the extent of my verbal contribution for the rest of the evening.

"Well, *that* was painful," I say to Miguel when we get back to our apartment. He shoots a look at me, then looks around for Marcus. "Don't worry. He's in the bathroom brushing his teeth. He can't hear us."

"It was okay," he says, sitting back on the couch with Jack on his lap. "I considered it downtime and used the time to relax."

"It wasn't relaxing for me," I say.

"I can see that. Andrea seems like she has something against you."

"She's still mad at me for abandoning Marcus when I took that magazine job in L.A. She thought I had left him for good. But my guess is that's only part of it. I don't think I'm living up to her expectations of the ideal daughter-in-law. It's bad enough that I'm not fluent in German—every time we see her she scolds us for not speaking German with each other—but God forbid we ever move to the States. She will never forgive me for taking her son away." I wait for his response, hoping for some comforting, brotherly advice.

"Oh, Bethacita," he laughs, "that's why I plan to stay single."

Not comforting.

By Day Eight of Miguel's visit we've logged enough miles on the Autobahn to wear down the tires and my energy reserves, but we press on. We drive two and a half hours to Schwangau for the day, climb up the trail to King Ludwig's Disneyland castle, grab a sandwich from the bakery, and get back on the road.

Over breakfast on Day Nine, Miguel delivers an assessment of his stay. "When I first got here people looked so hard to me, but everyone has been so nice. It's all in how you approach them; it's all about having a positive attitude," he tells me, smug for having avoided the public lashings I had warned him of. "No one has reprimanded me once since I arrived."

"Yeah, well, trust me," I say. "Life is a lot different here when you're not on vacation."

This is his last full day and we've scheduled it for souvenir shopping. I go through the list of my standard German gifts: hand-painted beer glasses, Dr. Hauschka skin care products, Stuttgart's VFB soccer team stocking hats, Ritter Sport chocolate, and edelweiss-print silk scarves. Nothing excites him enough to make a trip downtown, and I've already given these gifts to my family members, which are the same as his family members, so we just go to Aldi. There he can buy wine and *Sekt* (Germany's version of champagne), marzipan candies, and chocolate cookies imprinted with antique cars, which, I point out to him, are fitting since the automobile was invented here. Aldi also sells Ritter Sport chocolate in miniature squares. This Stuttgart-produced chocolate is available at American grocery and drug store chains, but only when you buy it Germany do you get labels printed with German words. I make this case to him as well. So we grab a few canvas tote bags and get in the car once again—though only to drive the two blocks to Aldi.

Schadenfreude is when you take pleasure in someone else's misfortune. I didn't fully grasp the sublimity of this German word until I had a first-hand experience. During my second month in Stuttgart, Marcus, who in spite of his engineering degree is not all that mechanically inclined, was trying to fix a windshield wiper on a friend's borrowed camper van. I could see the simple solution with my own layman's eyes and thus told him to feed the blade in from the *other* side of the wiper, but he wouldn't listen. He struggled for a few more fruitless minutes until the rubber blade snapped back, flying out of its forced (and incorrect) position, and smacked him on the forehead. I tried to hide my glee, but he caught me.

"I saw that," he said.

I burst out laughing, which luckily got him to laugh. We enjoyed our chuckle for a minute, then he fixed the blade—my way.

But my biggest and best *Schadenfreude* experience comes when grocery shopping with my brother.

After combing the aisles of Aldi, we take our full cart up to the checkout counter. Miguel unloads his boxes of chocolates and cookies, two bottles of the local *Trollinger-Lemberger* red wine, and two bottles of *Sekt* onto the conveyor belt. He doesn't lay his bottles down, but I don't say anything. I don't recognize the cashier, a meek-looking blond with wire-rimmed glasses, so I decide to do an experiment. Maybe it's only Barbara who has an issue about upright bottles. Maybe the lashing I took was a one-time phenomenon. Maybe Barbara was premenstrual that day or had been in a fight with her girlfriend, assuming she's a lesbian, though I can't be sure and I'm not about to ask her, but she does have a certain masculine look. I count four people in line in front of us, and so far at least five people have lined up behind us. The blond cashier is busy running items through her scanner, seemingly unaware of us. Then ever so suddenly, like a surprise sniper attack, she takes aim at my unsuspecting brother. "Blah blah blah blah blah!" she squawks.

I turn to look at him—as does everybody else in line. I don't catch the words—German is especially hard to understand when someone is firing it like a machine gun—but I know the drill. "She wants you to lay your bottles down," I tell him. And then I start laughing. And laughing. And laughing. I laugh until tears stream down my cheeks. Through my hysteria I can hear Miguel muttering under his breath. We move up the line and I collect myself enough to hand over the necessary euros to the cashier to pay for my milk, fighting back more laughter.

Miguel is up next. His body snaps back and forth as the cashier flings his purchases past her scanner for him to catch and put back into his cart. He fumbles with his wallet, while I stand by, wiping my tears of joy.

When we get outside I laugh some more, exclaiming, "That . . . ha ha ha!. . . was . . . ha ha ha!. . . classic! Ha ha ha ha ha!"

"I was just standing there minding my own business," he

says, annoyed. "And then suddenly everything went quiet and I could feel everyone staring at me. You could have told me."

"I thought about it. But then I wanted to see if she would say anything. *Now* do you see what I've been talking about?"

We drive home and settle back inside the apartment, but I can't stop laughing for the next full hour. Miguel thinks I am losing my mind. "It wasn't *that* funny," he says as I replay the scene again and again, doubling over with squeals of my delight in his misery.

"It's just that you have no idea how much this means to me," I tell him. "No one believes me when I tell them what my experience has been like here. Except for dad who was witness to several of my early encounters."

"It must be a sign that it's time for me to go home," he says, getting off the bar stool to start packing.

"I wish I could go with you," I reply. I think of why I wish I was leaving and Herr Schindler comes to mind, which in turn gives me a very naughty idea. My face lights up with a big smile as the devil horns sprout from my head. From the other side of the kitchen counter, I call over to him, "Hey, Miguel, how about grilling pork chops for dinner tonight?"

CHAPTER 16

How About Moving to Italy?

A T THE END OF AUGUST, RIGHT AFTER MIGUEL leaves, my dad comes for another visit. We rent a motorcycle for him as a seventieth birthday present and head south to Italy. We cross the cool, highest passes of the Alps—including climbing up and down the seventy-five hairpin turns on Italy's Passo dello Stelvio—to get to Lake Garda, Italy's largest lake. While we skirt the water's edge, moving at two miles per hour through the tourist traffic on a ninety-five-degree day, overheating in my padded leather gear on the back of Marcus' motorbike, I start having visions. Heat-induced hallucinations or not, there is one image that won't go away. I see myself moving back to Los Angeles. I picture a little guesthouse and Jack running on the beach.

On our Italian tour is a scheduled stop in Bologna—to visit the Ducati motorcycle factory. I use my journalist credentials to score us a private tour.

Marcus and I had traveled through Bologna on a winter road trip eight months earlier. When we passed the factory Marcus shrieked in my ear, "There it is! There it is!" I had never seen him so excited. But because the factory was closed for the New Year holiday, the closest we could get to a tour was the gear store across the street, which was open. "My dream is to work for a motorcycle company," he revealed to me that night over a plate of black truffle fettuccini. Yes, I could see it. His passion for motorcycles was obvious from the moment he picked me up that first night in Milan. And I had sat through numerous dinners listening to him extol the virtues of a trellis frame, a signature Ducati design. And, as far as his career dreams went, it sounded like more fun than working in a law office. Or, as in the case of his current reality, a truck factory.

"That's great, because I've always dreamed of living in Italy," I had responded. "You could get a job at Ducati."

Six months later he still hasn't contacted the company, but we have made it back to their Bologna headquarters, which I accept as progress.

Security guards in tailored suits and ties man the desk at the factory gate. Male and female employees enter the grounds on their scooters, laughing and talking like they're on their way to a party. We are escorted to the lobby—filled with race memorabilia—and welcomed by our host, Dan Van Epps. A tall, strapping blond from Connecticut, he looks more like a banker interested in literature than an executive who produces high-strung motorcycles, yet he's worked for Ducati for twenty-five years. I could spare us—myself, anyway—six hours of shop talk about lightning-speed pistons and the engineering brilliance of desmodromic valves if I cut right to the chase. "Dan, please save our marriage and hire my husband!"

It's not that things are so bad. I haven't had any recent confrontations—no harassment about stained wedding dresses, upright wine bottles, dogs peeing, or even about grilling. And Marcus has become more available, accessible. He has become the equal partner I had always hoped for, doing dishes, grocery shopping, mopping our wood floors, and making use of his ample vacation time to be with me. But I still feel out of place in Germany. My surroundings fit me like the waistband of my *Lederhosen*—a little too tight and restrictive; I need elastic not buttons. I am still biding my time until we can move somewhere else. Italy seems like a good option. Pasta instead of pork. A language full of musical words like *buongiorno* and *bellissimo*, instead of *Guten Tag* and *ausgezeichnet*. And, in keeping the parents happy too, a place within driving distance to Wolfgang and Andrea.

We are given a museum tour, a dissertation of the assembly line, and a private meeting with the marketing director. After that, we have a rigatoni lunch with Ducati's lead designer, Pierre Terreblanche from South Africa. Marcus whispers to me, "I can't believe we are sitting here with Pierre Terreblanche! He's a celebrity in the design world." Marcus is so enamored with the whole scene, I'm convinced he's ready to move here tomorrow. We drink a cappuccino in the employee cafeteria, a lively gathering spot decorated in Ducati's red and white logo colors. My dad and I linger over our coffee, while Marcus wanders off with Dan to tour the mechanics' workshop.

"I've been observing Marcus," my dad says, "and he doesn't seem interested in working here, Boo."

My dad is not always the most sensitive guy on the planet, but he makes up for it with his acute, almost psychic, sense of intuition. His statement—or is it a prediction?—haunts me the rest of the way back to Stuttgart.

But Marcus said it was his dream.

When summer turns to fall and Marcus still hasn't sent his résumé to Bologna—or any other place—I know my dad is right. Like a coiled sausage over the glowing coals of our cheap grill, I have been slowly burning, and by Thanksgiving, I have crossed the invisible threshold from a palatable medium to overdone—blackened, tough, inedible.

The next thing I know I am looking up a new word in my German dictionary. *Spedition.* Moving company.

It is merely a coincidence that my parents' studio apartment at the beach happens to be available again. Without considering the consequences, as if some higher power takes over my body, I drive down to the *Deutsche Post* and mail my dad a check for December's rent in L.A.—without telling my husband.

A week after mailing my dad the rent check, I break the news to Marcus. "I'm going back to L.A. Just for a while," I tell him.

"A while? Then why did you get all those shipping boxes?" he asks. His tone is terse, his fingers practically strangle his coffee mug. "And why did you take all your pictures off the walls?"

"I'm not *leaving* you," I insist as I separate my grandmother's silver from the sterling-plated pieces his mother had bought for him. "I just need to live in an environment where I can be the person I need to be. And we both know Germany is not that place. I wish I could find my way here. But I just can't." I look up at him with all the tenderness I can muster, my blue eyes silently pleading, *Please let me go; I feel so trapped here, so out of place, so tired.* "You're going to be coming over for vacations. We're still going to see each other."

He stands by quietly as I continue to pack. I wrap a sweatshirt around the candlesticks that were a wedding present. "Wait," he says. "You're not taking *both* candlesticks, are you?"

"They're a set."

"They were given to *us*. Let me keep one." I hesitate, then hand him one. Tears well up in his eyes as he cradles the heavy silver holder and says, "I have faith these will be reunited."

"They will be. *We* will be," I say. But I am not so sure.

The winter I move back, Los Angeles experiences one of its wettest periods in history. It doesn't stop raining from December to May. In typical Hollywood fashion, the local media names the winter weather pattern after a movie, a Tom Hanks film, *The Polar Express*. But it's mid-June now, the sun has finally come out, and I've swapped my rubber boots for flip-flops. Heading out with Jack for his morning beach walk, I squint toward the horizon, marked by the dark silhouettes of two sailboats claiming the whole sea to themselves. The sun's electrified reflection off the ocean is so intense that what normally looks blue is eye-blinding white. I trudge across the full width of the beach—warm grains of sand wedging themselves between my toes, Jack following at my heels—until I reach the high tide line. I sit down on the sand, inhale a long, salty gulp of this maritime tranquilizer, and press the speed dial on my cell phone.

"Marcus?"

"Hi," he says. "I was just about to call you."

"I've been thinking about your vacation and, well, I don't think it's a good idea for you to come to California," I say. I wait for the words to reach him, to sink in.

"Yeah, I was thinking the same thing," he responds.

We are silent for a moment. A gull swoops past me, landing on the rim of a garbage can. A tall woman with the body of someone who works out too much jogs by. "I'm going to New York," I say. "I'm going to housesit for Alayne and take a summer writing workshop. And I don't know how long I'm going to be there."

The waves, only "ankle high" in surfer terms, crash gently but relentlessly on the shore, their beauty reduced to static on the other end of the phone line, a continent and another ocean away. The sun beats down steadily, filling in the pale line on my ring finger where my wedding band sat until today. I am honoring the pact I made with myself: if he doesn't make a move from Germany in six months, then that's it, I move on. The pause continues, the ocean's constant purr fills the space and the growing distance.

"You should go," he finally says. "It will be good for you."

The day of my departure from L.A. to New York coincides with the arrival of Sigrid, my mother's German friend from Iowa. She lives in California, in Sonoma County, but has been visiting a friend in Laguna Beach, south of us. She's worked it out so she will meet my parents at the Long Beach airport where they are bringing me, so I will get to see her before my flight takes off. My dad hauls my well-traveled blue duffel bags to the ticket counter, while my mom parks the car. Check-in goes quickly. Jack charms the ticket agent with his wagging tail, but not enough for her to forget about checking his health certificate and charging me for his fare. We return to the curbside, where my mom is hurrying across the parking lot to reunite with us. "Have you seen Sigrid?" she asks, catching her breath.

After a quick perusal of the departure drop-off, my dad and I reply in unison, "No, not yet." But right then I see a familiar woman moving toward us on the crowded sidewalk. It's been fifteen years since I last saw her, yet I recognize her immediately, even at seventy years old. Dressed in a crisp, white blouse, a long strand of black pearls, and flowing black trousers, she still exudes an elegant European flair by the seemingly casual way she wraps her gray cashmere shawl around her shoulders. Hugs and happy greetings are exchanged.

"It's great to see you, Sigrid," I say.

"Oh, Bess!" she says, pronouncing my name—even after living in the U.S. for forty-five years—the same way my mother-in-law does. "You look exactly the same."

"So do you," I tell her.

But she is quick to point out her flaws. "No, dear. Look at all these wrinkles." She does have wrinkles. Creases, deep and ribbed like a compressed accordion, occupy the length of her face, attesting to a long life of hardship (losing her husband to cancer, raising seven kids as a single mom, and grieving a son killed in an unsolved murder). But there are lines of happiness too (authoring cookbooks, hosting glamorous cooking gigs in New York City, and doting on grandchildren). She may be self-conscious about her skin—particularly here in the land of Botox—but she radiates natural beauty and grace. Really, I never knew an aging face could look so pretty. I can only hope I wear my wrinkles as well when the day comes.

With twenty minutes to go before boarding, we park on a bench in the waiting area. "*So, jetzt du sprichst sehr gut Deutsch, oder*?" she asks.

I stare at her blankly while my brain unscrambles the code for "So, now your German is really good, right?"

I reply, "*Leider nicht so gut* (unfortunately, not so good)," adding the excuses, "I'm terribly out of practice. It's easier to speak it when I'm *in* Germany."

My parents don't understand our banter, but they smile proudly as their daughter communicates in this strange tongue with the family friend. "Don't worry, I've forgotten so much of it too," Sigrid says, switching back to English. "So what's happening with that German husband of yours?"

"He's still in Germany," I say. "And I'm not sure if he's ever going to leave."

"Why not?" she asks.

"Because he just bought a new motorcycle." The smiles of my parents change to raised eyebrows. I turn to my dad. "Yeah, I didn't have a chance to tell you yet. He traded in his Ducati for a BMW Enduro."

"Germans have a hard time with change," Sigrid says, nodding sympathetically.

"But *you* left."

She laughs, her wrinkles deepening. "I was young when I met Mark. He was in the military, and if I wanted to marry him I knew I would have to live in America." Her look turns serious and I steel myself for what she's going to say next; I already know, through my mother, her opinion of German men. She's going to seize the opportunity to tell me herself. Then again, she knows, also via my mom, what I've been going through. In the end, she says, "Marcus sounds like a good man. He should get himself over here. But it also sounds like you've done all you can."

She's right. I do feel like I've done all I can, short of getting a lobotomy and joining the ranks of The Stepford Wives. But since I can't drastically alter my personality—which, granted, leans a little too heavily toward impatient, intolerant, and willful—I am left to wonder if my German man would, in fact, prefer a more subdued, less demanding, less *independent* partner, someone more stable and structured like him. Still, he chose to marry me.

Likewise, I knew his pace of life was slower than mine—from that very first day in Milan when he wanted to linger over espresso instead of getting to Florence by motorcycle before dark—and that he was dedicated to his career, able to tolerate short-term dissatisfactions for the sake of the bigger picture. Still, I chose to marry him. It's true that opposites attract. And yet, here we are, like the wrong ends of a magnet, pushing each other away.

A voice over the loudspeaker announces, "Flight 221 to New York JFK is now ready for boarding."

My send-off crew stands in a receiving line and the salutations begin. I start with Sigrid. "It was wonderful to see you, Sigrid," I say.

"You keep in touch, now that you have my phone number," she replies. "And have Marcus call me so I can talk some sense into him."

Next, my mother. She is holding Jack so she hugs me with her free arm, both of us willing our tears into retreat. "You take care of *you*," she reminds me.

And finally, my dad. During his bear-like embrace he says, "I'm proud of you, Boo. You're a survivor."

I wave goodbye to the parental trio, continuing to wave until I am inside the terminal.

Survivor. I always cringe when my dad calls me that. I don't correct him and say "Why not a thriver?" because he's not wrong. He's simply paraphrasing Nietzsche (of course, it *had* to be a German!) who said, "That which does not kill us makes us stronger."

Well, I'm alive—and I'm ready to begin my next adventure.

CHAPTER 17

The Happily Ever After

I T'S TEN P.M. ON A MUGGY MANHATTAN NIGHT AND THE intercom in Alayne's Upper West Side apartment buzzes, its screen automatically displaying an image of the man who stands at the door. The security camera's severe angle and fish-eye lens make his face look distorted. The harsh lobby lights make his skin look ghostlike. And the backpack he wears, which I know is red, appears gray on the black and white monitor. He's dressed in his standard travel clothes—*Lederhosen* and hiking boots.

Marcus.

If only letting him back into my life, allowing for a fresh start, could be as easy as pressing a New York City door buzzer. Jack, as if he knows who waits down on the street, springs up and down, bouncing against my leg. We've lived apart for nine months and haven't seen each other in four (including the two months I've been in New York). The only thing that separates us now is three flights of stairs. My heart races, hope pulses in through my arteries, fear pumps out through my veins.

I push the little black button.

Our hug is awkward, cut short by Jack who demands to greet Marcus first. I study this stranger—*my husband*—as he bends down to get his face licked. He looks as handsome as he did the first time I saw him inside the Crater Lake Lodge. His body is trim. His hair is dark and smoothed back, though starting to thin. His smile is wide; his teeth, flossed daily, gleam white.

Okay, so I'm still attracted to him, but that doesn't mean it will work out between us. Calm down. Take a breath. You have two weeks together to figure this out.

"Jack learned to swim," I say, starting off with an easy subject. "We go to the pond at Central Park every morning."

"That's very cute," he says. But he's distracted; something urgent is on his mind. He breaks away from the dog's kisses. "I have some big news," he blurts out, leaping up like our energetic terrier. "I'm getting transferred to Portland."

He searches my face for my reaction, but he doesn't have to wait. My response is lightning-quick, my hands automatically clap together. "Are you kidding me? That is wonderful news!" In spite of this good news, an artillery of thoughts ricochets off the insides of my skull. *I always believed we would be happier together if our living situation were different . . . if we could live in a place where I could speak the language . . . someplace we could both be happy . . . I still love you . . . I want to stay married to you . . . But what if it's too late?* My internal drill sergeant

316

takes over and shouts, "STOP! JUST QUIET DOWN AND LISTEN!"

"You won't believe the story of how this came about," he continues, smiling and talking uncharacteristically fast. "I went to my boss to ask for a leave of absence. My plan was to take six months off to come and live with you and look for a job."

"You were going to leave your job to come here for me?"

I never really wanted him to quit his job; I just wanted to know that he would be *willing* to. Willing to make our marriage a priority. Willing to make the compromises necessary for our relationship to work. *Willingness*. The word tastes sweet, like an elixir, on my lips.

"Yes, but then Dr. Dostal heard I have an American wife. He said, 'If the reason you want to leave is to be with her, and you want to be on the West coast, that's good news, Herr Eisen, because your name just came up today for a new position in Portland.' And that's how fast it happened."

"I've never heard of anything happening that fast at your company. That's truly bizarre—I mean, in a good way. It's phenomenal, it's amazing, it's . . ."

"I know. This is really something." He takes my hands—he must notice my wedding band is missing—and swallows hard, his green eyes laser-focused on mine, his face set. "Do you want to be with me?"

My chest heaves up and down with heavy breaths as the question circulates through my body, checking in with every cell to find the answer.

Since I had come to New York, I wasn't sure when—or *if*—I

would see him again. The time and distance—and my refusal to live any longer in his homeland—had wedged its way between us. Though we still exchanged emails, they were becoming shorter and more restrained. And our daily phone conversations had dwindled to once a week. It was so incremental that we hadn't noticed at first, but we had begun moving on with our lives. Then, one week earlier, he called from Stuttgart. "I'd like to come to New York to see you," he offered cautiously. This was not an easy proposition for him, considering how I had rejected his plans to come to L.A. two months earlier.

Maybe my answer to his Portland proposal had already been clear in that phone call. I had admired his courage to reach out to me in New York, respected his strength to withstand my potential wrath and risk further rejection. My patience may have run out, but I had left the door open—or at least slightly ajar—and I said yes. "Yes. Please come."

Blowing my expectations for his visit to smithereens, he is next to me, dangling in front of me the news I had been wishing for for several years.

I let go of his hands and stand up. "Wait here. I'll be right back." I scurry off to the bathroom and rummage around in my toiletry bag until I find the small wooden box at the bottom. I open the box. Yes, it's still there.

I pick up the metal band. The faint drone of buses and honking taxis outside on Central Park West filters in through the window as I run my fingers across the ring, stroking the tiny nicks and dents in the outer gold ring that tell a story of the past. If only this ring could also tell the future.

But what if I could see what lies ahead? What if I knew that eighteen months after moving to Portland Marcus will be transferred to Saltillo, Mexico (the Stuttgart of Latin America!) and that we will be right back where we started—only my language classes will be in Spanish and the loose Mexican culture will make me miss the structure of Germany! What if I knew that the struggle to balance our disparate lives will be ongoing no matter where we live? What if I knew that happier times lie ahead, but also some of the darkest hours I will ever experience? Would I still want to stay with him? Would I want to put myself through the continuous and steep learning curve of marriage? Would I be willing to do the work? The question is: why wouldn't I? What kind of adventure would life be without climbing a few rocky peaks and paddling some white-water-filled valleys? Without the challenges, how would we ever gain strength and knowledge about ourselves? How would we tap into the deep, self-discovery kind of growth that creates wisdom? And isn't this wild journey all the richer when it is shared with a loving, sexy, smart partner who can help us navigate when we lose our way? I don't know yet how the rest of my life, or our marriage, will play out—no one knows for certain where their lives will take them—but I do know this: I want adventure! I want to be challenged! I want to be up in the mountains and down in the rivers! I want strength! I want growth! I want wisdom! I want a GPS who I can have sex with!

I slide the thick band onto my ring finger.

Returning to the living room, I crawl into Marcus' lap. I wrap one arm around his neck and gently shake my left hand next to his ear. The gold and steel bands, connected yet separate, rattle against each other making a soft clinking sound. "Does that answer your question?" I whisper.

He brings his right hand to my ear and jingles his ring in reply. "I love you," he says.

"*Ich liebe dich, auch.*" I love you, too, I answer. The words feel genuine, even when I say them in German. Ah, German. Staying married to Marcus means I not only have to keep working at the relationship, but also at his language. I rationalize the prospect—*We'll be living in Oregon so I'll only need to speak enough for polite conversation during holiday visits to the Omas and the in-laws*—thus subduing the potential panic. But just as I cannot know the future of our marriage, I also do not know that some years ahead I will find myself in circumstances that require me to speak German, and that my desperation to communicate will overpower my fear of embarrassment. In this unguarded, un-selfconscious state, my words will flow, my sentence structure will be accurate, my comprehension will be high . . . I will be nearly fluent. Miracles do happen!

Embracing each other tighter, we kiss—madly, deeply, powerfully. We kiss as if our love is breaking an evil spell. But in our story, there is no frog turning into a prince, and no princess is waking from a coma. This is no dream, there are no slippers of the glass or ruby kind; everything we've been going through—every messy, maddening, mercurial, imperfect thing—is real life. I have never needed rescuing from a locked tower; I have always had the freedom of choice and I continue to choose Marcus. Likewise, he is choosing me. Our kiss may not be the magic potion we ultimately need—if only such a thing existed!—still, it's a magical kiss that makes everything right with the world. A kiss that tells me no matter how frustrated I get with this man (or with his country), no matter what we've been through, no matter what's to come, I still love him beyond explanation.

And with that, just like all the other charmed characters in those romantic, idealistic—and yes, German!—fairy tales, we live happily ever after.

At least we keep trying.

– Das Ende –

EPILOGUE

"BUT WHAT DID YOU *LEARN* FROM YOUR TIME IN Germany?" readers have asked. "What *lessons* did you come away with?"

There is a German word to help answer that—a compound noun, naturally; it's *Sitzfleisch.* "Sit meat" is its literal translation, as in "keeping your butt in the chair." It's used to convey the ability to endure a situation. It's what authors need as it takes *Sitzfleisch* to write a book. But it's also what I relied on for enduring the many challenges I faced in Germany, whether they were cultural, lingual, marital, or all three at once. Living there was challenging in ways I had never experienced, but it was never boring! And "boring" is the one thing I cannot endure. I stayed in Germany until the meat I was sitting on was so pulverized I did something else: *Fersengeld*—"heel money"—an expression meaning "to turn tail and run." Because, while I learned the value of maintaining discipline to plow through difficult situations, I also learned the importance of self-preservation.

But that doesn't really answer the question of "What is the *lesson*? What is it that gave you an *understanding* of Germany?"

I don't have a concise answer. My feelings about Germany

continue to be as complex as the country itself. I witnessed first-hand how Germany is still trying to amend its transgressions from the last century. I experienced the kindness of strangers, like the time the man stopped by the side of the road to see if I was okay (see Chapter 13—The American Therapist). And I came to understand that just because Germany wasn't the right fit for me doesn't mean it's a bad place. My situation there was like being a fish out of water, but in reverse; I was in too deep and felt like I was drowning. I was a parrotfish from the shallows of the Caribbean (okay, maybe I was more like a piranha) trying to swim with the whales in the depths of the North Sea. The temperature wasn't warm enough for me, the light not the high wattage I needed to survive.

Perhaps the better question is, "If you had it to do over again, would you still move to Germany?" because that answer is an easy one: "Hell, yes!" Anytime you can immerse yourself in a different culture, study a new language, learn new customs, try new food, and stretch your comfort zone as far past the limits as you can go without breaking, the answer should always be yes, yes, yes! We live in a time when cultural tolerance has never been more important. Just because we speak different languages, have different rules for laying bottles down on grocery store conveyor belts, or drive at different speeds, we all share the same basic needs and desires—for food, shelter, and love. At the end of the day, we are all humans sharing one planet. I'm grateful to know other regions of it, to be educated about the myriad ways of life beyond our own borders. I'm *überglücklich*—which is to say, *very* happy *and* lucky—to have been able to experience the German part. My life is so much richer for it.

You may have been hoping this epilogue would reveal what happened with Marcus and me after our reunion in New York. Our story is a long and, I'm sorry to say, tragic one, and requires 320 pages to tell it. It's all in my book called *Making Piece*, and I hope you'll read it.

There may not be such a thing as a "happily ever after," but that should never stop us from striving for one.

Acknowledgements

Thank you to Nicole Gregory, for championing this book at the beginning and rallying again at the end.

Thank you to Andrew Salomon and the Summer Writers' Workshop at Hofstra University, including guest speaker, Alex Dinelaris, who schooled me on the three-act structure.

Thank you to my readers: Foong Broeker, Kee Kee Buckley, Susan Comolli, Kathy Eldon, Paul Galloway, Karen Karbo, Molly Moser, Joan Posch, and Lena Sintring. Reading doesn't begin to describe the contribution you made.

Thank you to the friends and family who supported me during various stages of this project: Colleen Coleman, Maggie Galloway, Sigrid Holland, Anne Howard, Tom and Marie Howard, Steve Johnson, Bibiana Overlack, Lyndsay Presthofer, Alayne Reesberg, Nan Schmid, and Doug Seyb.

Thank you to Morgan Krehbiel for your book design. And to Jane Friedman for the free tutorials on your blog.

And especially, thank you to Marcus—and to Germany—for putting up with me.

About the Author

BETH M. HOWARD is the author of *Making Piece: A Memoir of Love, Loss, and Pie* and *Ms. American Pie: Buttery Good Pie Recipes and Bold Tales from the American Gothic House*. Her work has appeared in *The New York Times, Real Simple, Country Living,* and *Guideposts*, among other publications. She has been featured on CNN's *Anderson Cooper 360*, CBS *This Morning*, BBC, NPR, and more. She lives on a farm in Southeast Iowa.